This book is dedicated to the memory of my son
Luke Razzell

Essays in Historical Sociology

Peter Razzell

Caliban Books

Published 2021
Caliban Books
30Ingram Road, London, N2 9QA
Copyright Peter Razzell.
ISBN 978-1-5272-8724-2

CONTENTS

PREFACE

The essays in this book were written in the period between 1963 when I was a lecturer in sociology until my retirement this year. A lot of the research was carried out with the support of fellowships from the Wellcome Trust and the Economic and Social Research Council. Seven of the eleven essays have not been published previously, and two of them were written jointly with my colleague Christine Spence and one with Emily Grundy.

I have slightly re-edited the essays which were previously published, to make them consistent with the other papers in the book.

The essays have benefitted from some lively debates with colleagues too numerous to enumerate. Many of the papers break new ground and are yet to be accepted in the mainstream of historical demography and historical sociology. My hope is that the book will provoke debate on the issues raised, allowing their eventual resolution.

I believe that history is a central discipline in the social sciences, and is indispensible for an understanding of our current economic, social, cultural and political life.

Peter Razzell

Chapter 1: The Problem of Determinism: A Sociological Solution.[1]

Contemplating the possibility of determinism, the social philosopher, Isaiah Berlin, wrote:

> ... the changes in the whole of our language, our moral terminology, our attitudes toward one another, our views of history, of society, and of everything else will be too profound to be even adumbrated. The concepts of praise and blame, innocence and guilt and individual responsibility ... are but a small element in the structure, which would collapse or disappear. If social and psychological determinism were established as an accepted truth, our world would be transformed more radically than was the teleological world of the classical and middle ages, by the triumphs of mechanistic principles or those of natural selection. Our words – our modes of speech and thought – would be transformed in literally unimaginable ways; the notions of choice, of responsibility, of freedom, are so deeply embedded in our outlook that our new life, as creatures in a world genuinely lacking in these concepts, can, I should maintain, be conceived by us only with the greatest difficulty.[2]

Although written perhaps with a touch of hyperbole, this quote indicates the seriousness with which some philosophers have viewed the problem of determinism, a concern which has not abated in the last number of years since the above passage was written. The number of publications on the issue has if anything increased, partly due to the growing success of the natural sciences, particularly in the fields of genetics and human biology. However, in spite of the proliferation of writing on the subject, one leading authority – J.O. Urmson – has concluded, that 'no solution to these problems has been

---

[1] Unpublished paper.
[2] I. Berlin, *Four Essays on Liberty,* 1969, p. 113.

found which commands anything approaching general consent.'[3]

The nub of the problem has been very succinctly summarised by J.R. Lucas in his book, *The Freedom of the Will.*

> We have a profound conviction of freedom. We know we are free. Yet when we think of ourselves from a scientific point of view, we do not see how we can be free. It would be a denial of science, we feel, to make man an exception to the universal laws of nature, and say that although everything else could be explained in terms of cause and effect, men were different, and were mysteriously exempt from the sway of natural laws.[4]

From the vast literature on the subject, and from everyday experience, it does seem that the majority of people do have a sense that both determinism and free-will are true, in spite of what appears to be a fundamental contradiction between them. The aim of this paper is to put forward a sociological resolution to this apparent contradiction. This will necessarily only touch on topics of great complexity, and will cover material from a number of disciplines, without being able to do full justice to any of them. The problem has of course had profound impact on the development of the social sciences, starting with the application of Kant's distinction between the 'laws of freedom' and 'laws of nature' in the nineteenth century. This led to the creation of the two separate disciplines *Geisteswissenschaften* and *Naturwissenschaften,* phenemonological and positivistic sociology respectively. Additionally there have been a number of sociologists who have attempted to integrate these two perspectives, including Max Weber and Talcott Parsons. This proliferation of approaches has generated much controversy.

---

[3] J.O. Urmson and J. Rie (eds.), *The Concise Encyclopaedia of Western Philosophy*, 1989, p. 113.
[4] J.R. Lucas, *The Freedom of the Will,* 1970, p. 1.

Determinism first became an issue in its modern form in the seventeenth century, although even then, Hobbes could write that the problem had already given rise to 'vast and insoluble volumes'.[5] Although it had been discussed in fragmentary form by some of the early Greek philosophers – particularly Epicurus – its first major presentation was in a religious context. A number of early Christian thinkers tried to reconcile the paradox of an omnipotent and omniscient God, who both predetermined the fate of the universe – including that of man – and created at the same time the capacity for free-will.[6] This led to numerous controversies in Christian theology, culminating in a polarisation of doctrine between the Calvinist belief in predestination, and the free-will Arminianism of the Quakers and Universal Baptists.

The success of the natural sciences in astronomy and other areas, led Descartes to adopt a mechanistic view of the material universe, which inevitably raised the question of the application of this mechanical principle to man himself. Descartes' solution to this problem was his well-known dualism, between mind and matter. Mind – or consciousness – was the basis of an 'I' that was capable of acting freely, independently of the laws of nature. The body was seen by Descartes as a part of the material world, raising the issue of the relationship between mind and body – a problem he never successfully resolved. This dualism was rooted in Greek and Christian thinking, and Descartes' 'mind' was the notion of the soul written in new language.

The major difficulty faced by Descartes was how could the non-material substance of mind interact with and influence the material body? Descartes argued that the mind was equivalent to an internal pilot guiding the machinery of the body, operating in the pineal gland, the seat of the mind-body interaction. The unsatisfactory nature of this solution

---

[5] Quoted in T. Honderich, *The Consequences of Determinism,* 1990, p. 84.
[6] B.A.O. Williams, 'Freedom and the Will', in D.F. Pears (ed.), *Freedom of the Will,* 1963, pp. 5, 6.

was clear even to Descartes himself, but he defined the problem in terms familiar to us today, largely because of his understanding of the principle of causality as applied to the natural sciences.[7]

As a part of this dualism, Descartes postulated a thinking 'I', a self which was the origin and basis of all free action. He was influenced by Aristotle's notion of an 'originating principle of action', capable of generating its own actions. This idea of an 'originator' has been key in all the discussions on free-will and determinism; most defenders of free-will have argued for a human capacity for originating totally free action, and rooted this capacity in a 'self', 'mind', 'person' or other form of individual identity. All these concepts arose historically out of the notion of an individual soul, which was central to both Greek philosophy and Christian theology. The soul was an essential and substantial spiritual self, created by God – and thus lying outside of the realm of nature, with its deterministic laws. In practice, there was a great deal of controversy about the nature of the soul, both in Greek and Christian thinking, a subject which we will return to later.

With the rise of science, it became necessary to substitute secular for religious language. The concepts of the mind and the self replaced that of the soul, although they involved the use of the same basic assumptions: that the self/mind was a simple, unitary essential 'I', capable of initiating free action. This change in language did not resolve the basic contradiction – the mind/body problem – and in fact raised new difficulties by postulating the self as an empirical reality subject to scientific scrutiny. It was Hume who first rigorously examined the concepts of the self and mind from an empirical point of view. From an analysis of mind, he concluded that 'what we call a *mind*, is nothing but a heap or collection of different perceptions, united together by certain

---

[7] J. Cottingham (ed.), *The Cambridge Companion to Descartes,* 1992.

relations, and supposed though falsely, to be endowed with a perfect simplicity and identity.'[8] Similarly, with the concept of self, he argued that 'when I turn my reflection on *myself,* I never can perceive the *self* without some one or more perceptions, nor can I ever perceive anything but perceptions.'[9] He criticized Descartes for his assumption that the mind was a substance of unitary identity, pointing out that 'everything that exists, is particular: and therefore it must be our several particular perceptions that compose the mind.'[10] A similar conclusion has been reached in our own day by Ryle who has argued that the conventional notion of the mind/self is nothing but the 'ghost in the machine'.[11]

Hume and subsequent thinkers saw that when the mind and self were analysed empirically they dissolved as unitary entities, and became sets of highly complex particular perceptions lacking any observable unity. Hume based his conclusions on subjective introspection, but an objective neurological and biological analysis involves equal difficulties for the concepts of a unitary mind and self. The same conclusion applies to existing sociological and social-psychological analyses of the mind and self; for example, in Mead's work, both mind and self arise out of a process of social interaction, and originate through a pattern of role taking and linguistic communication. The self is seen as being constituted as an 'I', defined as the spontaneous, unique individual, and the 'Me' which is a reflection of the 'Generalized Other', the composite of all social expectations. When Mead's work is examined in detail, it turns out that the 'Me' and 'Generalized Other' are not unitary phenomena, but are concepts reflecting specific roles that individuals enter in to, giving multiple sets of self-definitions.[12] It is for this and

---

[8] D. Hume, *A Treatise of Human Nature* [Book 1], 1962, p. 258.
[9] Ibid, p. 329.
[10] Ibid, p. 349.
[11] G. Ryle, *The Concept of Mind*, 1949, pp. 15, 16.
[12] See G. H. Mead, *Mind, Self and Society,* 1934.

other reasons that contemporary philosophers – even those sympathetic to arguments of indeterminism – have referred to the idea of a self, ego or mind as 'dreadful and bizarre' and 'extravagant'. This scepticism about the self has reached a point where a *Dictionary of Philosophy* has referred to it as 'an obsolescent technical term.'[13]

Hume was aware of the practical difficulties that ensued from this dissolution of the unitary self and mind. He had argued that causality could not be validated through inductive analysis: a perceived regularity could not guarantee the existence of a causal pattern outside acts of perception. His way of dealing with all these problems was his well-known resort to everyday life: 'It is not ... reason, which is the guide of life, but custom.'[14] Elsewhere he appealed to nature as a practical guide: 'Nature has ... doubtless esteemed it an affair of too great importance, to be trusted to our uncertain reasonings and speculations.'[15] Hume himself thus was able to accept the disturbing consequences of his own analysis with some equanimity, but his contemporaries were less happy with his conclusions. In particular, Kant concluded that Hume's work had undermined the philosophical basis of all knowledge, including the foundations of morality and individual freedom.

Kant's reaction to the problems raised by Hume was to resort to the two realms defined by Descartes, but to refashion this duality in a much more subtle and complex way. He postulated a phenomenal world of experience, not unlike Hume's, which was subject to the empirical laws of science and the principles of causality. All that could be observed and experienced was a part of this realm of nature, but in order for knowledge of this realm to be valid, Kant argued that it was necessary to postulate certain *a priori* categories of knowledge which could only be understood through the

---

[13] A. Flew (ed.), *A Dictionary of Philosophy,* 1979, p. 299.
[14] Hume, *A Treatise,* p. 343.
[15] Ibid, p. 238.

faculty of reason. Reason is the ultimate grounding and source of all continuity in human existence: 'Reason is present in all the actions of men at all times and under all circumstances, and is always the same.'[16] It was through reason that man could find a point of fixture, a principle invoked as a bastion against the flux of experience that Hume had discovered in his philosophy. Almost as important for Kant was the *a priori* category of freedom, that lay at the core of his moral ideas. All these categories were of a transcendental nature, and could not be derived from experience or empirical evidence. It was impossible according to Kant to know anything about the metaphysical content of these transcendental categories, as they could only be apprehended by rational understanding and not through empirical experience. The ultimate basis for all the categories was *practical necessity*: without them, it was impossible to establish a philosophical basis for either knowledge or moral freedom.[17]

Kant had succeeded in removing some of the more obvious difficulties in Descartes' dualism, but at the cost of transferring the ultimate realities – noumenal self, reason and freedom ('things-in-themselves') – to the empty realm of the transcendental. Although Kant's solution was radically different to Hume's, they both shared an appeal to practical necessity as a final resting point, although for Kant it was a formal part of his philosophy, whereas for Hume it was a form of almost perplexed resignation. Kant's postulate of the two realms of 'nature' and 'freedom' was associated with appropriate forms of causation – natural necessity and the causality of freedom. All empirical human acts were subject to the laws of nature, and according to Kant there were no exceptions to this rule. All acts could however be viewed from both standpoints, so that an act was both naturally caused, while at the same time originating from a free choice

---

[16] I. Kant, *Critique of Pure Reason*, 1933, p. 478.
[17] Ibid, p. 343; I. Kant, *Critique of Practical Reason*, 1956, pp. 5, 6.

of the noumenal self.[18] The former was empirically observable, but the latter could only be abstractly postulated through transcendental reason.

Kant's solution to the problem of determinism – the creation of two realms – was unsatisfactory on a number of accounts. Firstly, it was a transcendental solution, and therefore had an obscure, remote quality. Secondly, and most importantly, the noumenal self which was the originating source of freedom, was a non-empirical postulate, and therefore subject to the same objection as Descartes' original formulation. Kant had initially seen the self as 'a spiritual, enduring, incorruptible being'[19] – the soul – but later in his philosophy was content to postulate it merely as a transcendental category. Kant defined the soul as having the following qualities: '1. The soul is substance. 2. As regards its quality it is *simple*. 3. As regards the different times in which it exists, it is numerically identical, that is, *unity* (not plurality). 4. It is in relation to *possible* objects in space.'[20] The fourth point was necessary to deal with the problem of the soul interacting with the empirical world of nature, but it was in effect self-contradictory: Kant had defined the noumenal soul as being outside space and time, so how was it possible for it to influence the material world of nature? Kant's retreat into the transcendental postulate does not in any way solve this problem, and the formulation has failed to satisfy most philosophers. However, I will be arguing later, using sociological arguments, that it is possible to restate Kant's thesis in a much more acceptable and valid form.

* * * * * * * *

Most philosophers writing on determinism have recognized that it is not a theory which can be proved true or false, but

---

[18] Kant, *Critique of Practical Reason*, pp. 464, 467.
[19] K. Ward, *The Development of Kant's View of Ethics*, 1972, p. 72.
[20] Kant, *Critique of Pure Reason*, pp. 330. 331.

rather is a set of heuristic assumptions making possible the practice of science, at least in its classical form. It is impossible to falsify its premises, as any falsification of a particular hypothesis or theory, leads to further attempts to give causal explanations of the phenomenon in question. It is the source of the fruitfulness of science, that it never abandons its quest for explanation on the grounds of a particular failure. It is the basis of its aggressiveness, laying claim to all areas of experience, and given the hypothetical nature of scientific truth, it is unlikely to ever lose this dynamic quality, at least in the foreseeable future.

The reason why determinism has been taken so seriously is not because its major thesis has been proved to be true, but rather because of its successes in the natural sciences. In particular, the spectacular results in research in genetics and human biology in the last thirty or forty years, has given rise to the unease expressed by Berlin and quoted at the beginning of the paper. The explanations given by biology and genetics are in classical causal form, e.g. some of the recent work on genetic diseases such as muscular dystrophy, specifically defining muscular degeneration as an effect of a particular defective gene. In sociological terms, deterministic assumptions can be said to be a 'functional pre-requisite' for the practice of classical science, a pre-requisite which is in the form of fundamental premises rather than testable hypotheses.

The major difficulty with this line of argument is the emergence of quantum mechanics in twentieth century physics. This is subject of much controversy and obscurity, so that Feynman, one of the leading contributors to the development of relativistic quantum field theory, could write, 'nobody really understands quantum field theory'.[21] Physicists have been unable to agree amongst themselves whether or not quantum mechanics is fundamentally indeterminist, as Bohr and Heisenberg, two of the authors of the Copenhagen

---

[21] Quoted in E. Squires, *The Mystery of the Quantum World,* 1986, p. 122.

Statement, argued, or whether as Einstein believed 'God does not play dice with the universe'. The dispute continues unabated, and a number of physicists have continued to search for 'hidden variables' in order to give a complete deterministic account of quantum mechanics. It is clearly beyond the competence of an outsider to comment on what is such highly specialized and difficult work.

However, a number of scholars have pointed out that the problems of interpreting the behaviour of sub-atomic phenomena do not appear to apply to the macroscopic level of reality.[22] And this is ironically confirmed by Heisenberg: in describing the death of a physicist colleague, he stated that 'I cannot doubt but that the beginning of his illness coincided with those unhappy days in which he lost hope in the speedy completion of our theory of elementary particles. I do not, of course, presume to judge which was the cause and which the effect.'[23] So in practice, Heisenberg was forced to resort to deterministic language when talking about his own experience. As indicated·by Hume, we assume the principle of determinism applies to our everyday lives, particularly in its physical aspect. And it is for this reason that the problem of determinism will not go away, in spite of the emergence of quantum mechanics in contemporary physics.

The success of biology and neurology as disciplines in recent decades has led to a great deal of discussion of the mind/body problem, focussing on the brain and its relationship to consciousness. This has become a matter of some controversy, but it is universally agreed that there is a very close relationship between brain and mental activity. The most coherent and consistent explanation of this relationship is that known as identity theory. There are a number of variants, but I will confine myself to a discussion of the form which I believe can lay the foundations for a solution to the mind/body problem. The starting point is Frege's doctrine that

---

[22] See for example T. Honderich, *Mind and Brain,* 1990, p. 105.
[23] W. Heisenberg, *Physics and Beyond,* 1971, p. 236.

certain terms of language have both reference and sense. The most familiar example is the relationship between the Morning Star and the Evening Star; they are in fact the same star (having the same reference) but because they are perceived at different times (morning and evening), they have a different sense. In other words, the same phenomenon is described in a different language because it was viewed from different perspectives, the identity of the two stars not being realized when the two separate names were coined.

Similarly, it is argued by identity theorists that brain processes and consciousness are identical, the one being viewed from the outside, the other from inside. Consciousness is the process of the brain – it is merely that which is experienced from the inside. The term coined by the analytical behaviourists – privileged access – is germane to this formulation; the person in question has a privileged access to the private experience of consciousness because it can only be experienced from the inside. From the outside, this experience will be described in neurological and biological terms, and so we have the language of the subject·(inner consciousness) and that of the objective observer (neurology and biology) – both referring to the same, identical phenomena.[24]

This deceptively simple formula raises a host of problems, but I believe all these can be solved through careful analysis. Firstly, the most simple types of identity – for example pain – can clearly be seen to refer to the same phenomena. A toothache arising from caries caused through bacteriological infection and transmitting information to the brain (biology and neurology) is subjectively experienced as pain (consciousness). The first is an objective explanation in causal language, made by the outside observer; the second is a subjective account of consciousness made by the person undergoing the biological experience from the inside – and of

---

[24] See E. Wilson, *The Mental as Physical*, 1979 and D.M. Armstrong, *A Materialist Theory of Mind*, 1968.

course, they refer to the identical phenomena. Similarly with hunger and sexual desire (subjective experiences) – they are identical to certain physiological and neurological states which can be defined objectively and scientifically. Acts of cognition likewise can be readily analysed in this way; for example, a person opening his eyes from sleep and seeing an object (a picture) – this can be described either as: 1. an act of consciousness or 2. a physiological movement of the eyes and the activation of certain brain processes. (Patterns of sleep, dreaming etc have been analysed through encephalograph measurements.) Both these descriptions refer to an identical event, merely using different language, depending on perspective.

These examples do not pose major problems for identity theory, but there is more difficulty with subjective phenomena such as intentions, purposes and facts of choice. Identity theory works well with obvious physical events, but becomes more difficult to accept with subtle and complex phenomena of a less obviously physical nature. There are two reasons for this: 1. The difficulty of locating the phenomena in question or, 2. The problem of giving any kind of coherent explanation of them. Although it is not possible to precisely locate a subjectively described phenomenon such as (say) an intention, it is clear that it must be located in principle in the brain, even it is not possible (at least not on current knowledge) to identify it with a specific neurological process. Empirically, we can address this point by asking, if not in the brain, where else would it be located? And we may add from a scientific point of view, if it is located in the brain, it must necessarily be a physical phenomenon.

The second point is more serious. One of the major criticisms of identity theory is that it does not do justice to 'the indispensability of the mental'.[25] It is unclear exactly what this phrase refers to – possibly the sheer subjective

---

[25] Honderich, *Mind and Brain*, p. 105.

conviction of consciousness and mental experience. This itself is no objection to identity theory, but it does contain an implication which is valid. 'The indispensability of the mental' implies a Cartesian insistence on consciousness as the basis of knowledge and individual identity, with the tacit assumption that it is the foundation of a self capable of moral choice. Most accounts of identity theory, are unable to give a coherent explanation of what we might call the moral dimension of experience, so that for example, one of the most persuasive recent expositions of the theory, virtually eliminates moral choices and intentions from its analysis.[26] We are thus returned to the central dilemma of this paper: how can a deterministic account of human behaviour – such as identity theory – be reconciled with notions of free-will?

The answer is contained within identity theory itself. There are two ways of describing events: one in the language of the subject, the other in the language of the objective observer. This has most eloquently been summarized by J.R. Lucas:

> Free-will belongs to the agent's language, determinism to the spectator's. I, as an agent, perform some actions freely: he, as a spectator, may predict events correctly. But I am not he; to be an active participator is not the same as to be an observer from the sidelines, and actions and events are logically very different; and therefore ... no conflict can arise between my belief as an agent that I am acting freely and his certainty, as a spectator, that events will follow their pre-established course; since the key concepts of the opposition must be formulated in different languages, no contradiction between them can arise.[27]

Lucas was writing from the perspective of analytical philosophy, with its emphasis on 'linguistic games', and the function of language regarding the activities of separate

---

[26] Wilson, *The Mental.*
[27] Lucas, *The Freedom*, p. 17.

linguistic communities. Kant's distinction between the phenomenal and noumenal self is very similar, referring to the separate realms of natural necessity and freedom. None of these accounts give a satisfactory explanation of the existence of these separate modes of experience, but they all agree that they are based on *practical necessity*. For Hume it was the inevitability of nature and communal living; for Kant it was the necessity of practical reason; and for Wittgenstein and his followers, it was the functions of language for social life. Kant had summarized his philosophy when he wrote: 'Two things fill the mind with ever new and increasing admiration and awe ... the starry heavens above me and the moral law within me.'[28] This way of viewing the problem points us in the direction of a correct solution to the problem of determinism: the existence of two separate *social roles* – that of the *objective observer* and that of the *moral self.*

* * * * * * * *

There are innumerable and conflicting definitions of social role in the literature, but it can be defined as a set of normative expectations (obligations and rights) structured around a particular social position. In modern society, it is virtually impossible to escape the tensions which arise out of the above two role perspectives. This is not only because of the ubiquity of activities influenced by the natural sciences, but also because of the growth of bureaucratic and legal procedures which give rise to a rationalizing perspective linked with the objective attitude. In law it is now common to appeal to deterministic criteria in mitigating the consequences of criminal behaviour; the law is of course the main area in which the notion of personal responsibility is activated, but appeals to mitigating medical and psychological handicaps have become increasingly common in the last few decades. The debate about capital

---

[28] Kant, *Critique of Practical Reason*, Conclusion.

punishment illustrates this theme: those who view it as a deterrent see it in term of objective consequences, whereas those demanding revenge and punishment are adopting the moral and subjective perspective. In legal situations, whether to define behaviour morally or medically is largely a question of choosing the language and assumptions of the two role attitudes. There is no intrinsic or technical criteria for making this choice, it must by the very different nature of the two perspectives, be a matter determined by other criteria: sympathy, social position, power and the ability to manipulate others to give favourable definitions.

The attitudes and behaviour in the two role situations will be fundamentally different: in one sense, we can say that the person fulfilling these two roles will feel him or herself to be a different person in the two situations. The two roles will elicit distinctive perceptions, emotions and physical responses, and if required to describe role behaviour, will generate different languages.

Of course, there are many considerations other than role behaviour in these situations, and in any one instance there will inevitably be a mixture of role responses. Social roles are clusters of ideal, normative expectations, which in practice are hardly ever enacted in pure form. There are innumerable other variables which determine any one type of behaviour, but for our purposes, it is sufficient to note that the distinction between objective observer and moral self is both logically valid and empirically fruitful. The role of the moral self is however more significant than that of objective observer, and is the most fundamental role in human society, with universal applicability. We are here dealing with matters of great complexity, and it will only be possible to touch on the most significant features of the moral self.

One complication in the analysis of the objective observer and the moral self roles is the prevalence of magical thinking in the earliest stages of human cultural evolution, which inhibited objective realism as well as complicated the analysis of the moral self. For example, James Morrill, who spent thirteen years living with the aborigines of Queensland in the middle part of the nineteenth century, described some of their beliefs as follows

> The moon *(werboonburra)*, they say is a human being, like themselves, and comes down on the earth, and they sometimes meet it in some of their fishing excursions. They say one tribe throws it up and it gradually rises and then comes down again, when another tribe catches it to save it from hurting itself ... They think the falling stars indicate the direction of danger, and that comets are the ghosts or spirits of some of their tribe, who have been killed at a distance from them, working their way back again ... They think all the heavenly bodies are under their control; and that when there is an eclipse, some of their tribe hide it [the sun] with a sheet of bark to frighten the rest ... But they are very uneasy during its continuance. They pick up a piece of grass and bite it, making a mumbling noise, keeping their eyes steadily fixed on it till it passes over, when they become easy again and can go to sleep comfortably. They think they have power over the rain *(durgun)* to make it come and go as they like.[29]

There is no doubt that magic was ubiquitous in tribal societies, although a number of anthropologists have pointed out that a belief in magic was limited by the existence of economic technology, which ensured a degree of objectivity. However, the existence of magic affected both the practice of objective realism and the attribution of personal responsibility. We are told of the Australian aborigines that 'they do not suppose that any one dies from natural causes, but [always] from human agencies', with a number of examples given of individuals punished and killed on account of the alleged use of magic.[30] Additionally, magic was frequently used as a mode of punishment or retaliation. If as Levy-Bruhl and

---

[29] J. Morrill, *Sketch of a Residence Among the Aboriginals of Northern Australia*, 1864, pp. 19, 20.
[30] B. Malinowski, *Magic, Science and Religion*, 1948.

others have argued, the ubiquity of magic eclipsed the distinction between individual self and a universal, spiritual and mystical reality, personal responsibility would be impossible. In practice, all tribal peoples do make such distinctions, so that for example, as Evans-Pritchard tells us of the Azande, 'if you tell a lie, or commit adultery or steal ... you cannot elude punishment by saying that you were bewitched.'[31] Tribal peoples do universally ascribe spiritual qualities to the self, but it is the necessity of individual responsibility which limits the extent of magical belief, and, along with technology, is responsible for the beginnings of objective realism.

However, some anthropologists – in particular Levy-Bruhl – have argued that no distinction was made in tribal societies between the individual self and other subjectively defined realities, and an authority of the stature of Marcel Mauss, has concluded that a full sense of the individual self only arose in the modern period. This is a matter of some controversy, and Mauss, who was very familiar with the anthropological evidence, qualified this conclusion by writing that

> In no way do I maintain that there has ever been a tribe, a language, in which the term 'I', 'me' *(je, moi)* ... has never existed, or that it has not expressed *something* clearly represented ... it is plain, particularly to us, that there has never existed a human being who has not been aware, not only of his body, but also at the same time of his individuality, both spiritual and physical.[32]

Steven Lukes has pointed out, if we leave aside more arcane theoretical considerations, there is a parallel in 'everyday

---

[31] E.E. Evans-Pritchard, *Witchcraft, Oracles and Magic among the Azande*, 1937, p. 74.

[32] M. Mauss, 'A category of the human mind: the notion of the person, the notion of the self', in Michael Carrithers et.al. (eds.), *The Category of the Person*, 1985, p. 3.

conceptions of the person', in our own culture and those ranging from classical China through· to tribal Africa.[33] The notion of an individual self is universal, and is as important and significant in tribal societies, as it is elsewhere. Reactions to death of a particular individual indicate that people in tribal societies display as much, if not more, grief than do modern Europeans. However, many tribal societies appear to confer less status on very young children and to some extent the very elderly, and therefore less importance is attached to loss of life in these categories than with other persons.

The pervasiveness and ubiquity of the concept of self requires special explanation. Our starting point must be the analysis of practical necessity, or to use a sociological term, functionality. Functionalism has been criticized because of the teleological nature of much of its argument, as well as its conservative ideological bias. It is however possible to restate the tenets of classical functionalism so as to overcome these objections. The seeds of this restatement are to be found in a passage by one of the founders of modern functionalism, Wilbert E. Moore:

The explicit introduction of system survival as a test of necessary consequences of human action and the structural mechanisms for producing those results perforce appealed to an evolutionary perspective. The argument must essentially be that various behaviours appear in human aggregates, some of which support or improve the viability of those aggregates and others that do not. Through natural selection those that contribute to system operation survive, and others are rejected. The same argument can be made for whole societies, whether in competition with other societies or simply coping with the challenges of the nonhuman environment. In the early explicit formulations of what came to be called 'functional requisite analysis' this evolutionary assumption was not articulated.[34]

---

[33] S. Lukes 'Conclusion', in Carrithers, *The Category*, p. 297.
[34] W.E. Moore, 'Functionalism', in T. Bottomore and R. Nisbet (eds.), *A History of Sociological Analysis*, 1978, p. 342.

This formulation of functionalism places it squarely in the Darwinian tradition, removing its teleological aspect, and allowing for objective causal analysis. Socially structured behaviour is seen as analogous to a biological structure; its existence is explained through natural selection, so that only those behaviours which enable social systems – and their individual members – to survive, will be selected. This process of selection is independent of human intention or meaning, although obviously human beings can rationally assess the probability of a particular mode of action ensuring their survival. The latter is associated with the role of the objective observer, which also ensures the survival of both individuals and societies. But much human social behaviour will not fall within this rational category, and this will include aspects of the role of the moral self. Given the non-rationality of much of the behaviour associated with this role, its universality must be explained in terms of its capacity to meet certain fundamental functional pre-requisites.

This approach can be linked with the revival of interest in cultural evolution, as well as the more recent development by Popper and others of evolutionary epistemology. Popper and Eccles have touched on the evolution of consciousness and the self as follows:

What is usually described as the unity of the self, or the unity of conscious experience, is most likely a partial consequence of biological individuation – of the evolution of organisms with inbuilt instincts for the survival of the individual organism. It seems that consciousness, and even reason, have evolved very largely owing to their survival value for the individual organism. ... The activity of the self, or the consciousness of self leads us to the question of what it does; of what function it performs, and so to a biological approach to the self.[35]

---

[35] K. Popper and J. Eccles, *The Self and Its Brain*, 1977, pp. 108, 114.

Popper and Eccles are undoubtedly correct in emphasizing the biological basis of the self, and it is the physical separateness· of individuals which forms the primary condition for an individual self. It is this biological fact which makes individuals crucial for all social structures and their functioning; the individual necessarily is the focus of all social action, and it is this fact which lays the foundation for the universality of the individual self. Popper has quite correctly pointed out the need to look at the functions of the self to fully understand the phenomenon, but his biological emphasis only provides an initial statement of the problem, and what is required to complete the analysis is a sociological perspective.

* * * * * * * *

The reference to the unity of the self must be our starting point. All the concepts that have been discussed in this regard – self, soul, ego, personal identity – are essentially the same phenomenon. It is only with such a category and social role, that continuity and consistency in thinking is possible, and this forms the basis of 'a thinking, willing I ... an essence that 'posits' its own acts, 'generates' and possesses psychic realities as its very own and is responsible for them ... the abiding and supporting principle of all ... conscious life.'[36] The fundamental function of such a unified self is that it enables individuals to be held responsible for their actions, and thus forms the basis of all moral and social action. A self which can be held responsible for its actions constitutes the indispensible functional pre-requisite for all normative and social behaviour, and without meeting this pre-requisite, it would be impossible for any group or social system to survive. It is thus for this reason that the concept of a private self or soul is found in all societies, for without this concept

---

[36] W. Brugger, K. Baker, *Philosophical Dictionary*, 1976, p. 381.

and primary social role, no society could continue to exist. The moral self is a social role which creates the coherent and organized set of attitudes which constitutes individual identity, the ego and the self. The major obligation attached to the role is the personal responsibility which underpins all normatively regulated social life; the major right, is the capacity for personal freedom. In order to be held personally responsible, it is necessary to have the freedom to enact that responsibility.

The anthropologist, Paul Radin, has perhaps most clearly recognized the importance of personal responsibility and freedom in tribal societies:

> Now the concept of *person* in aboriginal society involves a number of definite things. This is not due to any mystical or philosophical interest on the natives' part, but flows from the purely practical consideration that they wish to know with whom they are dealing and the nature of the person's responsibility. In civilizations where a belief in reincarnation, ancestor-identification, transformation, multiple souls, etc., is involved in the concept of personality, the nature of an individual's responsibility for a given act is of paramount importance.[37]

This tacitly concludes that language used is secondary to the social reality; the assumption of individual responsibility exists even where it is not articulated explicitly.

According to Radin, although it is social groups who have formal legal responsibility in tribal society, it is individuals who in practice are held responsible, particularly for those most highly personal of activities, murder and marriage.[38] These are the most dramatic examples, but in fact, the concept of personal responsibility is ubiquitous, as without it, even minor forms of social life would be impossible. This can be illustrated through Colin Turnball's study of the Mbuti

---

[37] P. Radin, *The World of Primitive Man*, 1953, p. 114.
[38] Ibid, p. 290.

pygmies. Turnball describes an incident in camp late one evening:

> Moke, very quietly, and talking as if only to the hunters but never lowering his arm or taking his eyes off Asuk, said, 'That is a completely bad man. I have been watching and I have seen with my eyes, and my spirit (*roho*) makes me speak. He makes noise all the time, and he is the cause of all the noise in the camp. I would like to throw him out forever.'[39]

Although responsibility is individual, the quality and context of it is different in tribal societies to what it is in modern European societies. Radin tells us

> That there is a 'spiritual' side to a wrongdoer's state of mind is obvious but no feeling of sin, in the Hebrew-Christian meaning of the term, is present. All that is demanded is the realisation that an individual has offended against the harmony of communal life. His punishment means the harmony has been re-established ... Human beings can disport themselves as they will. If they are ridiculous, they will be laughed at; if they commit crimes, they will be punished and then, if they wish, they may commit some more.[40]

This should not be read to imply that there is a lack of internalisation of moral codes amongst tribal peoples. Radin specifically tells us while discussing a myth, in which a man kills his wife and child during a period of famine, that 'he judges and punishes himself. It must be so if society is to persist.'[41] Individual responsibility is found in all societies, it is its quality and context which differs: tribal societies emphasize social harmony to a much greater degree than do contemporary European ones. Radin probably over-estimates the degree of individual responsibility in such societies; even in marriage and murder where he believes it to have been

---

[39] C. Turnball, *The Forest People,* 1961.
[40] Radin, *The World*, pp. 249, 257.
[41] Ibid, p. 330.

particularly strong, it was often the family or wider social unit which took responsibility, and certain categories of individual – for example women – lacked the power and personal independence necessary for the exercise of full responsibility. However, Radin is probably correct in his conclusion that all individuals, with full adult status, were held responsible for their actions in the last resort.

This transition from the status of childhood to that of adulthood is universal, and is linked to becoming a responsible subject:

> Full status was conferred on an individual at puberty and we all know the .elaborateness of these rites and their ubiquity. A person was then truly functioning sociologically. He was responsible for his actions; he had to face life independently, and he could marry and raise children.[42]

To hold someone responsible for their actions implies that the person in question is capable of independent action. It has been generally recognized that this form of voluntary action must entail an absence of physical constraint, and also an assumption of personal causality. The term causality is not used here in the classical mechanical sense, but rather with the primary meaning given to it by Aristotle: an attribution of motivation to independent agents. Nevertheless, we can say historically, the assumption of personal causality laid the foundation for the eventual development of objective realism, with its complete separation of subject and object.

This separation was only fully achieved with the development of modern science, which was a part of that process of rationalization which eclipsed magical thinking, at least in the mainstream of European culture. This has led to a crystallisation of the modern self, with the virtual elimination of the projected subjectivity which was involved in animism and magic. But this in no way diminishes the underlying

---

[42] Ibid, p. 80.

continuity of the moral self found throughout human history, based on the necessity of individual responsibility. Perhaps the greatest difference between the tribal and modern self is the extension of the category of personhood to very young children. In some tribal societies, young children are not considered full persons, and are sometimes killed during periods of great scarcity, through infanticide and other practices. This is consistent with our definition of a person in terms of responsibility, which in turn is linked to a capacity for practical action in economic and other spheres. The extension of personhood to young children is itself a sociological phenomenon, but that takes us away from our main concern, which is the analysis of the role of the moral self and its relationship to determinism.

* * * * * * * *

In 1962, Peter Strawson wrote, 'Freedom and Resentment', a paper which initiated the modern debate about the problem of determinism. It is impossible to do justice to the complexity and subtlety of Strawson's argument with a brief summary, but an indication of its central theme is given in the following quotation:

> What I want to contrast is the attitude (or range of attitudes) of involvement or participation in a human relationship, on the one hand, and what might be called the objective attitude (or range of attitudes) to another human being, on the other. Even in the same situation, I must add, they are not altogether *exclusive* of each other; but they are profoundly opposed to *each other*. To adopt the objective attitude to another human being is to see him, perhaps, as an object of social policy; as a subject for what, in a wide range of sense, might be called treatment; as something certainly to be taken account, perhaps precautionary account, of; to be managed or handled or cured or trained ... The objective attitude ... may include repulsion or fear; it may include pity or even love. But it cannot include the range of reactive feelings and attitudes which belong to involvement or

31

participation with others in inter-personal human relationships; it cannot include resentment, gratitude, forgiveness, anger, or the sort of love which two adults can sometimes be said to feel reciprocally, for each other.[43]

Strawson's contrast between the objective and participating attitudes is very similar to the distinction between the roles of objective observer and the moral self, except that Strawson emphasizes intentionality rather than personal responsibility, and he is not interested in a formal analysis of the two sets of attitudes. For Strawson, individuals can engage in emotionally reactive relationships because of their capacity to express intended and meaningful behaviour as free agents. To adopt the objective attitude towards a person is to remove their capacity to be fully human, to depersonalize them, and to reduce them to the status of objects. Strawson recognises that adoption of this objective attitude can allow the suspension of normal moral responses which might have humane consequences depending on the situation, but his main interest is the indispensability of the reactive attitude for the continuation of human relationships.

This analysis of the objective attitude has led to what Honderich has termed dismay at the consequences of determinism.[44] Honderich has extended Strawson's analysis to include the 'life hopes, personal feelings, knowledge, moral responsibility, actions and principles, and the general moral standing of agents.'[45] It is beyond the scope of this paper to discuss these themes, but it sufficient to note that all these problems, like those outlined by Berlin earlier, stem from a belief that determinism undermines the possibility of free, independent action. Only the existence of a self acting as an ultimate 'originator', without the interference of the mechanical effects of determinism, can guarantee the individual freedom which will

---

[43] P.F. Strawson, 'Freedom and Resentment' in Gary Watson (ed.), *Free Will*, 1982, p. 66.

[44] Honderich, *Mind*.

[45] Ibid, p.3.

not result in dismay. Anything else will reduce man to the status of a depersonalized object, incapable of genuine humanity. Honderich has attempted to solve this problem by postulating the possibility of self-affirmation, but this very solution requires the assumption of a self which is at the very centre of the problem itself.

The solution to the problem is contained in the recognition that the moral self is a social role that is totally distinct from that of the objective observer. Although both these social roles are subject to deterministic analysis – as are all forms of empirical reality when viewed from the perspective of the objective observer – the roles themselves generate entirely different modes of experience.

It might be argued that from the point of view of the objective observer the postulate of a moral self is an illusion, because it assumes a freedom of action which conflicts with the assumptions of determinism. And it is the scrutiny of the role of the moral self from the viewpoint of the objective observer that has given rise to the problem of dismay, outlined by Honderich and others. But the problem only arises through role confusion: from the viewpoint of the moral self, freedom is not an illusion – it is an indispensible necessity of personal and social life. In our roles as moral selves, determinism is irrelevant, and as reality is shaped largely by our role experiences, it is with the acceptance of this reality that the problem of dismay disappears. This has some similarity with Hume's acceptance of the reality of everyday life, except the dimension of role analysis allows us to understand much more clearly and profoundly the nature of this solution, and in certain respects it is closer to Kant's postulate or two realms than Hume's voluntaristic position.

In practice, role confusion is not just a personal matter, but is also sociologically determined. The role of objective observer has become much more prominent in our society through the growth of science, technology and medicine, and this almost inevitably has led to role conflict. In contemporary psychiatry, the mainstream theoretical perspective is deterministic, both in the biological/behavioural schools, and psychoanalytical/psychodynamic ones. The language used is that of the objective observer, but inevitably the terminology of the moral self is introduced because of the nature of the disciplines. Strawson observed this when noting

> ... the strain in the attitude of a psychoanalyst to his patient. His objectivity of attitude, his suspension of ordinary moral reactive attitudes, is profoundly modified by the fact that the aim of the enterprise is to make such suspension unnecessary or less necessary. Here we may and do naturally speak of restoring the agent's freedom.[46]

The aim of the psychoanalyst is to restore the capacity of the patient to become an independent person, to cease being a clinical object, but to become a full subject, capable of free and responsible action. This illustrates that most psychiatric disciplines use the concepts and assumptions of both role models in their work, but this is not inevitable. Behavioural therapy tends to deny the subjectivity of the patient, and sees its work in purely objective, physiological terms,[47] whereas existentialist therapy almost exclusively emphasizes the freedom of the subject. In this sense, existentialist therapy is a contradiction in terms, as in its pure form, it refuses to acknowledge terms such as mental illness, patient cure and the concept of therapy itself.[48] Definitions will of course vary depending on which role model is adopted, so that for example during the First World War, soldiers who refused to stay and fight in the trenches were either classified as malingerers and therefore punished, or defined as suffering from shell-shock and given medical treatment. The first treated the individual as a moral self, the second viewed him as a clinical object.

---

[46] Strawson, *'Freedom'*, p. 75.

[47] B.F. Skinner, *Beyond Freedom and Dignity*, 1971.

[48] T. Szasz, *The Myth of Mental Illness*, 1962.

From the army's point of view – leaving aside ethical considerations – there is the practical question as to which role definition was most effective in getting soldiers to return back to the trenches. Likewise we can ask whether psychoanalysis or the existentialist attitude – or a combination of both – is more effective in bringing about personal independence. The psychoanalyst will classically take the former role and concentrate on the causally determined sequence of events which take place in childhood; the existentialist will adopt the position of the moral self, and emphasize freedom and personal responsibility. In practice, the effectiveness of the different role definitions will depend on a number of factors, including the expectations of patients and persons concerned.

It has become a commonplace to see bureaucracy as a source of the type of alienation that can be associated with the objective attitude. The dominance of bureaucracy and the devaluation ·of individual responsibility, may have been one of the factors in the collapse of Soviet Communism – all systems need to attribute personal responsibility to function effectively.

Kafka's description of the bureaucratic nightmare is reminiscent of Heidigger's notion of 'unauthenticity' – a depersonalized and objectivised mode of being – a concept not all that different from Marx's alienation and Weber's 'disenchantment of the world'. The existentialists have given some of the most persuasive descriptions ·of personal alienation, and to quote Galen Strawson on Camus, 'When *l'etranger* alludes to one of his desires, it is half as if he were recounting a fact about a feature of the world which is extraneous to him – a spectator to his own actions.'[49] For existentialists the immediate resolution of this type of alienation is the restoration of the potency associated with a full acceptance of personal responsibility and the freedom of the moral self.

Sociological factors are of course crucial in both determining patterns of alienation and the conditions necessary

---

[49] G. Strawson, *Freedom and Belief*, 1986, p. 234.

for their resolution. A capacity for freedom is inextricably linked with the structure of power in any society which in turn is shaped by its economic and social conditions. For example, in order for women to be full and free subjects, they not only have to achieve equal status with men, but also have to acquire the freedom which comes with the abolition of economic scarcity and political oppression. The same would apply to slaves, lower castes and all oppressed groups.

Power is a critical dimension in the overcoming of this form of alienation, as power is intrinsically linked with the capacity for self-determination and the independence necessary for full personal responsibility and individual freedom. Ultimately the freedom of any one individual is linked with the freedom of all, but this is to raise a theme beyond the scope of the present paper. However it is appropriate to end with a positive conclusion: the distinction between the objective observer and the moral self resolves the problem of determinism, and in doing so, provides a clear intellectual foundation for the existence and practice of individual responsibility and freedom, along with the personal self-affirmation which flows from it.

Chapter 2: The Protestant Ethic and the Spirit of Capitalism: a Natural Scientific Critique.[50]

Max Weber's *The Protestant Ethic and the Spirit of Capitalism* is widely recognised as one of the most outstanding contributions made by a sociologist to the understanding of the origins and development of modern capitalist society. Yet Weber himself felt towards the end of his life that his thesis had been fundamentally misunderstood. Critics such as Sombart and Brentano had mistakenly assumed that he was concerned with the impact of religious ethical teaching on the development of practical economic conduct:

> We are interested rather in something entirely different: the influence of those psychological sanctions which, originating in religious belief and the practice of religion, gave a direction to practical conduct and held the individual to it ... This is, to speak frankly, the point of the whole essay, which I had not expected to find so completely overlooked.[51]

Since Weber's death the same kind of fundamental misinterpretation has repeatedly recurred: for example, two of the most important historians to comment on his work – R.H. Tawney and Kurt Samuelsson – have both assumed that it primarily concerned the ethical doctrines preached by the leaders of the Reformation,[52] rather than the psychological effects of

---

[50] First published in the *British Journal of Sociology,* Volume 28, Issue Number 1, 1977.

[51] M. Weber, *The Protestant Ethic and the Spirit of Capitalism*, 1930, pp. 97, 197, 217, fn 3. Weber also felt he had been misrepresented on the role of ethical doctrines on usury – this had not been a part of his main argument and has been a further source of misunderstanding of his work. See Ibid, pp. 200. 201.

[52] R.H. Tawney, 'Forward' to Weber, *The Protestant Ethic*; K. Samuelsson, *Religion and Economic Action*, 1957.

theological ideas propounded by them.[53] Much of this misunderstanding of Weber's thesis is due to its notoriously fragmented nature: not only did he develop it in a number of sociological works other than *The Protestant Ethic* but he made some of his most important analytical statements in the rather obscure footnotes that he later attached to this work. In some respects virtually all of his writings can be seen as relevant to the thesis, which appears to have reflected certain central personal preoccupations.[54]

The major aim of this paper is to clarify the basic nature of Weber's substantive argument, and to critically evaluate its logical validity. In order to understand this basic argument, it is necessary to examine the methodological assumptions which form a concealed but important part of his analysis. The central methodological viewpoint of this paper is diametrically opposed to that adopted by Weber: whereas he rejected sociology as a natural science in favour of a definition of it as a historical cultural discipline dealing at the explanatory level in subjective meanings and values, the present work assumes that sociology is a natural science which treats social actions and behaviour as objects to be explained in a deterministic and causal manner. Weber objected to explanations made in the form of uniform or universal generalisations and was particularly averse to the application of evolutionary concepts of the kind employed in biology.

I will argue that Weber's methodology was incapable of explaining the results of his substantive work on the protestant

---

[53] Weber wrote that *The Protestant Ethic* thesis was 'a contribution to the understanding of the manner in which ideas become effective forces in history.' Weber, *The Protestant Ethic*, p. 90. Weber summarised his position about the role of ideas as follows: 'Not ideas, but material and ideal interests, directly govern men's conduct. Yet very frequently the 'world images' that have been created by 'ideas' have, like switchmen, determined the tracks along which action has pushed by the dynamic of interest.' H.H. Gerth and C. Wright Mills, *From Max Weber*, 1948, p. 280.
[54] See A. Mitzman, *The Iron Cage: An Historical Interpretation of Max Weber*, 1970.

ethic thesis, and that he was forced by the logic of his own analysis to continually resort to the evolutionary concept of rationalization. Weber's thesis, however, leads into complex areas beyond an evolutionary perspective, the most important being the psychological consequences of the growth of scientific thinking (anxiety and guilt resulting from disenchantment). Again, it is argued that only a natural scientific, psychological, perspective can adequately account for the results of his substantive work. However, no amount of further analysis can solve the problem posed at the beginning of the protestant ethic thesis: Why did the process of rationalization occur in so many different spheres of social life in the occidental world, and not elsewhere? No attempt will be made to discuss this question in this paper, except where it has a bearing on the mode of Weber's own analysis.

The above summary can only give the most important outlines of the arguments involved, and to fully understand the issues arising out of Weber's work it is necessary to carefully consider a wide range of his methodological and substantive writings. Weber can be classified as a neo-Kantian with respect to his most fundamental methodological assumptions. Kant's distinction between the realm of 'physical nature' and the realm of 'individual freedom' is reflected in the following statement made by Weber:

> ... every single important activity and ultimately life as a whole, if it is not to be permitted to run on as an event of nature but is instead to be consciously guided, is a series of ultimate decisions through which the soul – as in Plato – chooses its own fate, i.e. the meaning of its activity and existence.[55]

---

[55] M. Weber, *The Methodology of the Social Sciences*, 1949, p. 18. For a similar distinction made by Weber – between 'freedom of action' and the 'process of nature' – see D. Wrong (ed.), *Max Weber*, 1970, p. 111. Also J.P. Mayer, *Max Weber and German Politics*, 1956, p. 35.

Kant distinguished the science of physics from that of ethics, with the former formulating 'laws of nature' and the latter dealing with 'laws of freedom'.[56] This distinction was incorporated into Rickert's classification of the sciences into the 'natural' and the 'historical cultural' sciences – a classification accepted by Weber.[57] Although Weber was a thorough-going historical determinist,[58] the neo-Kantian distinction between the natural and historical cultural sciences had a fundamental influence on his methodological assumptions. He made a number of statements which reflected Rickert's influence in this respect:

> We can accomplish something which is never attainable in the natural sciences, namely the subjective understanding of the action of the component individuals. The natural sciences on the other hand cannot do this, being limited to the formulation of causal uniformities in objects and events and the explanation of individual facts by applying them ... subjective understanding is the specific characteristic of sociological knowledge.[59]

It is a commonplace in the sociological literature that Weber attempted to combine and integrate the methods of both the natural and historical cultural sciences, but, in fact, he attempted this integration only to a very limited extent. The natural scientific part of Weber's methodology was his acceptance of the necessity of empirical proof as a part of an historical determinist analysis; it was at the level of theoretical explanation, not the empirical testing of ideas, that he adopted the non-scientific methodology of 'subjective understanding'. The contradiction between the determinism of his empirical historicism and the voluntarism of his explanatory methodology seems to have

---

[56] T.K. Abbott (ed.), *Kant's Theory of Ethics*, 1927, p. 1.
[57] Weber, *Methodology*, p. 135.
[58] Ibid, p. 123; W.G. Runciman, *A Critique of Max Weber's Philosophy of Social Science*, 1972, p. 50.
[59] Max Weber, *Economy and Society*, 1968, Volume 1, p. 15.

escaped him, and the tension between a natural scientific explanation and a subjectivist methodology was never resolved:

> ... the more precisely they (uniformities) are formulated from a point of view of natural science, the less they are accessible to subjective understanding. This is never the road to interpretation in terms of subjective meaning. On the contrary, both for sociology in the present, and for history, the object of cognition is the subjective meaning complex of action.[160]

The polarity between natural scientific and meaningful explanations was reflected in the assertion that 'meaningfulness naturally does not coincide with laws as such, and the more general the law the less coincidence.'[61] Not only did Weber emphasize this contrast but in some sense defined the aim of his own work as combating the natural scientific method, particularly when applied to the study of human affairs.[62] The reasons for Weber's hostility to the natural sciences are complex. He had a dislike of the reduction of 'profound' metaphysical and religious preoccupations to questions answerable in terms of specialized technique and believed that the natural scientific attitude led to the 'disenchantment of the world':

> ... if these natural sciences lead to anything in this way, they are apt to make the belief that there is such a thing as the 'meaning' of the universe die out at its very roots.[63]

---

[60] Weber, *Economy and Society*, p. 13.

[61] Weber, *Methodology*, pp. 76-7.

[62] Ibid, pp. 186-7.

[63] Gerth and Mills, *From Max Weber*, p. 152. Weber's analysis of the 'disenchantment of the world' appears to have been grounded on changes in his own personal religious beliefs. Mayer, *Max Weber*, pp. 24, 25, 117. As a result of 'meaningfulness' associated with religious faith, 'the intellectual seeks in various ways, the casuistry of which extends into infinity, to endow his life with a pervasive meaning, and thus to find unity with himself, with his fellow men, and with the cosmos.' M. Weber, *The Sociology of Religion*, 1965, pp. 124, 125.

It was partly for this reason that he hated 'intellectualism as the worst Devil',[64] although his attitude towards scientific rationality was characterized by a complex and confused ambivalence.

His hostility to the natural sciences was linked to the belief that there was an inevitable quality to the development of the 'iron cage' of rationality; this largely explains his fascination with the distinctive rationality of the occidental world and his constant return to the impact of scientific thinking in his sociological work. But although this process of rationalization might appear to be itself a uniform generalisation of the type favoured by the natural sciences, Weber was concerned to combat just such an iron sense of scientific inevitability:

When modern biology subsumed those aspects of reality which interested us *historically,* i.e. in all their concreteness, under a universally valid evolutionary principle, which at least had the appearance – but not the actuality – of embracing everything essential about the subject in a scheme of universally valid laws, this seemed to be the final twilight of all evaluative standpoints in all the sciences ... the naturalistic viewpoint in certain decisive problems has not yet been overcome.[65]

From this point of view, it might be said that it was Darwin's ghost, and not Marx's, that most haunted Weber.

---

[64] Gerth and Mills, *From Max Weber*, p. 152. Weber's wife Marianne, in her biography of Weber, revealed a very important aspect of his attitude towards northern protestant culture as follows: 'Everywhere [in Sicily] she saw a sight not offered in the big cities in the north: families with a childlike happiness despite their poverty. Of course the travellers [the Webers] could not really feel at home among these people who lived in the present, enjoyed their brief lives unquestionably, and apparently desired only to be happy. They simply took things as they came and did not seem to struggle or to strive for higher things.' See M. Weber, *Max Weber: a Biography*, 1975, p. 364.
[65] Weber, *Methodology*, pp. 86, 87.

The above passage indicates Weber's own interest in the study of history: 'the understanding of the characteristic uniqueness of the reality in which we move'.[66] The historical cultural sciences were primarily interested in the unique and concrete flow of particular historical events; analytical uniformities and generalizations might be occasionally useful as heuristic devices for understanding historical reality but this was rarely the case as 'the specific meaning which a phenomenon has for us is naturally not to be found in those relationships which it shares with many other phenomena'.[67] It is for this reason that the ideal types employed by Weber are not analytical concepts but are 'ideal' categories used for understanding the concrete motives of individuals in the actual historical process. This emphasis on individual action explains the sociological testament written by Weber towards the end of his life:

> ... if I have become a sociologist (according to my letter of accreditation) it is mainly to exorcise the spectre of collective conceptions which still lingers among us. In other words, sociology itself can only proceed from the actions of one or more separate individuals and must therefore adopt strictly individualistic methods.[68]

One of the most important of these individualistic methods is of course the ideal type. In order to understand Weber's use of this much abused term it is necessary to see it not only in terms of his individualism but also his 'idealistic' concern for subjective meanings and value commitments. His problem was the construction of conceptual tools and methodological assumptions which would allow him to undertake an analysis of social meanings and cultural values 'logically in exactly the

---

[66] Ibid, p. 72.

[67] Ibid, pp. 76, 77.

[68] W. Mommsen, 'Max Weber's political sociology and his philosophy of world history', *International Social Science Journal*, Volume XVII, 1965, p. 44, fn 2.

same way as causal analysis of personal actions.'[69] In this idealistic formula, Weber is attempting to bridge the gap between individual actions and social values, but we shall see there are good logical reasons why he failed in this. It is not possible here to discuss Weber's rather tortuous and confused analysis of ideal types but we may note the difficulty he had in constructing this conceptual bridge. He was forced to resort to metaphysical language to attempt to resolve this problem; e.g. in discussing ideal typical analysis of political structures he wrote:

I am making it explicit to myself and others in an *interpretative* way the concrete, individual, and on that account, in the last analysis, unique form in which 'ideas' – to employ for once a metaphysical usage – are 'incorporated' into or 'work themselves out' in the political structure in question ... [70]

This resort to metaphysical language was in spite of an explicit rejection elsewhere of metaphysical notions such as a 'group mind' and the 'Hegelian idea' from which the individual components 'emanate'.[71] Although Weber rejected such philosophical idealism, in practice he smuggled some of its assumptions back into his work through constructs like the ideal type – and in this respect he was a methodological rather than a philosophical idealist.

It was on the basis of these methodological assumptions that Weber undertook to explain the process of historical change in terms of the motivations of individuals, so that for example when he discussed the origin of socialist communities he formulated the problem as follows:

The real empirical sociological investigation begins with the question: What motives determine and lead the individual

---

[69] Weber, *Methodology*, p. 177.
[70] Ibid, p. 157.
[71] Weber, *Economy and Society*, p. xxxviii.

members and participants in this socialistic community to behave in such a way that the community came into being in the first place and that it continues to exist?[72]

The central logical difficulty of a sociological explanation made in terms of these methodological assumptions – what Parsons has called a voluntaristic theory of social action – was pointed out by Durkheim in his *Rules of Sociological Method*:

> Where purpose reigns, there reigns also a more or less wide contingency; for there are no ends, and even fewer means, which necessarily control all men ... If, then, it were true that historic development, took place in terms of ends clearly or obscurely felt, social facts should present the most infinite diversity; and all comparison should almost be impossible.[73]

Of course where ends and values are brought about by social or biological forces (environment and heredity) social facts can be the apparent result of purposive choices, but such choices simply become intermediary psychological processes between one social (or biological) fact and another. It is for this reason that Durkheim insisted that one social fact must be explained by another social fact, although he has other reasons for invoking the social which border on the metaphysical. In principle there is no logical reason why a social fact cannot be derived from a biological one, but given the fundamental biological similarity of human beings in all societies the only social facts to be explained by biological factors must necessarily be universally applicable to all social situations. (Perhaps an example of this type is to be found in universal differences in social role between the sexes – although there are some sociologists who would dispute the assumption that these differences are due to biological distinctions.)

---

[72] Ibid, p. 18.
[73] E. Durkheim, *The Rules of Sociological Method*, 1964, p. 94.

Whatever the role of biological factors in universal cultural facts, it is indisputable that societal *variations* cannot be explained by an unchanging *constant* factor such as man's biological nature (this assumes that there are no significant biological variations from one society to another). Similarly, voluntaristic choices made by individuals uninfluenced by environmental factors must necessarily result in a set of randomized personal aims. The most appropriate image to convey this effect is the statistician's scatter diagram: plot a number of individual points unrelated to each other and the result will be the absence of any focus or trend in the distribution of the points – in sociological terms an absence of a social fact involving shared expectations and social meanings.

Weber himself appears at times to have been aware of this logical difficulty in any voluntaristic theory of the origin of social factors. For example in The Protestant Ethic he wrote that

> In order that a manner of life so well adapted to the peculiarities of capitalism could be selected at all, i.e. should come to dominate others, it had to originate somewhere, and not in isolated individuals alone, but as a way of life common to whole groups of men.[74]

But it was at this point of trying to explain the origin of 'a way of life common to whole groups of men' that Weber had the greatest difficulty. With some perplexity he stated at the beginning of *The Protestant Ethic:*

> When we find again and again that, even in departments of life apparently mutually independent certain types of rationalization have developed in the Occident, and only there, it would be natural to suspect that the most important reason lay in differences of heredity. The author admits that he is inclined to

---

[74] Weber, *Protestant Ethic*, p. 55.

think the importance of biological heredity very great. But ... it must be one of the tasks of sociological and historical investigation first to analyse all the influences and causal relationships which can be satisfactorily explained in terms of reaction to environmental conditions.[75]

Elsewhere, Weber speculated on the possibility that 'there are typical relations between ... certain kinds of rationality and the cephalic index or skin colour or any other biologically inherited characteristic.'[76] We do not have to dwell on this flirtation with racialist ideas, but merely note here that most sociologists would now reject the notion of racially determined culture patterns on empirical grounds. However, in the present context, the importance of these statements is that they reveal Weber's uncertainty about explaining 'a way of life common to whole groups of men', such as the protestant ethic. His reference to an explanation in terms of environmental conditions is paradoxical, for he makes it very clear in his methodological writings that he is primarily interested in historical explanations – and although he occasionally invokes factors such as the geographical environment, this is seen by him as a heuristic device along with the other modes of natural scientific analysis for the main business of meaningful explanation of unique historical sequences. As one scholar of Weber's works has recently put it: 'Since he was concerned with the unique course of Western rationalization, he did not view it as a generic phenomenon ....'[77]

In a number of places however, Weber wrote of the growth of scientific rationality as if it were an inevitable general 'law of development':

---

[75] Ibid, pp. 30, 31.

[76] M. Weber, *The Theory of Social and Economic Organisation,* 1947, p. 85.

[77] R. Bendix, G. Roth, *Scholarship and Partisanship: Essays on Max Weber,* 1971, p. 114.

The increasing intervention of enacted norms is, from our point of view, only one of the components, however characteristic, of that process of rationalization and association whose growing penetration into all spheres of social action we shall have to trace as a most essential dynamic factor in development.[78]

We have already seen how Weber believed that the growth of scientific thinking applied to many spheres of life in the occidental world and there are a number of other references to this process of general rationalization in his work, e.g. his statement in *The Methodology of the Social Sciences* that rationalization applies 'not only to a history of philosophy and to the history of any other intellectual activity but ... to every kind of history.'[79] He was careful however, as we have seen, to dissociate himself from metaphysical notions of history embodying 'a group mind' or the development of the Hegelian 'idea', as well as rejecting the natural scientific conception of analytical laws of development.

This rejection of laws of development can be seen in part as a legitimate objection to the tendency of reifying the growth of scientific rationality into a metaphysical proposition – and Weber appears to have had Marx particularly in mind when he formulated this objection, as well as contemporaries of his such as Sombart.[80] But it is clear that Weber's position on this was also determined by his commitment to the historical cultural sciences and antagonism to naturalistic methodology.

However, Weber was forced by the logic of his own arguments to refer constantly to a 'law of development' in order to explain the process of rationalization. His most explicit reference to this is contained in the footnotes appended to *The Protestant Ethic* and is made in the context of a discussion of economic determinism:

---

[78] Weber, *Economy and Society,* Vol. 1, p. 333.
[79] Weber, *Methodology,* p. 34.
[80] Ibid, p. 103; Weber, *Protestant Ethic,* pp. 76, 77, 284.

... religious ideas themselves simply cannot be deduced from economic circumstances. They are in themselves, that is beyond doubt the most powerful plastic elements of national character, and contain a law of development and a compelling force entirely their own.[81]

Weber refers to 'autonomous laws' in other parts of his work and even uses evolutionary terminology, e.g. in his sociological study of music he states that 'rationalization proper commences with the evolution of music into a professional art', and this is only one of a number of references to evolutionary rationalization in the sphere of music.[82]

Although Weber was prepared to concede that any one historical development was the result of the interaction of a number of forces – economic, political, religious etc. – in practice his prime interest was in tracing the influence of religious rationalization. It is in this area of his work that he came nearest to formulating universal sociological principles:

Scientific progress is a fraction, the most important fraction, of the process of intellectualisation which we have been undergoing for thousands of years ... this intellectualist rationalization ... means that principally there are no mysterious incalculable forces that come into play, but rather that one can, in principle, master all things by calculation. This means that the world is disenchanted.[83]

This process of intellectualisation is based on

---

[81] Weber, *The Protestant Ethic*, pp. 277, 278.

[82] M. Weber, *The Rational and Social Foundations of Music*, 1958, pp. 40, 41, 106, 107.

[83] Gerth and Mills, *From Max Weber*, pp. 138, 139.

the metaphysical needs of the human mind as it is driven to reflect on ethical and religious questions, driven not by material need but by an inner compulsion to understand the world as a meaningful cosmos and to take up a position towards it.[84]

It is this rationalization of metaphysical ideas that presumably constitutes the law of development of religious ideas referred to above.

Although this law of development appears at first sight to be an example of a non-naturalistic 'idealistic' law, there is no reason why if it is stated in appropriate language it should not be accepted as a proper scientific proposition. The growth of scientific thinking can be defined as a variable in continuum form which characterizes the process of social change; it is possible to see rationality as an emergent property of the human mind based on the biological structure of the human brain, a product of the process of natural selection during man's biological evolution.

The theme of rationalization has played a dominant intellectual role since at least the period of the Enlightenment, and nearly all the classic theories of social change have either explicitly or implicitly invoked the principle. Perhaps the most important sociological exponents of this principle other than Weber were Comte and Marx: Comte used the principle and applied it to a notion of general cultural development primarily at the level of ideas; Marx applied it to developments of technology and the means of production. As we have seen, Weber himself was primarily interested in the rationalization of man's need to understand the meaning of his life at a metaphysical level – and these very metaphysical questions were seen by him even in the first instance, as a function of rationality itself.[85] None of these

---

[84] Weber, *Sociology of Religion*, pp. 116, 117.
[85] Ibid, pp. 3, 6.

theorists satisfactorily answer the fundamental question as to why the growth of scientific thinking takes place in one society rather than another – in Weber's case of course the question being why did it develop so markedly in the occidental world and not elsewhere.

This argument about Weber's use of the concept of rationalization does not mean that he had abandoned an attempt to overcome the 'naturalistic dogma'. As we have seen, he did not recognize the law of development of rationalization as being a natural scientific proposition, and it is clear that his neo-Kantian voluntarism profoundly influenced his analysis of the development of the protestant ethic. In his General Economic History he wrote:

> In all times there has been but one means of breaking down the power of magic and establishing a rational conduct of life; this means is great rational prophecy.[86]

And a prophet according to Weber was 'a purely individual bearer of charisma'[87] – and 'charisma knows only inner determination and inner constraint'.[88] Frequently Weber writes of charisma as if it were the source of the deep personal individual freedom that he admired so much; other times he sees it as a function of irrational forces often of a biological nature. The association of charisma with irrationality is seen by him as leading to unfreedom – and freedom here is seen as a function of a rationally developed ethic. This contradiction is the result of a marked ambivalence on Weber's part towards both rationality and charisma which come to have a different significance depending on the context in which he is using them.

---

[86] M. Weber, *General Economic History*, 1961, p. 265.

[87] Weber, *Sociology of Religion*, p. 46.

[88] S.N. Eisenstadt (ed.), *Max Weber on Charisma and Institution Building*, 1968, p. 20.

The two forces of reason and charisma between them account for all the most important historical and social changes:

> In traditionally stereotyped periods, charisma is the greatest
> revolutionary force. The equally revolutionary force of reason
> works from without by altering the situations of action, and hence
> its problems, finally in this way changing men's attitudes towards
> them; or it intellectualizes the individual.[89]

There are obvious difficulties with this idea of charisma bringing about accumulative social changes. Inasmuch as the concept is used to refer to the profoundly personal creation of ultimate values,[90] all the logical objections to voluntaristic theories of action discussed earlier in the paper would apply. Charisma in itself will over a, long enough period of time and from one social situation to another neutralize itself through a process of randomization, except where it is influenced by a socially structured set of influences. But pure charisma as such is an individual phenomenon and analytically must be sharply distinguished from socially determined facts. Of course it is possible to imagine a single individual's charisma being so powerful as to overwhelm all rival charismas, but this could only account for the influence of charisma on a limited single cultural situation defined by the immediate contacts of the charismatic leader. Any influence beyond this will be expressed through ideas and thus becomes subject to the principle of randomization in the absence of socially determined choices. Sociological facts of the stature of capitalist culture had to originate 'not in isolated individuals alone, but as a way of life common to whole groups of men'. In actual historical situations charisma is associated with the

---

[89] Ibid, pp. 53, 54.
[90] For an example of this see Weber's stress on Luther's personal experience and its importance for the disappearance of monasticism. Weber, *Protestant Ethic*, p. 121.

complete range of ideas and ethics, so that for example the charisma of the Protestant Reformers no doubt can be matched by that of their Jesuit opponents.

The analysis of the development of the protestant ethic appears to contain equal emphasis on the role of both intellectual growth and charismatic innovation. The former refers basically to the level of ideas and changes in theological thinking; the latter to innovations in ethical doctrine propounded by the charismatic leaders of the Reformation. In this context it is easy to understand how many commentators on Weber's work have mistakenly assumed that ethical teaching was the major variable in the analysis. The question must be raised as to why Weber insisted that theological ideas had causal priority over ethical doctrine. The answer lies, I believe, in his uneasy awareness of the logical problems of voluntaristic explanations including those made in terms of charisma. Of course the same problem could be raised with respect to theological ideas which can be said to also originate through the innovations of particular individuals.

The difference is that developments of ideas can be classified according to the principle of increasing rationality, whereas there is no obvious equivalent principle with which to classify changes in ethical doctrine. Weber did talk about the rationalization of ethical life, but although he is using the term rationalization here in a somewhat different sense to that used when applied to the level of ideas, in the last resort the concept returns the analysis back to the process of intellectualization associated with the development of ideas.

It is now possible to understand why Weber not only gave priority to theological ideas in his analysis of the protestant ethic but also why he laid so much stress on Calvinist theology. According to Weber, Calvin's doctrine is derived not, as with Luther, from religious experience, but from logical necessity of his thought; therefore its importance increases with every increase in the logical consistency of that religious thought.[91]

Logical consistency is one of Weber's main criteria of rationality and was viewed by him as the most important characteristic defining theological rationality. It might be thought that he chose Calvinist theology as a key starting point of his analysis on empirical grounds, i.e. that he believed it to be empirically the most important of the theological doctrines that he considered. But Weber showed an uneasy awareness of a major problem in this part of his analysis:

> ... the types of moral conduct in which we are interested may be found in a similar manner among the adherents of the most various denominations ... similar ethical maxims may be correlated with very different dogmatic foundations ... It would almost seem as though we had best completely ignore both the dogmatic foundations and the ethical theory and confine our attention to the moral practice so far as it can be determined.[92]

Weber went on to reject this difficulty on empirical grounds, although he produced no evidence in any of his work to show that the Calvinists were any more thoroughly committed to the protestant ethic than any of the other Puritan groups with different theologies – such as the Arminian Quakers and Wesleyan Methodists. In fact a cursory examination of the evidence reveals that if anything the contrary is true and it is difficult to believe that Weber was unaware of this. If Calvinist theology was not chosen on empirical grounds – and Weber does not cite any evidence in support of this – it is likely that it was selected on theoretical grounds, specifically because of Weber's pre-occupation with finding out 'whose intellectual child'[93] the

---

[91] Ibid, p. 102.
[92] Ibid, p. 97.
[93] Ibid, p. 78.

protestant ethic was in terms of the dominant notion of rationalization.

The logical consistency of Calvinist theology was outlined by Weber in a brief passage in *The Protestant Ethic*:

> To assume that human merit or guilt played a part in determining; this destiny (of man) would be to think of God's absolute free decrees, which have been settled from eternity, as subject to change by human influence, an impossible contradiction ... His quite incomprehensible decrees have decided the fate of every individual and regulated the tiniest details of the cosmos from eternity.[94]

In other words, if God is viewed as being totally omnipotent and omniscient – as Christians have traditionally assumed – it is logically impossible by definition for him not to know the results of his creative activities before the actual creation of the universe. It is also by definition impossible for such a God to diminish his own power and transfer part of it to man in the form of free-will – such a transfer would limit his power, contradicting his total omnipotence. Weber's arguments about the psychological consequences of the Calvinist belief in pre-destination are very familiar and need only be touched on briefly here. The Calvinist is faced with the problem of reconciling his need for salvation with his belief that it is impossible for him either to know or to be able to influence his salvation in any way. This creates acute metaphysical anxiety which is dealt with (this solution evolves over time) through using the ethical notion of success in one's calling as a 'sign' of salvation.

Weber goes to great pains to point out that this solution is a psychological not a logical one to the problems posed by a belief in predestination – according to him, the logical outcome is 'fatalistic resignation', but the Calvinist does not follow this path because of his

---

[94] Ibid, pp. 103, 104.

overwhelming need to 'prove' himself in the face of his omnipotent God (the Calvinist's economic interests and social class position also predispose him to accept this illogical solution).[95] The doctrine of predestination creates a decisive psychological motive in the form of anxiety which is channelled into the active performance of a calling through the need of the Calvinist to prove himself.

The doctrine of proving oneself before God was postulated by Weber as being common to all Puritan groups[96] – and inasmuch as it was a part of the Christian ethic it was a doctrine common to all Christians.[97] This however poses a problem in Weber's analysis, for on the one hand he states that the doctrine was a part of the 'Christian ethic' and on the other that 'the actual evolution to the proof of faith through works, which is the characteristic of asceticism, is parallel to a gradual modification of the doctrines of Calvin'.[98] Implicit in the latter statement is the idea that the Calvinist's belief in predestination had somehow led to a natural development of evolving the doctrine of proof – yet this doctrine would have been associated with Calvin's original body of ethics as a part of the 'Christian ethic'. Weber's analysis could always be rescued from this objection by emphasizing the role of 'practical interests' in determining the ethical consequences of the Calvinist's belief in predestination,[99] but this begins to shift the emphasis heavily away from a 'spiritualistic' explanation towards an economic one.

Weber does however at one point relate the doctrine of proof to the mainstream of his sociological analysis:

---

[95] Ibid, p. 232.
[96] Gerth and Mills, *From Max Weber*, p. 321.
[97] Weber, *Sociology of Religion*, p. 203.
[98] Weber, *Protestant Ethic*, p. 228.
[99] Ibid, p. 232.

Grace could not be guaranteed by any magical sacraments, by relief in the confession, nor by individual good works. That was only possible by proof in a specific type of conduct unmistakably different from the way of life of the natural man. From that followed for the individual an incentive methodically to supervise his own state of grace in his own conduct, and thus to penetrate it with asceticism.[100]

This returns the discussion of rationalization – the elimination of magical sacraments and religious ritual through the growth of scientific rationality. Weber distinguished a 'subjectively rational' action from 'one which uses the objectively correct means in accord with scientific knowledge'.[101] Although he did not explicitly state that the elimination of magic is due to the growth of scientific rather than subjective rationality, this is implicit in his analysis, i.e. it is the development of a rational scientific emphasis on empirical observations rather than the internal logical rationalization of magic itself, which is important in its disappearance.

Weber believed that this process played a key role in cultural development:

the complete elimination of salvation through the Church and the sacraments (in Puritanism) ... was what formed the absolutely decisive difference from Catholicism. That great historic process in the development of religions, the elimination of magic from the world which had begun with the old Hebrew prophets and, in conjunction with Hellenistic scientific thought, had repudiated all magical means to salvation as superstition and sin, came here (in Puritanism) to its logical conclusion. The genuine Puritan even rejected all signs of religious ceremony at the grave and buried his nearest and dearest without song or ritual in order that no superstition, no trust in the effects of magical and sacramental forces on salvation, should creep in.[102]

---

[100] Ibid, p. 153.
[101] Weber, *Methodology*, p. 34.
[102] Weber, *Protestant Ethic*, pp. 105, 106.

The consequence of the elimination of magic was that

> There was no place for the very human Catholic cycle of sin, repentance, atonement, release, followed by renewed sin. The moral conduct of the average man was thus deprived of its planless and unsystematic character and subjected to a consistent method for conduct as a whole.[103]

This displacement of magic was not confined to any one Puritan denomination; according to Weber they were all equally affected by the process.[104] One of the most important features of the elimination of magic was the disappearance of the confessional: 'it was a psychological stimulus to the development of their (the puritans') ethical attitude. The means to a periodical discharge of the emotional sense of sin was done away with'.[105]

Although Weber did not develop this theme about the psychological consequences of the disappearance of institutional magic, he made a number of isolated points which are capable of being formulated more systematically. One of the consequences of the diminution of the role of the church and its administration of sacred ritual was that the puritan's 'intercourse with his God was carried on in deep spiritual isolation'[106] and there 'was a feeling of unprecedented inner loneliness'.[107] The elimination of 'the doctrine of salvation through the Church' culminated in the Quaker doctrine of the 'significance of the inner testimony of the Spirit in reason and conscience'.[108] The final result of this process is

---

[103] Ibid, p. 117.
[104] Ibid, p. 119.
[105] Ibid, p. 106.
[106] Ibid, p. 107.
[107] Ibid, p. 104.
[108] Ibid, p. 149.

that distinctive type of guilt and, so to speak, godless feeling of sin which characterises modern man precisely as a consequence of his organisation of ethics in the direction of a system based on an inner religious state, regardless of the metaphysical basis upon which the system was originally erected.[109]

The similarity of this part of Weber's analysis with that made by Durkheim in *Suicide* is too striking to be ignored. The elimination of institutionalized magic and ritual activities was seen by Durkheim as leading to an increase in the rate of 'egoistic' suicide – an increase due to a decline in the amount of integration between the protestant individual and his religious institutions (using this term to refer to both belief and activity). Integration protects the individual from excessive reliance on himself which when carried to the extreme produces deep feelings of melancholy and eventually suicide. Weber and Durkheim disagreed about the role of the growth of science in bringing about these results: Durkheim saw the intellectualism of the 'egoist' as a by-product of general social disintegration rather than as a causal factor in the process. Neither Weber nor Durkheim gives an adequate account of how religious institutions function to protect individuals from these feelings of anxiety, guilt and depression, for they both lacked a satisfactory psychological framework necessary to achieve such an explanation.

Although Weber's interpretations of social psychological situations are couched exclusively in ordinary language, it is possible to trace a set of psychological assumptions about the nature of the protestant ethic which are very similar to the postulates of psychoanalysis. When discussing puritan attitudes towards sport Weber wrote:

> Sport was accepted if it served a rational purpose, that of recreation necessary for physical efficiency. But as a means for the spontaneous expression of undisciplined impulses, it was

---

[109] Weber, *Sociology of Religion*, p. 206.

under suspicion; and in so far as it became purely a means of enjoyment, or awakened pride, raw instincts or the irrational gambling instinct, it was of course strictly condemned. Impulsive enjoyment of life, which leads away from work in a calling and from religion, was as such the enemy of rational asceticism ...'[110]

The contrast between rational self-control on the one hand and the irrational acting out of impulses on the other is very similar to the distinction made by Freud between the super-ego and the id. The similarity is perhaps more clearly revealed by a comment by Weber on the relationship between the protestant ethic and sexuality:

Rational ascetic alertness, self-control, and methodical planning of life are seriously threatened by the peculiar irrationality of the sexual act, which is ultimately and uniquely unsusceptible to rational organisation.[111]

The language used by Weber in these passages reveals a meaning of the word 'rational' which extends that already discussed in connection with intellectual rationality: ethical rationality is the equivalent of the constraint of biological and emotional impulses which by their very nature threaten the deliberate and conscious reflection of intellectual rationality. From the other side, intellectual rationality is in part responsible for the suppression of sexual spontaneity; historically there had been

a gradual turning away from the naive naturalism of sex. The reason and significance of this evolution, however, involve the universal rationalization and intellectualization of culture.[112]

---

[110] Weber, *Protestant Ethic*, p. 167.
[111] Weber, *Sociology of Religion*, p. 238.
[112] Gerth and Mills, *From Max Weber*, p. 344.

Weber saw the results of this 'turning away from the naive naturalism of sex' in very much the same way as did Freud: the sublimation of sexual energy into work and rationality. Weber summarized his position when writing that

> the rejection of all naive surrender to the most intensive ways of experiencing existence, artistic and erotical, is as such only a negative attitude. But it is obvious that such a rejection could increase the force with which energies flow into rational achievement, both the ethical as well as the purely intellectual.[113]

Weber (like Freud) was ambivalent about this process of sublimation of sexual and emotional energy, for rationality can proceed in a variety of directions; positively in that of a conscious intellectualization of ultimate values; or negatively, at the expense not only of custom, but of emotional values.[114] It was presumably these negative consequences that led Weber to· view 'intellectualism as the worst devil'.[115]

The characteristics of the protestant ethic – 'rational ascetic alertness, self-control, and methodical planning of life' – are not according to Weber confined specifically to a religious context but are also the ethical qualities included in the definition of the secularized spirit of capitalism. The title of Weber's thesis is rather misleading in this respect: it suggests that the protestant ethic is a causally significant determinant of the independent spirit of capitalism, but it is clear from his methodological writings that they do not have a 'determinate' relationship but rather have a 'measure of inner affinity'.[116] The spirit of capitalism is nothing but a more secularized version of the protestant ethic which

---

[113] Ibid, p. 350.
[114] M. Weber, *Theory of Economic and Social Organisation*, 1947, p. 112.
[115] There is some evidence that Weber failed to consummate his marriage because of sexual impotence. See Mitzman, *The Iron Cage*, p. 276.
[116] Weber, *Economy and Society*, p. xxxviii.

develops over time through the process of rationalization. Perhaps this is revealed most clearly in Weber's summary of the nature of the spirit of capitalism:

> the *summum bonum* of this ethic, the earning of more and more money, combined with the avoidance of all spontaneous enjoyment of life is above all completely devoid of any eudaemonistic not to say hedonistic, admixture ... it expresses a type of feeling which is closely connected with certain religious ideas.[117]

Weber went to great pains to dispel the idea (which some of his critics had mistakenly attributed to him) that the spirit of capitalism was the same thing as acquisitiveness and greed for gain:

> Unlimited greed for gain is not in the least identical with capitalism, and still less its spirit. Capitalism *may* even be identical with the restraint, or at least a rational tempering of this irrational impulse.[118]

The language of this passage – 'the restraint, or at least a rational tempering of this irrational impulse' – indicates the identical ethical and psychological nature of the protestant ethic and the spirit of capitalism. Both essentially are ethics which oppose what Freud called the pleasure principle and institutionalize ego and super-ego psychological forces. Weber does however qualify this point about acquisitiveness in stating that the puritans did not struggle against rational acquisition, but against the irrational pursuit of wealth.[119] The result of this ethic was that

---

[117] Weber, *Protestant Ethic*, p. 53.
[118] Ibid, p. 17.
[119] Ibid, p. 171.

When the limitation of consumption is combined with the release of acquisitive activity, the inevitable practical result is obvious: accumulation of capital through ascetic compulsion to save.[120]

The combined results of the 'compulsion to save' and diligent activity in a calling led, in interaction with economic and other forces, to the development of modern capitalism.

Although the overwhelming emphasis of Weber's empirical analysis is on the causal influence of religious forces on economic development, he did also discuss the effect of economic factors on religious ideas and ethics. He explicitly stated that he believed this latter type of causal relationship to be of great importance:

> For those to whom no causal explanation is adequate without an economic (or materialistic as it is unfortunately still called) interpretation, it may be remarked that I consider the influence of economic development on the fate of religious ideas to be very important.[121]

Weber's references to the economic determination of religious ideas are to be found scattered in rather piecemeal fashion in a number of his works. He located the protestant ethic in a Christian tradition associated distinctively with an urban status group of craftsmen and small traders:

> The wandering craftsman first appears at the beginning of our era. Without him the spread of Christianity would have never been possible; it was in the beginning the religion of the wandering craftsmen, to whom the Apostle also belonged, and his proverb 'he who does not work shall not eat' expressed their ethics.[122]

Not only was this social group associated with the birth of Christianity, but during the Middle Ages it 'remained the

---

[120] Ibid, p. 172.
[121] Ibid, p.277, fn 84.
[122] Weber, *General Economic History*, p. 111.

most pious, if not always the most orthodox, stratum of society.'[123] It was the same group who formed the backbone of puritanism:

> With great regularity we find the most genuine adherents of Puritanism among the classes which were rising from a lowly status, the small bourgeois and farmers.[124]

Weber gave a number of reasons as to why this social group should be so predisposed towards puritanical Christianity. Primary among these reasons was the personal economic self-interest contained in the ownership of small amounts of property:

> The appropriation of the means of production and personal control, however formal, over the process of work constitute among the strongest incentives to unlimited willingness to work. This is the fundamental basis of the extraordinary importance of small units in agriculture, whether in the form of small-scale proprietorship or small tenants who hope to rise to the status of owner.[125]

The acquisition of wealth destroys this ethic of work among this lower-middle class group; Weber illustrated this point by quoting Wesley's famous statement that 'wherever riches have increased, the essence of religion has decreased in the same proportion'.[126] The other major reason for the puritanism of this stratum lay according to Weber in its elimination of magical and traditional styles of thought (we have already discussed the ethical consequences of this intellectual development) – and the growth of scientific rationality was essentially a function of the urban style of life of the lower-middle classes:

---

[123] Weber, *Sociology of Religion*, p. 95.
[124] Weber, *Protestant Ethic*, p. 174.
[125] Weber, *Theory*, p. 242.
[126] Weber, *Protestant Ethic*, p. 175.

When one compares the life of a lower-middle class person, particularly the urban artisan or the small trader with the life of the peasant, it is clear that middle class life has far less connection with nature. Consequently, dependence on magic for influencing the irrational forces of nature cannot play the same role for the urban dweller as for the farmer. At the same time, it is clear that the economic foundation of the urban man's life has a far more rational essential character, viz., calculability and capacity for purposive manipulation.[127]

Weber's willingness to consider economic explanations is further illustrated by his position on the relationship between science and the process of rationalization: in his essay on science he summarized this when stating that 'intellectualist rationalization' had been 'created by science and scientifically oriented technology'.[128] It is here that we see Marx's greatest influence over Weber. The location of religious ideas and ethics in an economic context does not however solve the fundamental problem that Weber set out to solve: 'the special peculiarity of Occidental rationalism'. Neither the emphasis on intellectualist or economic rationalization can explain why it was in the occidental world that rationality developed particularly in either or both these spheres. As we have seen, Weber attempted to give an historical answer to the problem but raised a further difficulty which he never resolved: in criticising a Marxist speaker at the first meeting of the German Sociological Association, Weber revealed his own position on the nature of historical explanation:

> I would like to protest against the statement made by one of the speakers that some one factor, be it technology or economy, can be the 'ultimate' or 'true' cause of another. If we look at the causal lines, we see them run, at one time, from technical to

---

[127] Weber, *Sociology of Religion*, p. 97.
[128] Gerth & Mills, *From Max Weber*, p. 139.

economic and political matters, at another from political to religious and economic ones etc. There is no resting point.[129]

It is for this reason that he accepted that in the analysis of cultural phenomenon 'the appearance of the result is, for every causally working empirical science determined not just from a certain moment but from eternity.'[130]

This infinite causal regress is clearly a very unsatisfactory mode of explanation, for in the last resort it explains both everything and nothing. Although in principle Weber was prepared to accept that causal explanation could be regressed infinitely, in his substantive work on the development of the protestant ethic he was 'not primarily interested in the origin, antecedents, or history of these ascetic movements, but (took) their doctrines as given in a state of full development'.[131]

It must be asked what principle enabled Weber to decide the point of departure for his analysis. In practice it was the principle of understanding which allowed him to meaningfully explain the 'inner affinity' of the protestant ethic with the spirit of capitalism. The function of understanding in empirical causal analysis was 'to establish the really decisive motives of human actions'[132] – and to enable Weber to break into the 'eternal stream' of history for a point of departure of analysis. This point is necessarily a

---

[129] Bendix & Roth, *Scholarship*, p. 242.

[130] Weber, *Methodology*, p. 187.

[131] Weber, *Protestant Ethic*, p. 220. Weber did however make a number of substantive references to earlier historical developments and stated elsewhere that the 'causal regress' of 'present-day Christian capitalistic culture' might have to extend back 'into the Middle Ages or Antiquity.' Weber, *Methodology*, p. 155.

[132] Weber, *Methodology*, p. 14. This notion that it is possible 'to establish the really decisive motives of human actions' is reflected in Weber's conclusion that 'the real roots of the religious ethics which led the way to the modern conception of calling lay in the sects and heterodox movements, above all in Wyclif.' Weber, *Protestant Ethic*, p. 203.

subjective rather than a material factor of analysis: Weber's methodology inescapably involved the understanding of subjective meanings. Material circumstances cannot be 'understood' – a statement about them can only be invoked on Weber's methodology as a subsidiary heuristic device. The selection of puritan theology and the protestant ethic as a point of departure for Weber's analysis of the emergence of modern capitalism is therefore an example of a deeply partisan idealistic methodology.

The fundamental analytical problem that Weber set out to solve thus remains unanswered: what were the sociological factors responsible for the pervasive and systematic growth of scientific thinking in occidental culture? Clearly Weber's references to a racial explanation of this cultural development form no basis whatsoever for a solution to this problem (the development of Japanese capitalism is by itself sufficient to discredit this purely speculative notion). Its solution lies beyond the scope of this paper, although it is intended to return to this question in future work. Weber's greatest achievement was to analyse the relationship between the disenchantment flowing from the process of rationalization and the evolution of the protestant ethic. This involved the sublimation of anxiety and guilt resulting from the destruction of protective belief and institutional magic (e.g. the elimination of the confessional), into the rationalized, methodical and sober ethic associated with both puritanism and certain aspects of occidental capitalism. Further work is required to elaborate the nature of the psychological forces that were involved in this process and why they took the form that they did. Although the protestant ethic has come to influence cultures outside of its area of origin, the question raised by Weber for comparative sociology still remains: why did the process of rationalization first develop in Western Europe, and not elsewhere?

Chapter 3: Max Weber and Environmental Determinism.[133]

The process of rationalization was seen by Weber as occurring within the occidental world at periodical intervals: in ancient Greece, Renaissance Italy, Puritan Holland and England. It is not therefore in practice conceived by him as a linear cultural development or a series of unique accidental events, but a process which perennially but cumulatively repeats itself in the occident. And it was this which led him against his own methodological inclinations to refer to the process of rationalization as a 'law of development'.

Weber was also forced by the logic of his own analysis to raise the possibility of a racial determination of occidental culture, but at the same time indicated what the only alternative explanation was an environmental one. In practice he conceived environmental explanations as being historical and these cannot solve 'the special peculiarity of occidental rationalism.' Yet in principle the nature of a satisfactory solution to Weber's problem is to be found through the logic of scientific analysis. If social science is viewed as a natural scientific discipline which gives an objective casual account of social reality – as this paper does – then in the last resort this environmental factor must be a geographical one.

The logic is this assertion is as follows: 1. Heredity and environment exhaust the range of possible natural scientific explanations. 2. Subjective voluntaristic theories of social action are logically incapable of explaining systematic societal variations because of randomization of individual action. 3. Heredity also cannot explain societal variations because of this process of randomization – this assumes that biological race does not determine culture. 4. The only remaining factor which is both environmental and objective is geographical environment.

---

[133] Unpublished paper.

Weber himself did not discuss the nature of sociological explanations in terms of the environment. Talcott Parsons has attempted however to develop Weber's theory of social action in a more systematic fashion and has dealt with the problem of environmental explanations at a general theoretical level. In the summary of his theoretical position in *Societies: Evolutionary and Comparative Perspectives*, Parsons distinguished two 'environments of action': the 'physical-organic environment' and 'ultimate reality'[134] The former refers essentially to the geographical environment but would also include all forms of biological life other than man himself.

The latter is so ambiguous as to require clarification. At first sight 'ultimate reality' might appear to refer to ideas that men have about such a reality, but Parsons makes it very clear that his referring to an 'environment of action', i.e. an environment external to all modes of social action inducing religious ideas. That this is not an accidental use of words but a fundamental part of Parsons' analysis is revealed in his earlier writings. The most telling summary of these is his discussion of Durkheim's ideas on religion in *The Structure of Social Action*:

> Religious ideas, then, may be held to constitute the cognitive bridge between men's active attitudes and the non-empirical aspects of their universe ... The specific content of religious ideas is no more completely determined, probably not nearly as much, by the intrinsic features of the non-empirical than is scientific knowledge completely determined by the 'external world'.[135]

What Parsons is saying here is that the 'non-empirical world' is in part a determinant of men's religious ideas – not exactly

---

[134] T. Parsons, *Societies: Evolutionary and Comparative Perspectives*, 1966, p. 20.

[135] T. Parsons, *The Structure of Social Action*, Volume 1, 1968, p. 424. See the discussion of Durkheim's treatment of religious ideas by Parsons: Ibid, pp, 411-429. For his position on the role of non-empirical reality in explaining cultural facts, see also his article 'The place of ultimate values in sociological theory', *Ethics*, Volume 45, 1934-1935.

Hegel's 'God in History', but at least an indeterminant supernatural/metaphysical force at work. This explicit supernatural idealism at least has the merit of pointing out the logic of Parsons' 'cultural determinism', and it allows us to decisively reject such idealism as being incompatible with sociology as a natural scientific discipline. However, it must be pointed out that it has been possible for Parsons to present such an argument as a scientific one, because his theory of social action has the authority of research derived from Weber. Parsons erroneously confuses a scientific analysis of social action with a particular kind of scientific orientation on the part of the social actor himself. In fact it is in principle just as valid to give a scientific explanation of 'irrational' non-scientific ideas and orientations as it is of 'rational' scientific ones. If we eliminate Parsons' 'ultimate reality' as a causal variable in sociological analysis – and if we subscribe to the notion of sociology as a natural social science we must – the only theoretically valid part of his analysis of environments is that part which deals with the objective observable 'physical-organic environment'.

Both Marx and Durkheim came near to applying this principle of objective environmental analysis in their sociological work. Marx's 'materialism' and emphasis on the economic determinants of social life is compatible with geographical determinism, although he only occasionally located his analysis in a specific geographical context. Environmental determinism is also compatible with non-economic explanations of social facts, in particular those made in terms of political structures. Durkheim accepted in principle the sociological importance of geographical environment but in practice was much more interested in another objectives determinant of social life – changes in population density. However, alterations in population density can account for historical processes of change but not for systematic variations in the development of different societies. For the question must be always raised: as to why population grew in one type of society and not another?

Of course population does change in a particular society for 'accidental' reasons – perhaps an example of this is the appearance and disappearance of the plague in Europe – but this kind of change cannot account for systematic changes in the social structure in a number of different contexts that interested Weber. Rationality appears and reappears so systematically in occidental societies that he was forced to search for some 'fixed' factor which was a 'constant' in the historical process – and if we reject the constant factor of biological race, as we must, the only other factor which is both objective and relatively unchanging is geographical environment.

It might be objected that geographical environment cannot be a 'determining cause of social development, for that which remains almost unchanged in the course of tens of thousands of years cannot be the chief cause of development.'[136] This is certainly the case, but what can be explained by geographical environment is variations in the process of development between different societies – historical development itself is brought about by factors such as technological innovation and the process of intellectual rationalization. The logic of this type of distinction is identical to that employed by biological evolutionary theory which locates biological changes in the context of geographical environments. The genetic mechanisms of biological change are quite distinct from the process of natural selection: the former is primarily a function of 'random' genetic mutations, the latter a function of adaptations to geographical environments.

Although Weber rejected the above kind of argument on account of his methodological idealism, in practice he came near to applying it in his actual attempt to explain cultural variations between one society and another. For example his explanation of the emergence of the free artisan in northern Europe:

---

[136] A statement made by Stalin quoted in K.A. Wittfogel, *Oriental Despotism*, 1957, p. 408.

In antiquity the slaves remained in the power of the lord, while in the middle ages they became free. In the latter there is a broad stratum of free craftsmen unknown to antiquity. The reasons are several: the difference in the consumptive requirements of the Occident as compared to all other countries of the world ... The contrast rests on climatic differences. While in Italy heat is not indispensable, even today, and in antiquity the bed counted as a luxury – for sleeping one simply rolled up one's mantle and lay down on the floor – in Northern Europe stoves and beds were necessities. The oldest guild document which we possess is that of the bed ticking weavers of Cologne ... again in consequence of climatic relations, the German appetite was greater than that of the southerner.[137]

And in this context, Weber might have added the commonplace observation that the temperate climate of the northern European countries is much more conducive to the protestant ethic of work than that of the hot southern countries. Weber's most comprehensive statement concerning the environmental determinant of cultural variations is to be found in his study of the religion of China:

In sharp contrast with the Occident, but in harmony with Indian conditions, the [Chinese] city as an imperial fortress actually had fewer formal guarantees of self-government than the village ... This can be explained in terms of the different origins of the occidental and oriental city. The polis of antiquity originated as an overseas trading city, however strong its base in landlordism, but China was predominantly an inland area ... On the other hand, the characteristic inland city of the occidental Middle Ages, like the Chinese and the Middle Eastern city, was usually founded by princes and feudal lords in order to gain money rents and taxes. Yet at an early date the European city turned into a highly privileged association with fixed rights. These could be and were extended in a planned manner because at the time the lord of the city lacked the technical means to

---

[137] M. Weber, *General Economic History*, 1961, p. 107.For other examples of Weber's analysis of cultural facts in terms of the climate see M. Weber, *The Sociology of Religion*, p. 98; M. Weber, *The Rational and Social Foundations of Music*, 1958, p. 24.

administer the city. Moreover, the city represented a military association which could successfully close the city gate to an army of knights. In contrast, the great Middle Eastern cities, such as Babylon, at an early time were completely at the mercy of the royal bureaucracy because of canal construction and administration. The same held for the Chinese city despite the paucity of Chinese central administration. The prosperity of the Chinese city did not primarily depend upon the citizen's enterprising spirit in economic and political ventures but rather upon the imperial administration, especially the administration of rivers.

This statement of Weber's could very easily be mistaken for one made by Marx on the theme of 'oriental despotism', with its emphasis on the role of economic factors and its general geographical materialism.[138] Weber was very aware of the possibility of an 'explanation of a political structure from its geographical background.'[139]

> Royal bureaucracies (in the East) were developed to carry out the regulation of river traffic and execution of irrigation policy with the consequent establishment of a process leading towards the bureaucratization of the entire administration. This permitted the king through his staff and revenues supplied them to incorporate the army into his own bureaucratic management ... No political community of citizens could arise on such a foundation for there was no basis for military independence of royal power.[140]

This emphasis on irrigation management for explaining 'oriental despotism' has been developed in detail by Wittfogel in his

---

[138] For Marx's analysis of 'oriental despotism' see Wittfogel, *Oriental Depotism*, especially p. 374.

[139] The example of this in the text refers of course to the geographical determination of political structure via economic forces. Weber was also aware of the direct effect of geographical environment on political structure, e.g. his comments on the peculiar geographical position of Germany and the consequent effects on its political life. J.P. Mayer, *Max Weber and German Politics*, p. 20.

[140] M. Weber, *The City*, 1968, pp. 119, 120.

Oriental Despotism. The thesis has been subsequently attacked on empirical grounds that the administration of irrigation systems did not always require large-scale bureaucratic structures but in many cases was organized on a small-scale local basis.[141] However, it is possible to restate the hypothesis in a much more acceptable form, whereby the regional management of irrigation is only a stage, although a significant one, in the development of 'oriental despotism'. Julian Steward has come near to restating the hypothesis in this form and has added to it by invoking military conquest as a further variable in the analysis.[142] In the context of the present paper's emphasis on geographical determinism, military conquest would have to be analysed in terms of physical accessibility of one region to another through factors such as navigable seas, lakes, rivers and canals. It is likely however, that other geographical variables are also important in explaining the emergence of 'oriental despotism' in particular societies.

Emerging out of this part of Weber's work which deals with the geographical determinants of culture, is the theme that some geographical environments through economic and political forces create the social conditions which free men for independent action, whereas others force men into personal dependency. The former was seen by Weber in terms of the occidental city where 'city air makes man free'.[143] The latter was viewed by him mainly in the context of 'oriental despotism' which arose out of the 'iron cage' of bureaucratic control. Freedom was the crucial factor in the development of rationality. This was true according to Weber in three major contexts: 1. 'A powerful organization of priests' possessing 'the greatest

---

[141] See for example R.M. Adams, *The Evolution of Urban Society*, 1966, pp. 15, 66-68, 74, 76; *International Encyclopaedia of Social Sciences*, 1968, Volume 1, p. 424 and Volume 16, pp. 204, 210.
[142] See J. Steward (ed.), *Irrigation Civilizations: a Comparative Study*, 1995, pp. 1-5, 58-78.
[143] Ibid, p. 94.

measure of independence from political authorities'.[144] 2. Prophets as lay preachers with powers of 'sovereign independence'.[145] 3. 'The peculiar freedom of urbanites' in the occidental city.[146]

Weber never spelt out the reasons for this association between freedom and rationality but there are suggested explanations in negative statements such as he made in his study of methodology:

> The points of departure of the cultural sciences remain changeable throughout the limitless future as long as a Chinese ossification of intellectual life does not render mankind incapable of setting new questions to the eternally inexhaustible flow of life.[147]

His reference to 'a Chinese ossification of intellectual life' is of course employed here as a metaphor for what Weber feared would be the consequence of the spread of bureaucratic control in modern life. Rationality results from freedom through the critical questions that individuals are naturally predisposed to ask through the 'metaphysical needs of the human mind as it is driven ... to understand the world as a meaningful cosmos.' The 'iron cage' of bureaucracy inhibits the development of rationality because it stereotypes the questions that men ask through the process of routinization and centralised control.

The process of rationalization was illustrated by the poet John Milton, who described in 1641 his fellow Londoners 'sitting by their studious lamps, musing, searching, revolving new notions and ideas ... reading, trying all things, assenting to

---

[144] Weber, *Sociology of Religion*, p. 73.
[145] Ibid, p. 78.
[146] Gerth and Mills, *From Max Weber*, p. 269.
[147] Weber, *Methodology*, p. 84. Weber recognized of course that there was a significant amount of rationalization in Chinese and other oriental cultures, but it was his view that it had become 'ossified' in the oriental world in a way that it had not in the occident.

the force of reason ...'[148] It was possible for Milton and others to pursue the freedom to explore 'the force of reason' because of a culture of individualism which had developed in England.[149] This was linked to the growth of capitalism, and Weber briefly explored its geographical basis:

'As a result of its insular position [as an island] England was not dependent on a great standing army.' On the continent it was possible for the state to protect its peasantry through its standing army, but in England this was not possible. As a result, England 'became the classical land of peasant eviction. The labour force this threw on the market made possible the development of the domestic small master system ... Thus while in England shop industry arose, so to speak, by itself, on the continent it had to be deliberately cultivated by the state ... This is by no means fortuitous, but is the outcome of continuous development over centuries ... the result of its [England's] insular position.'[150]

Recent Research on Environmental Determinism.

Although environmental determinism and cultural evolutionary theory became unfashionable during the first half of the twentieth century, there has been a significant revival of interest in both these approaches, particularly in the writings of American anthropologists.[151] The most important attempt to revive

---

[148] Worden, *The English Civil Wars*, p. 79. In 1650 Wallington a London artisan noted in his diary that he had not only written 'above forty books and read over the Bible many times,' but had also read 'above two hundred other books'. P.S. Weaver, *Wallington's World: a Puritan Artisan in Seventeenth Century London*, 1985, p. 5.

[149] See my paper on the sociological basis of the English civil war.

[150] M. Weber, *General Economic History*, 1961, pp. 129, 130; M. Weber, *Theory of Social and Economic Organization*, 1964, p. 277.

[151] For writings on evolutionary theory see L. White, *The Evolution of Culture*, 1959; M.D. Aahlins, E.R. Service (eds.), *Evolution and Culture*, 1960; M.H. Fried, *The Evolution of Political Society*, 1967 and M. Harris, *The Rise of Anthropological Theory*, 1969. For recent publications on

geographical determinism was Julian Steward's work on cultural ecology.[152] There has not yet however been a successful integration of the evolutionary and ecological approaches comparable to the synthesis achieved by biological theory.

There has been a recent resurgence of interest in environmental determinism which has been conveniently summarized and detailed by Wikipdia as follows:

1. Ibn Khaldun has argued that soil, climate, and food determined whether societies were nomadic or sedentary, shaping their customs and ceremonies.[153]
2. Ellen Churchill Semple's case study focused on the Phillipines, where she analysed patterns of civilization and wildness in relation to the topography of its islands.[154]
3. Daron Acemoglu, Simon Johnson and James A. Robinson concluded that geography was the most important influence on institutional development during early state formation. However, they argued that geographic factors cannot directly explain differences in economic growth after 1500 A.D., except through their effects on economic and agricultural productivity.[155]
4. Jeffrey Sachs and John Luke Gallup have examined the role of geography on coastal trade and access to markets, as well as

---

environmental determinism see R. Kaplan, *The Revenge of Geography*, 2013; T. Marshall, *Prisoners of Geography*, 2015; L. Dartnell, *Origins: How the Earth Shaped Human History*, 2019.

[152] J.H. Steward, *Theory of Culture Change*, 1963; M.D. Coe, C.P. Kottak, 'Social typology and tropical forest civilizations', *Comparative Studies in Society and History*, Volume 4, 1961-1962.

[153] See A. Hannoum, *Translation and the Colonial Imaginary: Ibn Khaldun Orientalist*, 2003.

[154] J. Painter, *Political Geography: an Introduction to Space and Power*, 2009, p. 177

[155] D. Acemoglu, J. Robinson, *Why Nations Fail: The Origins of Power, and Poverty*, 2012.

its impact on disease environment and agricultural productivity.[156]

5. Jared Diamond has concluded that early states located along the same geographical latitude made it easier for the spread of crops, livestock, and farming techniques. Regions suitable for the cultivation of wheat and barley saw high population densities and the growth of early cities. Resulting writing systems gave people the ability to store and build knowledge. A surplus of food enabled craftsmanship to flourish allowing some groups the freedom to explore and create, which led to the development of metallurgy and advances in technology. The close proximity in which humans and their animals lived led to the spread of disease across Eurasia. Europeans took advantage of their environment to build large and complex states with advanced technology and weapons. The Incas and other native groups in South America did not have these advantages, and suffered from a north-south orientation that prevented the flow of goods and knowledge across the continent.[157]

6. Dr Marcella Alsan argued that the prevalence of the tsetse fly hampered early state formation in Africa. Because the tsetse virus was lethal to cows and horses, communities afflicted by the insect could not rely of agricultural benefits provided by livestock. The disease environment hindered the formation of farming communities, and as a result, early African societies resembled small hunter-gatherer societies rather than centralized states.[158]

7. Stanley Engerman and Kenneth Sokoloff examined the economic development of the Americas during colonization. Specific factor endowments in each colony affected their growth. The development of economic institutions, such as

---

[156] J.D. Gallup, J.D. Sachs, A.D. Mellinger, 'Geography and economic development', *International Regional Science Review,* Volume 22, 1999.
[157] J. Diamond, *Guns, Germs and Steel,* 1997.
[158] See M. Alsan, 'The effect of the tsetse fly on African development', *American Economic Review*, Volume 105, 2015.]

plantations, was caused by the need for a large amount of land and a labour force capable of harvesting sugar and tobacco, while smallholder farms thrived in areas where large scale economies were not suitable for the environment. They also found smallholder economies to be more equitable since they discouraged an elite class forming, and distributed political power democratically to most land-owning males. Colonies with educated and free populations were better suited to take advantage of technological change during the industrial revolution, granting country wide participation into the booming free-market economy.[159]

8. Historians have also noted that population densities seem to concentrate on coastlines and that states with large coasts benefit from higher average incomes compared to landlocked countries. Coastal living has proven advantageous for centuries as civilizations relied on the coastline and waterways for trade, irrigation, and as a food source. However, factors including fertile soil, nearby rivers, and ecological systems suited for rice or wheat cultivation can give way to dense inland populations.[160]

9. Nathan Nunn and Diego Puga note that rugged terrain usually makes farming difficult, prevents travel, and limits societal growth. Harsh terrain hampered the flow of trade goods and decreased crop availability, while isolating communities from developing knowledge and capital growth. However, harsh terrain had positive effects on some African communities by protecting them from the slave trade. Communities that were located in areas with rugged features could successfully hide from slave traders and protect their homes from being destroyed.[161]

---

[159] S. Engerman, K. Sokoloff,, *Economic Developments in the Americas since 1500: Endowments and Institutions*, 2011.
[160] J.D. Gallup, J.D. Sachs, A.D. Mellinger, 'Geography and economic development', *International Regional Science*, 22, 1999.
[161] N. Nunn, D. Puga, 'Ruggedness: The blessing of bad geography in Africa', *The Review of Economics and Statistics*, Volume 94, 2012

10. Locations with hot tropical climates often suffer underdevelopment due to low fertility of soils, excessive plant transpiration, ecological conditions favouring infectious diseases, and unreliable water supply. These factors can cause tropical zones to suffer 30% to 50% decrease in productivity relative to temperate climate zones.[162]

Conclusion

There are a number of critical questions which can be asked of Weber's argument about the social process of the development of freedom and rationality which are beyond the scope of this paper. In conclusion however, it is necessary to point out that Weber's analysis lacked depth in certain areas because of the neglect of the details of what might be termed the 'materialistic' dimension. Not only did he fail to discuss in detail the effect of geographical environments on social structure and cultures, but he also neglected the analysis of the most important factor in the evolution of culture: the development of technology.[163] His methodological idealism did however allow him to develop an analysis of the process of intellectual rationalization. His great achievement was to establish the cultural conditions necessary for freedom and the development of rationality, and the psychological consequences of the process of rationalization which led to a sublimated ethic of work. However, he only hinted at the links between geographical environment and economic and political structures and their impact on cultural development.

---

[162] Gallup, Sachs, Mellinger, 'Geography'; W. Easterly, R. Levine, 'Tropics, germs, and crops: how endowments influence economic development', *Journal of Monetary Economics,* Volume 50, 2003.]
[163] Weber did however analyze in some detail the development of economically more rational forms of social organization. He correctly saw the process of bureaucratization as a form of 'social technology'. For Weber's belief in the inevitable evolution of society towards a structure built on 'mechanized foundations' see Mayer, *Max Weber*, pp. 126, 127.

Weber's emphasis on freedom is consistent with the growth of capitalism, which occurred particularly in England, Holland and elsewhere where there was an absence of major political constraints. This occurred as a result of environmental factors which hampered the growth of standing armies, with a reliance on navies and militias for defence. Weber's methodological idealism was probably responsible for his relative neglect of the role of material and geographical conditions. However, he laid the groundwork for the further scientific work necessary for answering the fundamental question as to why the process of rationalization first occurred in the occident than elsewhere.

Chapter 4: A Sociological Analysis of the English Civil War.[164]

Geography and the Civil War in England.

England experienced the growth of capitalism earlier than most European powers, which along with the prevalence of individual freedom, is central for an understanding of the civil war. Luciani Pellicani in his discussion of the history of capitalism, has emphasized the importance of political and military constraints on personal freedom:

> The *consumer's freedom* is as essential for the functioning of capitalism as the *entrepreneur's freedom* ... The emancipation of the urban communities marks the beginning of the genesis of modern capitalism. Its roots are political and military, not economic. Cities were able to inject dynamism and rationality into the stagnant rural world only to the extent to which they succeeded in withdrawing from the effective jurisdiction of their lords and the spiritual control of economic obscurantism centred around the condemnation of profit and trade. They were successful precisely because they were opposed by a crumbling public power, lacking as never before the military and financial means to compel its subjects to obedience.[165]

As we saw earlier, Max Weber argued that England had developed capitalism as a result of its insular position as an island, resulting in dependence on naval power rather than a standing army. In the absence of a standing army, the crown was unable to control the development of the economy. These changes occurred as a result of 'a continuous development over centuries'[166] consistent with Alan Macfarlane's thesis that 'the

---

[164] Unpublished paper.

[165] L. Pellicani, *The Genisis of Capitalism and the Origins of Modernity*, 1994, pp. 10, 123.

[166] M. Weber, *General Economic History*, 1961, pp. 129, 130; M. Weber, *Theory of Social and Economic Organization*, 1964, p. 277.

majority of ordinary people in England from at least the thirteenth century were rampant individualists, highly mobile both geographically and socially, economically "rational", market-oriented and acquisitive, ego-centred in kinship and social life.'[167] This indicates that English individualism existed well before the late fifteenth century, which is when most historians have dated the emergence of capitalism in England.[168] This suggests that something fundamental in English society – 'its insular position' – was responsible for this cultural development.

England's geographical situation as an island meant that it was relatively free from the wars occurring on the continent, relying mainly on a navy for defence and resulting in periodic recruitment of militias rather than the establishment of a permanent army. France, Germany and most continental powers were vulnerable to military attack because of the threat from other land based societies, and therefore were forced to develop armies in order to survive. According to Jane Whittle

> The lack of prosperity [in France was due to] ... the wars conducted on French soil from the fourteenth to the sixteenth centuries, and the heavy royal taxation to which French peasants were subjected from the late fifteenth century onwards ... That English peasants were not subjected to a similar level of taxation was not a matter of chance. There were rebellions against taxation in 1489, and 1497 and 1525, as well as 1381 ... Yet because of the low level of taxation, English governments could not afford to keep a standing army to put down these rebellions.[169]

Whittle does not explain the relative success of rebellions in England, and why it was so difficult to suppress them. The absence of a permanent national army was the result of England's geographical position as an island, not allowing it as

---

[167] A. Macfarlane, *The Origins of English Individualism*, 1978, p. 163.

[168] Ibid, pp. 34-48.

[169] J. Whittle, *The Development of Agrarian Capitalism: Land and Labour in Norfolk 1440-1580*, 2000, pp. 18, 19, 311.

in France, to introduce high taxes. This resulted in a vicious circle: no standing army, low taxation, no standing army.

The exceptions to the vulnerability of continental powers were Holland and Venice, which were protected from attack by their geographical location. In the case of Holland, the canals and marshes allowed them to create flood barriers against enemies, and they established a Water Line in the early seventeenth century which was used to almost transform Holland at times into an island. The Water Line was used for example in 1672, where it prevented the armies of Louis XIV from conquering Holland.[170] Venetian power was derived from its fleet and linked military forces, and its control of its lagoons provided protection from military attacks.[171] It is perhaps no accident that both states became republics with early forms of capitalist development,[172] illustrating Pellicani's thesis about the centrality of military and political factors in creating the freedoms necessary for entrepreneurial growth.

The lack of a permanent national army in England meant that the English crown, as well as the aristocracy, was dependent on the population at large for the creation of military force.[173] This absence of a standing army made it difficult for the government to impose taxes, and eventually resulted in the development of markets relatively free of political and military control. England's reliance on its navy for defence included its merchant fleet – and this partly explains its active involvement in world trade, an important dimension in the growth of English capitalism.

There were also important internal geographical factors associated with the development of capitalism in England. It was a country with plentiful coal and iron deposits, internal rivers and good coastal harbours, and a location between Europe and the Americas. However, there were internal environmental

---

[170] Wikipedia: *Dutch Water Line.*
[171] Wikipedia, *Military History of the Republic of Venice.*
[172] See M. Lincoln, *London and the 17th Century*, 2021, p. 134.
[173] Ibid, pp. xvii-xx, 3-37.

conditions which also facilitated the growth of individual freedoms:

> ... [there was] a growing distinction between working communities in forest and in fielden areas. In the nucleated villages characteristic of the latter ... manorial customs [were] fairly rigid, political habits comparatively orderly, and the labourer's outlook deeply imbued with the prevalent preconceptions of church and manor-house. In these fielden areas labourers often ... more or less freely [accepted] their dependence on squire and parson ... In the isolated hamlets characteristic of forest settlements ... the customs of the manor were sometimes vague or difficult to enforce ... and the authority of church and manor house seemed remote. In these areas [the population was] ... more prone to pick up new ways and ideas. It was primarily in heath and forest areas ... that the vagrant religion of the Independents found a footing in rural communities.'[174]

The areas outside of manorial control consisted 'mainly of towns, the pasture and woodland areas linked to an expanding market economy, and the industrializing regions devoted to cloth-making, mining, and metal-working ...'[175] Many of these districts were 'perceived as being lawless ... Few gentry families lived there to supervise the behaviour of the 'common' people and ... [they] proved to be one of the areas of considerable religious independence and dissent.'[176]

---

[174] A. Everitt, 'The marketing of agricultural produce' in J. Thirsk (ed.), *The Agrarian History of England and Wales, 1500-1640*, 1967, pp. 462, 463. See also the discussion of the contrast between pastoral and arable areas in D. Underdown, *Revel, Riot and Rebellion: Popular Politics and Culture in England 1603-1660*, 1987, p. 5; J. Thirsk, 'The farming regions of England' in Thirsk, *The Agrarian History*, p. 14; K. Wrightson, *English Society, 1580-1680*, 1982, p. 171; S.B. Jennings, *The Gathering of the Elect: The Development, Nature and Socio-Economic Structures of Protestant Religious Dissent in Seventeenth Century Nottinghamshire*. (D.Phil. Thesis, Nottingham Trent University), p. 270.
[175] Underdown, *Revel*, p. 18.
[176] Jennings, *The Gathering*, p. 17.

Given the importance of the cloth industry in England, the support of clothing districts for parliament was a key factor in the civil war.[177] The attempts at political control by Charles I extended to the power of the guilds, which were seen by him, along with monopolies, as 'one of the traditional instruments of industrial control'.[178] However, much economic development took place in rural areas, where the power of the guilds was progressively weakened:

> ... during the thirteenth century there was an increasing shift of industry away from urban areas to the countryside ... The growth of the rural cloth industry was partly enabled ... by a rural location ... [which] permitted cloth producers to take advantage of cheap labour away from the prohibitive restrictions of the guilds ... the very existence of craft guilds or endeavours to establish them might encourage merchants to transfer their entrepreneurial activities to the countryside. Textile skills were traditional there and rural overpopulation made labour available ... [179]

The Role of Armies on the Political Development of France and England.

In order to fully understand the civil war in England it is necessary to compare it with events in France during the sixteenth and seventeenth centuries. The French 'Wars of Religion' were a period of war between Catholics and Huguenots in France in the latter half of the sixteenth century. This included the destruction of images in Catholic churches, which resulted in

---

[177] Underdown, *Revel*, pp. 220, 231-32, 275-78; J. Morrill, *The Nature of the English Revolution*, 1993, p. 235.
[178] R. Ashton, 'Charles I and the City', in F.J. Fisher (ed.), *Essays in the Economic and Social History of Tudor and Stuart England*, 1961, p. 145; L. Stone, *Causes of the English Revolution, 1529-1642*, 1986, p. 126
[179] P.T.H. Unwin, 'Town and trade 1066-1500' in R.A. Dodgson, R.A. Butlin (eds.), *A Historical Geography of England and Wales*, 1978, p. 136.

Catholics attacking Protestants, including the St. Bartholomew's Day Massacre in 1572.

Correlli Barnet contrasted the military developments in England, France and Germany during the sixteenth and seventeenth centuries as follows:

> An army had indeed been 'standing' in France almost continuously throughout the sixteenth century; an emergency force to meet continuous emergency. Since 1569 there had been permanent regiments of native-born infantry. France's rise to greatness as a modern military power dates, however, from about 1624, during Cardinal Richelieu's administration ... In 1628 the twelve oldest regiments were given a permanent status ... By 1635, when France entered the war [the Thirty Years War], she had five field armies numbering 100,000 men, including 18,000 horsemen ... Men were now to be paid not by their captains but by state commissioners, one per regiment ... In France under Louis XIII and Richelieu royal authority rested on the army – in the 1630s and 1640s taxes were even collected by armed force. In Germany, where some states enjoyed greater formal powers than the English Houses of Parliament, the princes could plead the emergency of the Thirty Years War to make a convincing case for emergency taxation on royal authority and for raising standing armies ... [180]

Fourteen regiments of the French Army were used to persecute the Huguenots, the major Protestant group in France. Louis XIV instituted a campaign of harassment, which included the occupation and looting of Huguenot homes by military troops, attempting to forcibly convert them. In 1685, he issued the Edict of Fontainebleau, revoking the Edict of Nantes and declaring Protestantism illegal. Huguenots made up to as much as ten per cent of the French population; but by 1685 it had reduced to no more than 1,500 people.[181]

---

[180] C. Barnett, *Britain and Her Army, 1509-1970*, 1970, pp. 69-73.
[181] Wikipedia Huguenot.

The impact of the suppression of the Huguenots and the control of French society by the military has been summarized by Hatton:

> the monarchy followed the policy of state support, regulation and economic control ... To live nobly, in other words in the manner of the nobility, idly without following a trade or craft, was in itself a claim to honour and social esteem. Colbert and his contemporaries did not realise the advantages which would derive from a general system of freedom of labour.[182]

The incidence of taxation was very high in France, but by contrast the level of taxation in England before the civil war resulted in the emergence of an independent group of prosperous yeomen, artisans and traders.[183] The presence of royal troops in France led to the decimation of the rural population, described by Sir John Fortescue in an account written as early as the 1460s, and summarized by Perry Anderson as follows:

> ... Sir John Fortescue, Lord Chancellor to King Henry VI, fled into France with Henry in 1461 and during the next ten years of exile he wrote his *Learned Commendation of the Politique Laws of England* ... Fortescue noted the oppressions of the rural population by royal troops in France ... 'so that there is not the least village there free from this miserable calamity, but that it is once or twice every year beggared by this kind of pilings (pillage).' This and other exactions, such as the salt tax, led to great poverty of the rural inhabitants which Fortescue observed around him ... In England, on the other hand, the position of rural inhabitants was very different. The absence of heavy taxation, of billeted soldiers, and of internal taxes, meant that 'every inhabiter of that realm useth and enjoyeth at his pleasure all the fruits that his land or cattle beareth, with all the profits and commodities which by his own travail, or by the labour of others he gaineth by land or by water ...' Neither are they sued in the law, but only before

---

[182] R. Hatton (ed.), *Louis XIV and Absolutism*, 1976, pp. 227, 240.
[183] T.H. Aston, C.H.E. Philpin, *The Brenner Debate: Agrarian Class Structure and Economic Development in Pre-Industrial Europe*, 1987, p. 89.

ordinary judges, whereby the laws of the land they are justly intreated.[184]

A similar account was given by John Aylmer, later Bishop of London, who lived in exile on the continent and in 1559 published a pamphlet entitled *An Harborowe for Faithfull and Trewe Subjects*. He claimed that the impoverishment of the rural French population was due to the frequency of wars – 'as they are never without it' – resulting in the king's soldiers entering 'the poor man's house, eatheth and drinketh up all that he ever hath'.[185]

Barnett has summarized the role of the army on political developments in England during the outbreak of the civil war:

> In England ... Charles I endeavoured from 1629 to free himself from the Commons' control over taxation by virtually abandoning any foreign policy, with all its implications in terms of costly armies. However, he could not then plead national emergency to raise an army. The Commons were well aware of the danger to their position which a royal army would represent ... No funds were available to pay an army ... Charles had nothing except the militia system ...[186]

As a result of an absence of a permanent national army, Charles was unable to arrest the rebellious five Members of Parliament, precipitating the civil war. Thomas May's two publications, issued in 1647 and 1650 ... [claimed] 'what the parliamentarians were defending, as they saw it, was the ancient constitution, the common law which had existed (so Coke said) since time immemorial, and the rights and liberties of all free-born Englishmen,'[187] which Levellers and other radicals believed had been subverted by the Norman Conquest. Sir John Strangways writing in the Tower in the 1640s concluded 'that if the gentry were not universally Anglican high-flyers, neither were they

---

[184] P. Anderson, *Lineages of the Absolute State*, 1974, pp. 179-181.
[185] Ibid, p. 178.
[186] Barnett, *Britain and Her Army*, pp. 69-73.
[187] R. Richardson, *The Debate on the English Revolution*, 1998, p.15.

supporters of any supposed scheme to establish a despotism on the French model – most of the Cavalier gentry were as attached to the liberties of the ancient constitution as their old enemies had been.'[188] This emphasis on civil liberties rather than religion was confirmed by Cromwell when he said that at the beginning of the civil war 'religion was not the thing first contended for, but God hath brought it to that issue at last.'[189]

The Political History of London.

The City of London was by far the biggest urban area in England, and became one of the largest cities in Europe. It was the capital of a major sea power, and through its trade had grown immensely powerful. This was illustrated by the Venetian ambassador when he 'reckoned that twenty thousand craft, small and great, were to be seen from London in a day.'[190]

It was relatively immune from the control of the monarchy because of the crown's lack of a standing army. Also, its inland geographical location in the Thames gave it a degree of protection from outside invaders. Its population had grown rapidly during the late sixteenth and seventeenth centuries, reflecting its commercial and financial success and growth.

---

[188] Underdown, *A Freeborn*, p. 115. See also H. Perkin, *The Origins of Modern English Society, 1780-1880*, 1969, pp. 52, 53.
[189] Morrill, *The Nature*, p. 394.
[190] C.V. Wedgwood, *The King's Peace, 1637-1641*, 2001, p. 30.

Table 1: Estimated Population Size of London, 1520-1700.[191]

Approximate Date	Estimated Population of London	Period	Estimated Population of England	London's Population as a Proportion of England's Population
1520	55,000		2,600,000	2.1%
1600	200,000	1520-1600	4,300,000	4.7%
1650	400,000	1600-1650	5,250,000	7.6%
1700	575,000	1650-1700	5,100,000	11.3%

In 1650 towns with a population of over 10,000 numbered about 494,000 people in England, of which about 400,000 – 81% – were living in London.[192] This indicates the overwhelming importance of London in the civil war, dominating the urban landscape and its support for parliament.

Historically, London had formed the centre of opposition to the crown's attempts to control the country through its use of the prerogative. As early as the tenth century the City resisted the invasion of the Danes through its defensive fortifications and its military power:[193] Later in the twelfth century Fitz-Stephen described in some detail the military strength of London:

> ... the city mustered, according to estimation, no less than sixty-thousand foot and twenty thousand horse ... the city was possessed of very considerable military strength, the only efficient source of power in those days ... its wall was strong and lofty, adorned with seven gates, and having all along the north side turrets at equally

---

[191] P. Razzell, C. Spence, 'The history of infant, child and adult mortality in London, 1550-1850', *London Journal*, Volume 32, p. 25.

[192] M. Anderson (ed.), *British Population History*, 1996, p. 122.

[193] G. Norton, *Commentaries on the History, Constitution and Chartered Franchises of the City of London*, 1829, p. 29.

distances. Within it and its immediate suburbs were ... one hundred and twenty-six parish churches.[194]

London formed alliances with barons and others in conflict with the crown, but also supported the crown on occasions, and because of its financial and military power this formed the basis of the City's relative independence and autonomy.[195]

Under a Royal Charter of 1067 the crown had granted London certain rights and privileges, which were confirmed by Magna Carter. These privileges were given on the basis of loans and taxes that the City granted to the crown. However this charter and later ones were frequently abolished by the crown, often requiring major loans and taxes in order to obtain renewals.[196]

The Role of London in the Civil War

London was seen by contemporaries during the civil war as the chief centre of resistance to the crown. Clarendon called London 'the sink of the ill-humours of this kingdom',[197] and a royalist writer declared: 'If (posterity) should ask who would have pulled the crown from the King's head, taken the government off the hinges, dissolved Monarchy, enslaved the laws, and ruined their country; say, 'twas the proud, unthankful, schismatical, rebellious, bloody City of London.'[198] The Venetian ambassador in one of his summaries of events in the civil war claimed 'London was the chief and most determined hot bed of the war against the King. Countless treasure was poured out of the purses

---

[194] Ibid, pp, 76, 83.
[195] Ibid, pp. 75, 156, 158, 204, 211.
[196] Ibid, pp. 70, 96, 97, 115, 156, 157, 282.
[197] V. Pearl, *London and the Outbreak of the Puritan Revolution: City Government and National Politics, 1625-43,* 1961, p. xi; see also T. Hobbes, *English Works,* Volume VI, 1839-45, pp. 191-92.
[198] Pearl, *London,* p. xi.

of private individuals for the support of their armies. The goldsmiths alone are creditors for a loan of 800,000 crowns made to Parliament ...'[199]

At the beginning of the civil war, the Earl of Holland told London's aldermen that 'Your City is the strength of the Kingdom indeed; it is not only the life, but the soule of it; if they [the royalists] can destroy you here, the rest of the Kingdom must all submit and yield.'[200]

London was the biggest manufacturing centre of England during the sixteenth and seventeenth centuries, much of it in the suburbs beyond the control of the City authorities:

From at least the early sixteenth century ... there had been a tendency for domestic industry to establish itself in the suburbs where it was often possible to escape the powers and penalties of the Livery Companies. By 1600, nearly all the leatherworkers and makers of felt hats had left the city and were living in Bermondsey, Southwark and Lambeth ... Many of the newer industries of the period were being attracted to the liberties and out-parishes: sugar-refining and glass-making around Stepney and Islington, alum and dye works to the north and east of the city, and copper and brass mills at Isleworth. Large-scale industrial enterprises, such as ship-building at Rotherhithe and Deptford, and brewing in Clerkenwell and Holborn, were also migrating to the suburbs. There were older industries too: brick-and tile-making in the northern outskirts ... clock-making in Holborn and Westminster; bell-founding in Whitechapel; paper-making in Middlesex, while St. Giles, Cripplegate, was crowded with artisans of the weaving, printing and paper-making trades. Thomas Mun, writing in the sixteen-twenties, described the concentration of workers in the silk industry and recalled how in the past thirty-five years, the winding and twisting of imported raw silk, which previously had not more than 300 in the city and suburbs, had

---

[199] E. and P. Razzell (eds.), *The English Civil War: A Contemporary Account*, Volume 5, 1657-1675, *Relatzione of England by Giovanni Sagredo*, 1656, p. 4.
[200] Lincoln, *London*, p. 106.

now 'set on work above fourteen thousand souls'. The great majority of these would have been workers in the outskirts of London.[201]

These manufacturing areas included Southwark which had long been an area beyond the control of the City – brothels, bear baiting and illegal theatrical productions[202] – but also attracted unregistered artisans and foreigners who brought with them a range of industrial skills:

> The more the city became the commercial centre of England, the more the actual industries moved beyond the walls. The poorer craftsmen who did not have the money to set up shop within the city, and the 'foreigners' or unfree men – often including aliens – who were not qualified to do so, not having served an apprenticeship, tended to settle in the suburbs. Over such recalcitrant workers the [guild] companies found it difficult to assert any control, even when empowered to do so by statute or charter.[203]

This was partly the result of the growth of London's population, which undermined the capacity of the City authorities to regulate industry in the suburbs.[204] The City authorities attempted to exonerate itself from blame for the disorders in the City, writing to the king that 'many of the trouble-makers, they thought, came from the unregulated and disorderly suburbs' which were beyond their control.[205] The radicalism of the suburbs was displayed in 1647 when the inhabitants of Southwark opened the gates of London Bridge to Fairfax's army, resisting the City's attempt to oppose the New Model Army.[206]

---

[201] Pearl, *London*, p. 16.
[202] Anonymous, *The City Laws Showing the Customes, Franchises, Liberties, Priviledges, and Immunities of the Famous City of London*, 1658.
[203] D.J. Johnson, *Southwark and the City*, 1969, p. 313.
[204] P. Wallis, 'Controlling commodities: search and reconciliation in the early modern livery companies', in I.A. Gadd, P. Wallis (eds.), *Guilds, Society and Economy in London, 1450-1800*, 2002, p. 87.
[205] Pearl, *London*, p. 129.
[206] Ibid, p. 28.

Given London's high mortality rate, much of its growth was fuelled by migration from elsewhere in Britain. One of the best sources for data on migration is apprenticeship records. According to Brian Manning, most apprentices were 'of good parentage' whose families 'lived honestly and thriftily in the country.'[207] Only a minority of apprentices came from London and the cosmopolitan nature of the City meant its population came from all areas of the country and with fathers in all occupational groups.[208] The majority of apprentices were from 'middle sort' backgrounds, and it was this group who provided the main support for parliament in London.[209]

Table 2 Apprentices' Fathers: Occupations and Number from London.[210]

Occupation of Father	Total Number	Fathers Residing in London	% Fathers Residing in London
Gentlemen, Esquires & Clerks	33	2	6%
Yeomen	51	0	0%
Artisans. Tradesmen & Merchants	90	38	42%
Husbandmen & Labourers	26	2	8%
Total	200	42	21%

---

[207] B. Manning, *Aristocrats, Plebeians and Revolution in England, 1640-1660*, p. 89.

[208] For data on migration patterns of apprentices see Razzell and Spence, 'The history', p. 27. For confirmation of the very high levels of in-migration to London in the seventeenth century see V.B. Elliott, *Mobility and Marriage in Pre-Industrial England*, Cambridge University Ph. D. thesis, 1978.

[209] B. Manning, *The English People and the English Revolution*, 1991.

[210] Data from C. Webb, *London Livery Apprenticeship Registers*, Volumes 2, 33, 43 and 48, tylers & bricklayers, plumbers, vintners, grocers. First 50 cases were selected from each volume, 1640-1660

As C.V. Wedgewood observed: 'In all the larger towns, and above all in London, the short-haired apprentices who thronged about the place counted among their number gentlemen's sons, yeomen's sons, the sons of professional men and of citizens ... all were alike apprentices, and common interests, hopes and pleasures broke down the barriers of inheritance.'[211] This illustrates the importance of social structures in unifying disparate individual differences, an important factor in the communities involved in the civil war.

London was both cosmopolitan in the origins of its residents, but also in its high degree of literacy. Evidence produced by David Cressy indicates that seventy per cent of men in England were unable to sign their names in 1641-42, whereas this was true of only twenty-two percent of Londoners, suggesting 'that the capital may have provided a uniquely literate environment.'[212] This high level of literacy was partly associated with the occupational structure of London, as indicated by Table 3.

Table 3 Social Structure of Illiteracy in the Diocese of London, City and Middlesex, 1580-1700.[213]

Fathers Occupation	Number Sampled	Proportion Signing with a Mark
Clergy & Professionals	168	0%
Gentry	240	2%
Apprentices	33	18%
Tradesmen & Craftsmen	1,398	28%
Yeomen	121	30%
Servants	134	31%
Labourers	7	78%
Husbandmen	132	79%
Women	1,794	76%

---

[211] Wedgwood, *The King's Peace*, p. 52.
[212] D. Cressy, *Literacy and the Social Order: Reading and Writing in Tudor and Stuart England,* 1980, p. 72; see also P.S. Seaver, *Wallington's World: A Puritan Artisan in Seventeenth Century London*, 1985, p. 5.
[213] Cressy, *Literacy*, p. 121.

There was a significant difference in the high literacy of the gentry, professionals, tradesmen & craftsmen on the one hand – who were in a majority in the sample – and the low literacy of husbandmen, labourers and women on the other.

London not only provided the bulk of the money, supply of weapons, ammunition, uniforms and other military equipment for parliament,[214] but in the early stages of the war also the majority of its soldiers from its trained bands.[215] As Clarendon wrote of the Battle of Edgehill, 'the London train bands, and auxiliary regiments ... behaved themselves to wonder, and were in truth the preservation of that army that day ...'[216] London not only supplied the bulk of the trained parliamentary troops, but also the City was central to the beginning of the war through its participation in mass demonstrations of parliament, as well as creating petitions for political and religious reform.[217] These demonstrations occurred virtually every day, constantly lobbying parliament in a threatening way.[218] The population also demonstrated through its actions its opposition to the crown and support of parliament:

In a desperate attempt to redeem his abortive coup, Charles went down to the city on 5 January [1642], 'the people crying 'Privilege of Parliament' by thousands ... shutting up all their shops and standing at their doors with swords and halberds ... the city was now in mortal fear of the king and his cavaliers. A rumour the next evening that Charles intended to fetch out his victims [five Members of Parliament] by force brought huge crowds into the streets, with whatever arms they could lay their hands on: women provided hot

---

[214] S. Porter, S. Marsh, *The Battle for London*, 2010, p. 41.

[215] J. Morrill (ed.), *Reactions to the English Civil War, 1642-1649*, 1982, p. 19.

[216] E. Hyde, Earl of Clarendon, *The History of the Rebellion and Civil Wars in England Begun in the Year 1641*, Volume 3, 1888, pp. 174, 175.

[217] Fletcher, *The Outbreak*, p. 128; See also R Ashton, *The City and the Court, 1603-1643*, 1979, p. 220.

[218] E. And P. Razzell (eds.), *The English Civil War: A Contemporary Account, Volume 2: 1640-42*, 1996, p. 142.

water to throw on the invaders, stools, forms and empty tubs were hurled into the streets 'to intercept the horse' ... the truth was dawning in Whitehall, between 4 and 10 January, that, for all their swashbuckling of the cavaliers and the protestations of young loyalists at the Inns of Court, the king had lost control of his capital.[219] The five members ... together with Viscount Mandeville [who the king attempted to arrest], embarked at the Three Cranes ... there was a fleet of boats, armed with muskets and ordnance ... Trumpets, drums and martial music accompanied the MPs all the way to Westminster ... More than 2000 men in arms and citizens thronged Westminster Hall ...[220]

The Venetian ambassador claimed in July 1643 that 'the support of this war rests upon the city alone ... [It] has already usurped practically absolute power. They have formed a council for the militia, composed of citizens with supreme authority to do what is considered necessary for self defence while, for the equipment of the Army and its despatch, they are raising money and men ...'[221] It was the absence of a standing army which led to the failure of Charles I to force parliament to comply with his demands, leading to his failure to arrest the five members in 1642. He was unable to force Londoners to reveal their whereabouts, and London turned out to be the chief centre of resistance to royal control.

The Venetian ambassador argued that the Puritans owed their success in the Short Parliament elections to their achievements in 'Swaying the Common votes', and Thomas Hobbes more or less concurred, asserting that 'tradesmen, in the cities and boroughs ... choose as near as they can, such as are most repugnant to the giving of subsidies'.[222]

---

[219] Fletcher, *The Outbreak*, p. 182.
[220] Ibid, p. 185. See Manning, *Aristocrats*, pp. 34-36 for a discussion of the role of London citizens in support of parliament.
[221] E. And P. Razzell (eds.), *The English Revolution: A Contemporary Study of the English Civil War*, 1999, p. 194.
[222] D. Hirst, *The Representative of the People? Voting in England under the Early Stuarts*, 1975, p. 68. See also Morrill (ed.), *Reactions*, p. 70 for a

This illustrates Pellicani's thesis about the role of towns and urban areas in injecting 'dynamism and rationality into a stagnant rural world', and laying the foundation for parliamentarian opposition to the crown. The Venetian Ambassador on the 24th January 1642 gave a further account of the popular support for parliament in London,[223] and on the 7th November described how the Londoners erected barriers to protect the City against the royalist army: 'There is no street, however little frequented, that is not barricaded with heavy chains, and every post is guarded by numerous squadrons. At the approaches to London they are putting up trenches and small forts of earthwork, at which a great number of people are at work, including the women and little children.'[224] On the 15th May the following year, the ambassador described the completion of these fortifications:

The forts round this city are now completed and admirably designed. They are now beginning the connecting lines. As they wish to complete these speedily and the circuit is most vast, they have gone through the city with drums beating, the flag flying to enlist men and women volunteers for the work. Although they only give them their bare food, without any pay, there has been an enormous rush of people, even of some rank, who believe they are serving God by assisting in this pious work, as they deem it.[225]

This was a revolutionary moment demonstrating fierce and violent opposition to the crown. This moment has been described in detail by Pearl as follows:

At the order of the Common Council, pulpits were to resound with the call to defend the city. Ministers were to 'stir up the parishioners' to complete the fortifications with the aid of their children and

---

discussion of the support of trading cities for parliament and the support of cathedral cities for the crown.
[223] Razzell, *The English Civil War,* Volume 2, 1640-42, p. 169.
[224] Razzell, *The English Revolution*, p. 173.
[225] Ibid, p. 188.

servants ... It is not surprising that Pennington's wife, the Lady Mayoress, was there (armed with an entrenching tool, said a Royalist ballad) – we have already encountered her staunch Puritanism. But ladies of rank were also present, as well as fish wives who had marched from Billingsgate in martial order headed by a symbolic goddess of war ... Columns with drums beating and flags flying were sent through the city to recruit more volunteers until 20,000 persons, it was said, were working without pay, drawing only their rations ... The work was allocated by whole parishes, and different trades and Livery Companies, who marched out with 'roaring drums, flying colours and girded swords': over fifty trades were said to have competed in friendly emulation: one day it was 5,000 Feltmakers and Cappers with their families: the next almost the entire Company of Vintners with their wives, servants and wine-porters; on another, all the 2,000 city porters 'in their white frocks', followed by 4,000 of 5,000 Shoemakers, a like number from St. Giles-the-Fields and thereabouts, and the entire inhabitants of St. Clement Dane. In this astonishing manifestation of unity, even the 'clerks and gentlemen' participated as a profession. Those belonging to Parliament, the Inns of Court, and other public offices, were mustered in the Piazza in Covent Garden at seven o'clock in the morning with 'spades, shovels, pickaxes and other necessaries' Popular enthusiasm for the fortifications could reach no higher pitch. Whatever the military value of the defences, the successful mobilization of a great mass of the ordinary people proved the power of parliamentary puritan organization and leadership ... The city had been united in one desire – London should not become a battlefield.[226]

London also had a major influence on provincial towns and urban areas. Clarendon concluded that the chief opposition to the king lay in 'great towns and corporations ... not only the citizens of London ... but also the greatest part of all other cities and market towns of England.'[227] This was mainly through trading

---

[226] Pearl, *London*, pp. 264, 265.

[227] Hyde, *The History,* Volume 2, 1888, pp. 226, 238. Hyde was quoting from Hobbes in this account. The Corporation Act passed in 1661 which prevented non-Anglicans from holding office in towns and corporations, is further confirmation of the role of towns in supporting parliament during the civil war.

links, as described by the Puritan clergyman Richard Baxter in his discussion of the support of tradesmen and artisans for parliament: 'The Reasons which the Party themselves gave was, Because (they say) the Tradesmen have a Correspondency with London, and so are grown to be far more Intelligent sort of Men ... '[228] The role of tradesmen in the civil war was confirmed by Parker, in his *Discourse of Ecclesiastical Politie* published in 1671: 'For 'tis notorious that there is not any sort of people so inclinable to seditious practices as the trading part of a nation ... And, if we reflect upon our late miserable distractions, 'tis easy to observe how the quarrel was chiefly hatched in the shops of tradesmen, and cherished by the zeal of prentice-boys and city gossips.'[229]

There was however internal opposition led by royalists in London to the Puritan takeover of the City.[230] On October 24, 1642 the Venetian ambassador wrote:

In this city a by no means negligible party is disclosing itself in his [the king's] favour, and a goodly number of men, anxious to make themselves known as such by those who inwardly cherish the same laudable sentiments, have introduced the practice, following His Majesty's soldiers, of wearing a rose coloured band on their hats, as a sign that they are his faithful servants. The Mayor, on the other hand, who is a Puritan, whose duty it is to superintend the government of the City, is endeavouring by vigorous demonstrations to prevent the spread of this custom ... [231]

The conflicts sometimes led to violence and the ambassador reported on an affray which took place in St. Paul's Cathedral on the 30th October 1653:

[228] R. Baxter, *Reliquiare Baxterianae*, Part 3, 1696, Part 1, p. 30.
[229] C. Hill, E. Dell (eds.), *The Good Old Cause: The English Revolution of 1640-1660, Its Causes, Course and Consequences,* 1969, p. 238. After the restoration, Bishop Hacket claimed that the 'Conveticles in Corporations were the seminaries out of which the warriors against King and Church came.' Stone, *Causes*, p. 103.
[230] Porter and Marsh, *The Battle*, p. 46.
[231] Razzell, *The English Civil War, Volume 2: 1640-42*, p. 312.

Last Sunday ... a riot took place in St. Paul's Cathedral to the consternation of all present. Among the various sects, of which more than fifty may now be counted in England, that of the Anabaptists which at present numbers many proselytes, had a place assigned it there for preaching purposes ... on the day in question, a considerable mob of apprentices appeared there on a sudden to oust the Anabaptists, whose preacher they began to insult. His followers took his part, but though the military were called in and quelled the tumult, some were killed and others maimed.[232]

But that London was the centre of opposition to the crown was reflected in political affiliation in the post-restoration period. In the 1661 election, it returned to parliament four MPs, two Presbyterians and two Independents.[233] Pepys records a conversation with a Mr Hill on 26th July 1661, telling him that 'the King now would be forced to favour the Presbytery, or the City would leave him.'[234] Later in 1663 Pepys claimed that the royalists were afraid of London and that 'they talk of rebellion, and I perceive they make it their great maxime to be sure to Maister the City of London.'[235] As a result of the fear of the City, in 1683 Charles II suspended the rights and privileges of the corporation, which were only restored by William and Mary in 1689.

Puritanism in the Civil War

---

[232] Razzell, *The English Civil War, Volume 4: 1648-1656*, p. 157. For other accounts of opposition to the radicalism of the sects see K. Lindley, 'London and popular freedom in the 1640s' in R.C. Richardson, G.M Ridden (eds.), *Freedom and the English Revolution*, 1986, pp. 127, 132.

[233] R.C. Thatham, W. Matthews (eds.), *The Diary of Samuel Pepys,* Volume 2, 1995, 20 March 1661, p. 57, fn.

[234] Ibid, p. 141.

[235] Pepys, Volume 4, p. 131.

Religion played a major role in the civil war, although it was not the first issue to provoke parliament in its opposition to the crown.[236] London had been the centre of separatist Puritan congregations from the fourteenth century onwards,[237] and according to Baxter, 'The remnant of the old Separatists and Anabaptists in London was then very small and inconsiderable but they were enough to stir up the younger and inexperienced sort of religious people.'[238] Contact with London influenced opposition to the religious policies of Laud, which was most vocal 'in great clothing towns, because they see no such thing, as they say, in the churches in London.'[239] London's influence on the spread of puritanism occurred through its trading links:

> The growth of puritanism, wrote a hostile critic, was by meanes of the City of London (the nest and seminary of the seditious faction) and by reason of its universall trade throughout the kingdome, with its commodities conveying and deriving this civil contagion to all our cities and corporations, and thereby poisoning whole counties.[240]

London merchants were also responsible for endowing lectureships in their home towns, encouraging the widespread spread of puritanism.[241] Baxter concluded 'that there was [not] in all the World such a City [as London] for Piety, Sobriety and Temperance.'[242]

---

[236] Baxter, *Reliquiare Baxterianae*, Part 1, p. 18.

[237] M.M. Knappen, *Tudor Puritanism*, 1965, pp. 8, 290; A. Woolrych, 'Puritanism, politics and society', in E.W. Ives (ed.), *The English Revolution, 1600-60*, 1968, p. 53; B. Manning, *The English People and the English Revolution*, 1976, p. 38; H. Barbour, *The Quakers in Puritan England*, 1964, pp. 21, 22.

[238] Woolrych, 'Puritanism', p. 53.

[239] Underdown, *Revel*, p. 78.

[240] R.H. Tawney, *Religion and the Rise of Capitalism*, 1936, pp. 203, 204. See also Hyde, *The History*, Volume 2, p. 226; Hirst, *The Representative*, p. 47.

[241] J.E.C. Hill, 'Puritans in the dark corners of the land', *Transactions of the Royal Historical Society*, 5th Series, Volume 13, 1963, p. 95.

[242] Baxter, *Reliquiare Baxterianae*, Part 3, 1696, p. 17.

Perhaps the essence of puritanism was summarized by Bishop Gardiner in the 1540s: 'They [the Puritans] would have all in talking, they speak so much of preaching, so as all the gates of our senses and ways to man's understanding should be shut up, saving the ear alone.'[243] This was the consequence of a 'rational' rejection of all magic and ritual, described so eloquently by Milton and central to Weber's thesis on the protestant ethic. Puritans placed great emphasis on individual conscience often linked to literacy and the reading of the bible.[244] However, much of puritanism was a reaction to the historical threat from catholicism, and one source noted that John Milton who 'was the oracular poet of the hard-working, godly, mercantile London citizenry, who saw themselves increasingly menaced by papists at court and abroad, and for him and his family and friends, the Gunpowder Plot was both the incarnation of their worst nightmares and solid proof that they were right to be afraid.'[245]

The Puritan reformation often created a hostile reaction among the general population, described by one apologist as the 'weeping and bewailing of the simple sort and especially of women, who going into the churches, and seeing the bare walls, and lacking their golden images, their costly copes, their pleasant organs, their sweet frankinsense, their gilded chalices, their goodly streamers, they lament in themselves and fetch deep sighs and bewail the spoiling and laying waste of the church, as they think.'[246]

By the 1620s Dorchester was in the grip of an authoritarian Puritan regime 'which regulated the most minute details of the residents' lives with fanatical rigour. Swearing, tippling, sexual irregularities, 'night walking' absence from church, feasting and merry making, and general idleness: these

---

[243] M.M. Knappen, *Tudor Puritanism,* 1965, p. 68.
[244] Woolrych, 'Puritanism', p. 87.
[245] D. Purkiss, *The English Civil War: A People's History*, 2007 p. 305.
[246] Ibid, pp. 435, 436.

were the common targets of reformers everywhere.'[247] The clothing industry was notorious for its puritanism and its support for parliament; for example, one contemporary noted that Colchester 'is a raged, factious Towne, and now Swarming in Sectaries. Their Trading Cloth ... '[248]

The bulk of London Puritans were made up of tradesmen and artisans:

> ... depositions of Francis Johnson's separatist congregation in London, when they were arrested in 1593, show that they included six shipwrights, five tailors, four servants, three ministers, three weavers or cloth-workers, three carpenters, three clerks, and scriveners, two fishmongers, two haberdashers, two shoemakers, two purse-makers, a glover, a cup-maker, a goldsmith, a 'scholler', a broad-weaver, an apothecary, a coppersmith, and two schoolmasters. Most were men under thirty-five years old.[249]

This socio-economic group has historically been the core group supporting puritanism, as pointed out by Weber: 'With great regularity we find the most genuine adherents of puritanism among the classes which were rising from a lowly status, the small bourgeois and farmers.'[250] The low status suburbs and some of the liberties very quickly earned a reputation for puritanism and after 1640, for radicalism. In 1642, the inhabitants of the eastern suburbs of London, 'mariners, soldiers, or private persons' petitioned against the removal of their own trained bands from the Tower and the violence which had been used against Puritans.[251] Southwark was another suburb with a radical reputation: 'Here, the tanners, glovers and brewery workers were notorious for lawlessness and sedition. In May

---

[247] Underdown, *Revel*, p. 52.
[248] E.S. De Beer, *The Diary of John Evelyn*, Volume 3, 1955, p. 177.
[249] H. Barbour, *The Quakers in Puritan England*, 1964, pp. 21, 22.
[250] M. Weber, *The Protestant Ethic and the Spirit of Capitalism*, 1930, p.174.
[251] Pearl, *London*, p.40.

1640 ... they joined with the sailors of Bermondsey in a great demonstration against Laud.'[252]

However, during the civil war period, puritanism appealed to a greater range of socio-economic groups:

> To contemporaries the chosen seat of the Puritan spirit seemed to be those classes in society which combined economic independence, education, and a certain decent pride in their status, revealed at once in a determination to live their own lives, without truckling to earthly superiors, and in a somewhat arrogant contempt for those who, either through weakness of character or through economic helplessness, were less resolute, less vigorous and masterful, than themselves. Such ... were some of the gentry. Such, conspicuously were the yeomen, 'mounted on a high spirit, as being slaves to none,' especially in the free-holding counties of the east. Such, above all, were the trading classes of the towns, and of the rural districts which had been partially industrialized by the decentralisation of the textile and iron industries.[253]

The leaders of the Puritan movement in parliament were members of the gentry and aristocracy – John Pym, the Earls of Warwick and Holland, Lords Saye, Lord Brooke and John Hampden – who were shareholders in the Providence Company, a trading company in the Caribbean.[254] In the early period of the civil war parliament attracted great support from the aristocracy and gentry on constitutional and economic grounds.[255]

The influence of puritanism on the support for parliament occurred not only in London, but also elsewhere such as in Lancashire, where Oliver Heywood noted in his diary:

> Many days of prayer, have I known my father keep among God's people; yea, I remember a whole night wherein he, Dr Bradshaw, Adam Faernside, Thomas Crompton, and several more did pray all

---

[252] Ibid.
[253] Tawney, *Religion*, p. 208.
[254] C.V. Wedgwood, *The King's War, 1641-1647*, 2001, p. 28.
[255] Baxter, *Reliquiare Baxterianae*, Part 1, pp. 30, 31.

night in a parlour at Ralph Whittal's, upon occasion of King Charles demanding the five members of the House of Commons. Such a night of prayers, tears, and groans, I was never present at all in my life.[256]

The parliamentary Puritans captured both the City government and its trained bands, so giving parliament its first soldiers. This preceded the king's early departure from Whitehall in January 1642, which prevented a successful counter-revolution in London.[257] There was however resistance to the imposition of Puritan discipline, as illustrated by events in London where many riots were touched off by attempts to suppress popular amusements. There were sporadic outbreaks in London, including an apprentice riot at Christmas 1645, and another in April 1648 when troops broke up a Sunday tip-cat game in Moorfields.[258]

There were also internal divisions within the Protestant movement, which eventually led to serious political conflicts. Presbyterians began to increasingly oppose the radicalism of the Independents, the Baptists and other religious sects which dominated the New Model Army, leading to differences in support for the monarchy. By June 1651 'many English Presbyterians were beginning to opt for monarchy ... A Presbyterian minister rejoicing in the name of Love was arrested in London during May for conspiring on behalf of the king. He and another minister were executed on Tower Hill at the beginning of August as a warning to all other Presbyterians sympathetic to Charles II.'[259]

This conflict between Presbyterians and Independents undermined London's central role in opposition to the crown. These political conflicts were partly the result of differences in socio-economic status:

---

[256] W. Haller, *The Rise of Puritanism*, 1957, pp. 297, 298.
[257] Pearl, *London*, p. 132.
[258] Underdown, *Revel*, p. 261.
[259] Ashley, *The English*, p. 173.

The general picture conveyed of Presbyterians in Nottinghamshire is of solid, respectable individuals drawn predominantly from the ranks of the 'middling sort'. Over half of the county's Presbyterians lived in the town of Nottingham. This very much reflects both the national and regional picture of Presbyterianism ... as a faith of the 'urban middle class' ... supporters were predominantly drawn from the upper 'middling sorts', minor or pseudo gentry and their servants. The pseudo-gentry consisted of wealthier merchants, lawyers, civil servants and the younger sons of gentry. Though not part of the landed elite, their status as gentlemen and esquires was increasingly recognized throughout the century and their greater wealth distinguished them from the 'middling sorts'.[260]

The variations in social status between the Presbyterians and the more radical sects was reflected in their appearance: 'While the one party retained the close-cropped and ungainly appearance of the Independents in the days of Cromwell, our Presbyterian clergy developed into full periwigs and flowing luxuriance of band and habit which usually characterized persons of their status after the Restoration.'[261]

Of the Nottingham Presbyterians Lucy Hutchinson wrote

the Presbyterians were more inveterately bitter against the fanatics than even the Cavaliers themselves ... and prayed seditiously in their pulpits and began openly to desire the king, not for good will to him, but only for the destruction of all the fanatics. In 1660, a confrontation occurred in Nottingham between the young men of the town who were demonstrating for the return of the King, and soldiers of Colonel Hacker's regiment ... Charles II's Declaration at Breda in 1660, which promised to allow a 'measure of religious liberty to tender consciences', encouraged many Presbyterians to actively campaign for his return.[262]

---

[260] Jennings, *The Gathering*, p. 244
[261] C.E. Whiting, *Studies in English Puritanism*, 1931, p. 44; Jennings, *The Gathering*, p. 244.
[262] Jennings, *The Gathering*, p. 160.

After the restoration settlement, the Puritan aristocracy and gentry abandoned religious dissent, which became dominated by the middle sort.[263] The middle classes were too influential to allow the eclipse of dissent, which eventually became embedded in English society.[264] The Compton Census of 1676 confirmed that dissenters were 'mostly found in towns with a strong puritan tradition, in centres of the cloth industry, and in places where the social and residential structures created conditions favourable to religious individualism.'[265]

Richard Baxter's Account of the Civil War

Richard Baxter, although a Puritan minister who had served in the New Model Army, was nearest to a contemporary with the most sociological understanding of the civil war. He summarized the role of religion as follows:

> ... the generality of the People through the Land (I say not *all* or every *one*) who were then called Puritans, Precisions, Religious Persons ... and speak against Swearing, Cursing, Drunkeness, Prophaness etc. I say, the main body of this sort of Men, both Preachers and People, adhered to Parliament. And on the other side, the Gentry that were not so precise and strict against an Oath, or Gaming, or Plays, or Drinking, nor troubled themselves so much about the Matter of God and the World to come, and the Ministers and People that were for the King's Book, for Dancing and Recreation on the Lord's Days ... the main Body of these were against the Parliament.[266]

Baxter elaborated on this analysis by stating that 'though it must be confessed that the public safety and liberty wrought very

[263] H. Perkin, *The Origins of Modern English Society, 1780-1880*, 1969, pp. 34, 42.
[264] Ibid; Jennings, *The Gathering*, p. 278
[265] Underdown, *A Freeborn*, pp. 120, 121.
[266] Baxter, *Reliquiare Baxterianae*, Part 1, pp. 30, 31.

much with most, especially the nobility and gentry who adhered to Parliament, yet it was principally the difference about religion that filled up the Parliament's armies and put the resolution and valour into their soldiers, which carried them on in another manner than mercenary soldiers are carried on.'[267] On the other side it was the 'ignorant rabble [who] are everywhere the greatest enemies against Godly ministers and people ... the Tinkers and Sowgaters and water carriers and beggars and bargemen and all the rabble that cannot reade, nor even use, the bible.'[268]

He described the puritanism of artisans, particularly weavers, who were literate and read the bible and other religious works, and how the occupational structure of Kidderminster aided his evangelism.

> A weaver or a Shoemaker or a Taylor can worke without the wetting or tiring his body, and can thinke and talke of the concerns of his soule without impediment to his labour. I have known many [at Kidderminster] that weave in the Long Loome that can set their sermon notes or a good book before them and read and discourse together for mutual edification while they worke. But the poor husbandman can seldom do ... Another help to my Success was, that my People were not *Rich:* There were among them very few *Beggars*, because their common Trade of Stuff-weaving would find work for all, Men, Women and Children, that were able ... The Magistrates of the Town were few of them worth 40 £ *per* An. ... The generality of the Master Workmen, lived but a little better than their Journey-men, (from hand to mouth) ... [269]

Baxter further elaborated the influence of socio-economic status on religious and political affiliation.

> And, which I speak with griefe, except here and there one (of the richer sort mostly that are not pincht with the necessity of others)

---

[267] Quoted in Woolrych, 'Puritanism', pp. 93, 94.

[268] R. Baxter, *The Poor Husbandman's Advocate to Rich Racking Landlords*, 1926, p. 24.

[269] Ibid, p. 26; Baxter, *Reliquiare Baxterianae*, Part 1, p. 94.

there is more ignorance of religion among them than among tradesmen and corporation inhabitants and poore men of manuall artificers. And yet they are not usually guilty of the sins of Gluttony, fornication or adultery, so much as rich citizens and great men's full and idle serving men ... But among merchants, mercers, drapers and other corporation tradesmen, and among weavers, taylors, and such like labourers, yea among poore naylors, and such like, there is usually found more knowledge & religion than among the poor enslaved husbandman. I may well say *enslaved*: for more are so servilely dependent (save household servants and ambitious expectants) as they are on their landlords. They dare not displease them lest they turn them out of their houses; or increase their rents. I believe the Great Landlords have more command of them than the King hath. If a Landlord be but malignant, and enemy to piety or sobriety or peace, his enslaved tenants are at his beck to serve him, in matters of any publike consequence.[270]

He wrote approvingly in 1673 of the presence 'in most places' of 'a sober sort of men of the middle rank, that ... are more equal to religion than the highest or lowest usually are ...'[271] Another Puritan, Nehemiah Wallington, in 1650 anticipated Wesley in his argument about the link between wealth and religious sobriety. He lamented that the 'great change in some men, for ... when they in mean condition, they were humble, and they were for God, but now they be rich ... [they have purchased] brave houses, fine apparel, or belly cheer, when the poor saints have perished in want.'[272]

The authority of a landowner over his employees continued to exist well into the nineteenth century and was illustrated by an account in a local Herefordshire autobiography as follows:

Every worshipper had to wait outside [the church] until the squire had walked to the widening of the path and had made that dramatic

---

[270] Baxter, *The Poor Husbandman's*, p. 27.
[271] J. Barry, C. Brooks (eds.), *The Middling Sort of People: Culture, Society and Politics in England, 1550-1800*, 1994, p. 48.
[272] Seaver, *Wallington's World*, p. 129.

flourish when he pulled out his gold watch and looked up at the church clock. When he was satisfied that the clock had not dared to contradict the time on his watch he would nod to the clock, smile at the admiring people, and hold out his hand to the vicar standing in the doorway to welcome him. Then the bells would ring merrily and then the other direction the staff of another big house marched to the church: the housekeeper and butler in front, two footmen next then about fourteen girls walking in pairs. They were paraded to church every Sunday, but were only allowed one free evening a month.[273]

By this period deference no longer had such a powerful hold as it did in the seventeenth century:

We paid three pounds an acre for our land [in Hertfordshire], and looked over fences at land held by big farmers for seventeen and sixpence an acre ... My father once asked a gentlemen farmer to rent him a piece of ground ... He was given a definite refusal: 'Certainly not' ... Some months later the same gentleman stopped my father and said, 'I suppose you have heard that I am standing at the next election. We've been neighbours for some years. Can I count on your vote?' It was not my father's way to avoid the truth. 'Certainly not', he replied; 'my vote is the most valuable thing I have got ...'[274]

The Role of the Navy.

Protestantism became embedded in the navy, partly as a result of the historical reaction against the threat from Catholic powers, particularly from Spain. This often took the form of Puritan worship:

When Drake set sail from Plymouth on November 15, 1577, on the voyage that was to take him around the world, he carried for the instruction of his men Bibles, prayer books, and Foxe's Book of Martyrs, and had, for chaplain, one Francis Fletcher ... Routine

---

[273] B.L. Coombes, *These Poor Hands: The Autobiography of a Miner Working in South Wales,* 2012. [First published in 1939], pp. 5, 6.
[274] Ibid, p. 4.

religious duties were as rigorously enforced as any other discipline of the ship, and in times of crisis the commander prescribed special religious exercises.[275]

This emphasis on worship also applied to private navies such as those of the East India Company. The Company 'saw to it that ships were amply provided with edifying reading matter. The essentials were a Bible and a Book of Common Prayer, John Foxe's *Book of Martyrs*'[276] and on 'the rare occasions when a ship's commander failed in his religious responsibilities, he was subject of complaints, not only from the chaplains but from the seamen themselves.'[277] The religious radicalism of mariners was sometimes found outside London. For example 'a gang of seamen battered down the images and glass of Rochester Cathedral, and destroyed the cherished library accumulated by the poet Dean Henry King.'[278]

This radicalism led to the participation of ordinary seamen in religious and political protests against the crown's attempt to suppress parliament:

When ... the Five Members returned to Westminster, some 2,000 sailors accompanied them, and their participation was explained in the anonymous *The Seamans Protestation Concerning their Ebbing and Flowing to ... Westminster*. The pamphlet maintained that the sailors had not been summoned but came 'of our own free voluntarie disposition ... as well to protect *White-hall* ... ' This publication too, blamed 'Papists' as the enemy, and concluded with an oath supposedly sworn by the mariners, closely modelled on Parliament's Protestation oath.[279]

---

[275] L.B. Wright, *Religion and Empire: The Alliance between Piety and Commerce in English Expansion, 1558-1625*, 1943, p. 1.
[276] Ibid, p. 71.
[277] Ibid, p. 68.
[278] Wedgwood, *The King's War*, p. 124.
[279] R.J. Blakemore, E. Murphy, *The British Civil Wars at Sea, 1638-1653*, 2018, p. 47.

Had the king held the fleet, it would have created major problems for parliament. He would have been able to blockade the Thames, starving London of trade, food and fuel. Such an outcome would probably have led to a major loss of support for parliament, changing the course of the civil war.[280]

Mariners lived in communities on both sides of the Thames, along the shipyards in Wapping, Shadwell, Limehouse, Rotherhithe and Southwark. [281] St Dunstans's Stepney, was one of the most staunchly protestant in London. This was partly because its congregation included a high proportion of Huguenot refugees.[282]

These areas also contained the artisans and tradesmen living in the suburbs, and they formed with the mariners the crowds who had lobbied and petitioned parliament for radical political and religious reform.[283] Much of the political and religious divide which shaped the civil war was based on communities which cut across individual differences of support, providing socially structured action groups.

Parliament's control of the navy was brought about by the Earl of Warwick who seized it in 1642, with only two captains refusing to surrender their ships.[284] The gentlemen commanders who had dominated the navy before the civil war were replaced by men who had been active in popular radical politics.[285] According to Bernard Capp only 20 of the 319 officers appointed by the Commonwealth and Protectorate, came from the gentry, mostly from younger branches which had gone into trade.[286]

Parliament used the navy to land forces and blockade ports held by the royalists, which played an important role in

---

[280] M.J. Lea-O'Mahoney, *The Navy in the English Civil War* (D.Phil. University of Exeter, 2011), p. 8.

[281] Wedgwood, *The King's Peace*, p. 29.

[282] Purkiss, *The English*, pp. 41, 42.

[283] C.V. Wedgwood, *The King's War, 1641-1647*, 1983, p. 61; Purkiss, *The English*, p. 470.

[284] Wedgwood, *The King's War*, p. 105.

[285] Blakemore and Murphy, *The British*, p. 95.

[286] R. Hutton, *The British Republic 1649-1660*, 2000, p. 12.

winning the civil war.[287] The navy also ensured that weapons could be imported from abroad – by 4 October 1642 these included 5,580 pikes, 2,690 muskets, 980 pairs of pistols, 246 carbines and 3,788 sets of armour.[288] Warwick's sailors – approximately 3,000 strong – were also organized into two regiments and played an important part in parliament's victory.[289] However, after the polarisation of the opposition into Presbyterian and Independent factions in 1648, there was a significant defection of ships and mariners from the parliamentary cause.[290]

Socio-Economic Status and the Civil War

An analysis of the socio-economic status of participants in the civil war is fraught with difficulty. Information on the elites is relatively easy to obtain, but data on rank-and-file members of political and religious groups is largely lacking.[291] Although statistical analysis is virtually impossible, literary evidence is abundant but often very partisan given the nature of the civil war. However, by adopting the principle of triangulation which uses sources from both sides of the conflict, it is possible to achieve a degree of consensus.

There is also the difficulty of significant changes in the adherents to parliament and the crown, so that for example more than two-fifths of the Commons and the majority of the Lords left Westminster for the king's cause in 1642.[292] Also there were major changes in the social structure of England during the

---

[287] Blakemore and Murphy, *The British*, p. 74.

[288] Porter and March, *The Battle*, p. 41.

[289] Ibid, p. 80.

[290] Blakemore and Murphy, *The British*, p. 137; Lea-O'Mahoney, *The Navy*, p.199.

[291] Underdown, *Revel*, pp. viii, 183-184; C. Holmes, *The Eastern Association in the English Civil War*, 1974, p. 172.

[292] R Richardson, *The Debate on the English Revolution*, 1998, p. 45.

sixteenth and seventeenth centuries which affected the social composition of supporters of the crown and parliament:

> ... between 1540 and 1640 ... The number of peers rose from 60 to 160; baronets and knights from 500 to 1400; esquires from perhaps 800 to 3,000; and armigerous gentry from perhaps 5,000 to 15,000 ... This numerical expansion was made possible mainly by the transfer of huge quantities of landed property first from the church to the crown and then from the crown to the laity, mostly gentry, in a series of massive sales to pay for foreign wars.[293]

The House of Commons itself changed during this period, 'so that it grew from about 300 to approximately 500, and the gentry component in it rose from about 50 per cent to approximately 75 per cent.'[294] Throughout the civil war there were major changes in the numbers of adherents to the parliamentarian and royalist armies, making it difficult to carry out statistical analysis of membership numbers. The alignment of forces of 1640 was quite different from that of 1642, by which time a large block of former Parliamentarians had moved over to reluctant Royalism.

There were changes again in 1648, when 'conservative elements among the Parliamentarians, misleadingly known as Presbyterians, swung back to the side of the king.'[295] Many of those who had supported parliament on constitutional grounds in 1640, like Sir Edward Hyde, transferred their allegiance in 1642, whereas those who supported parliament on religious grounds tended to continue to support the parliamentary cause.[296]

The most significant change in parliament occurred in December 1648 when 'under the command of Colonel Thomas Pride, the army purged the House of Commons of any opposition (some 100 MPs were excluded 45 who were actually arrested – others prudently removed themselves). It was the remaining

---

[293] Stone, *Causes*, pp. 72, 73.
[294] Ibid, p. 92.
[295] Ibid, p. 34.
[296] Ibid, p., 143.

"Rump" of around 70 MPs who would address the matter of bringing the King to trial.'[297]

Recent research by Alexandra Shepard using church court depositions indicates that wealth inequality increased markedly during the first half of the seventeenth century.

Table 4: Median Wealth in England, Deflated to 1550-1559 Values, by Social Group Over Time.[298]

	1550-74	1575-99	1600-24	1625-49
Gentry (N = 367)	£16.00	£8.00	£59.30	£50.00
Yeomen (N = 1104)	£5.34	£7.27	£23.92	£50.00
Craft/Trade (N = 2185)	£2.40	£1.40	£2.99	£5.00
Husbandmen (N = 2127)	£4.00	£3.37	£5.93	£5.00
Labourers (N = 273)	£1.58	£1.35	£1.36	£1.03

Although the gentry increased their wealth – increasing by about three times – the yeomen's wealth had grown nearly ten times, while labourers' worth decreased slightly. There was little change among husbandmen and a doubling of wealth among craft/tradesmen. This data suggests that this was a period of 'the rise of the yeomanry' during the first half of the seventeenth century. Wrightson has summarized the situation of yeomen:

Like the gentry, they benefited from low labour costs as employers, while as large-scale producers they stood to gain from rising prices ... Again like the gentry, they took a thoroughly rational and calculating attitude towards profit ... often ambitious, aggressive, [and] small capitalists ... [they experienced] gradually rising living standards, the rebuilding of farmhouses and their stocking with goods of increasing sophistication and comfort.[299]

---

[297] D. Flintham, *Civil War London*, 2017, p. 41.
[298] Data from *Perceptions of Worth and Social Status in Early Modern England*, ESRC Reference Number RES-000-23-1111.
[299] Wrightson, *English Society*, pp. 134, 135.

These changes had a significant effect on the relationships between different social classes. Village elites composed of local gentry and prosperous yeomen farmers and tradesmen began to attempt to control the impoverished and unruly elements of the poor.[300]

> Long before the civil war, especially in towns and pasture regions where cloth-working or other industrial pursuits were available, the growing gulf between the people 'of credit and reputation' and their less prosperous neighbours was reflected in the emergence of parish elites who saw it as their duty to discipline the poor into godliness and industriousness, and who found in puritan teaching (broadly defined) their guide and inspiration. Along with reformist elements of the gentry and clergy, they mounted a campaign against the traditional culture of the lower orders.[301]

The merging of interests between the gentry and prosperous yeomen and tradesmen makes it difficult to distinguish social statuses in this period.[302] One-hundred-and-two Yorkshiremen obtained coats of arms as gentlemen between 1558 and 1642 and roughly half of them were yeomen farmers. In Lancashire two-hundred-and-two families entered the gentry: ...'the majority were prosperous yeomen.'[303] Gordon Batho has concluded that 'there was no sharp distinction between lesser gentry and the richer yeomen ... In innumerable wills and legal documents of the age a man is described in one place as a yeoman and in another as a gentleman ... '[304]

Oliver Cromwell himself illustrates the ambiguity of status in this period. John Morrill has summarised the evidence as follows:

---

[300] Manning, *The English People*, p. 46; Wrightson, *English Society*, pp. 168-73, 181.
[301] Underdown, *Revel*, pp. 275, 276.
[302] Hirst, *The Representative,* p. 4; see also O'Day, 'Universities', p. fn 19, p. 100; Wedgwood, *The King's War*, p. 205.
[303] Manning, *1649: The Crisis*, p. 58.
[304] Ibid.

... his standing in St Ives was essentially that of a yeoman, a working farmer. He had moved down from the gentry to the 'middling sort' ... Despite his connections with ancient riches, Cromwell's economic status was much closer to that of the 'middling sort' than that to the country gentry and governors. He always lived in towns, not in a country manor house; and he worked for his living. He held no important local offices and had no tenants or others dependent upon him beyond a few household servants. When he pleaded for the selection of 'russet-coated captains who know what they are fighting for', and when he described his troopers as 'honest men, such as feared God', this was not the condescension of a radical member of the elite, but the pleas of a man on the margins of the gentry on behalf of those with whom he had had social discourse and daily communion for twenty years.

Cromwell had been elected to parliament in Cambridge in 1640 'by a godly clique of otherwise obscure individuals rather than as a result of aristocratic patronage.'[305] This illustrates the role of towns in shaping the English parliament, where 'between 1584 and November 1640 the proportion of all Commons' representation controlled by boroughs rose from 79% to 82%.'[306]

A further example of the blurring of statuses is to be found in Shakespeare's social circle in Stratford:

The Quiney family was one of the most respectable in the town; they bore arms, had been long settled in the community, and were influential members of the corporation. They were well-educated – Richard conducted much of his correspondence with Abraham Sturley, who had been educated at Queen's College, Cambridge, in Latin – and appears from the language of this correspondence, to have been strongly puritan. Nevertheless, along with all other leading

---

[305] J.C. Davis, 'Oliver Cromwell', in M.J. Braddick (ed.), *The English Revolution*, 2015, p. 224.
[306] P. Withington, 'Urban citizens and England's civil wars', Braddick, *The English*, p. 316.

townsmen, they frequently engaged in illegal speculative activity, particularly in corn and malt.[307]

Shakespeare's own family illustrates the ambiguities in status at the end of the sixteenth century. His father John, officially a glover, had illegally traded in wool, corn and money-lending, and had yet been granted a coat of arms in 1596, warranting the title and status of 'gentleman', in spite of an earlier bankruptcy.[308] Shakespeare himself also engaged in these illegal activities. Not only did local tradesmen engage in the hoarding of grain during a period of scarcity, but all four local landed magistrates had arrangements with the townsmen to illegally store large stocks of grain on their behalf.[309] In 1601 the poor of Stratford were 'in number seven hundred and odd, young and old – something like forty per cent of the total population.'[310] As a result, the hoarding of grain resulted in threatened violence and riot by the poor, but they unwittingly appealed to the magistrates without realising that they were some of the leading forestallers of grain.[311]

The conflicting and contradictory position of the townsmen and local gentry, many of whom were of the Puritan persuasion, left them exposed to the charge of hypocrisy. When a dispute over the appointment of the Puritan minister, Thomas Wilson, broke out in 1621, his supporters were satirized in the following verse: 'Stratford is a Town that doth make a great show. But yet is governed but by a few. O Jesus Christ of heaven I think that they are but seven Puritans without doubt? For you may know them. They are so stout. They say 'tis no sin, their neighbour's house to take. But such laws their father the devil did make ... One of the Chiefest hath read far in Perkin's works. The rest are deep dissembling hypocrites.'[312]

---

[307] P. Razzell, *William Shakespeare: The Anatomy of an Enigma*, 1990, p. 26.
[308] Ibid, p. 28.
[309] Ibid, p. 142.
[310] Ibid, p. 140
[311] Ibid, pp. 141, 142.
[312] Ibid.

There was a great deal of social mobility at this time, with many wealthy yeomen and tradesmen achieving gentry status during the first half of the seventeenth century.[313] Gentlemen and yeomen/tradesmen were educated together in local grammar schools and universities, and so shared similar cultural backgrounds.[314] There was also an increase in the literacy of both the gentry and the middle classes, whereas most husbandmen and labourers remained illiterate during this period.[315] Because of the fear of literacy amongst the 'lower sort', as early as 1543 parliament had stipulated that 'no women, nor artificers, prentices, journeymen, servingmen of the degrees of yeomen or under, husbandmen nor labourers shall read the Bible or New Testament in English to himself or any other, privately or openly.'[316] Hobbes had complained that 'after the Bible was translated into English, every man, nay every boy and wench, that could read English thought they spoke with God Almighty and understood what He said.'[317]

The fear that established authority had of the 'lower sort' obtaining literacy was probably well-founded. As early as the fourteenth and fifteenth centuries 'throughout southern and central England groups of Lollards met secretly in towns and villages to read or listen to readings of Scripture and to consider their contemporary application. Most of them came from the class of skilled, literate traders and craftsmen. They were masons, carpenters, wool-merchants and leatherworkers – men and women whose work took them long distances in search of employment and markets.'[318]

---

[313] Wrightson, *English Society*, p.27; see also Manning, *1649 The Crisis*, p. 51.
[314] R. O'Day, 'Universities and professions in the early modern period', *oro.open.ac.uk*, pp. 83, 87, 101; Wrightson, *English Society,* pp. 89; 186, 191-193; Stone, *Causes*, pp. 74.
[315] Wrightson, *English Society,* p. 191.
[316] D. Wilson, *The People and the Book: The Revolutionary Impact of the English Bible 1380-1611*, 1976, p. 87.
[317] Stone, *Causes*, p.101.
[318] Wilson, *The People*, p. 26.

This was as we have seen the classic socio-economic group associated with puritanism, but nevertheless there were many adherents of a higher status. When Prynne, Burton and Bastwick, martyrs to the protestant cause who had been punished and exiled by the king, returned to London on the 28th November 1640, 'some three thousand coaches, and four thousand horsemen' were included in the crowd that welcomed them back to London.[319] During the building of the defensive wall around London, the people helping to build the wall included 'a great company of the common council and diverse other chief men of the city'.[320]

Nevertheless the evidence suggests that wealthy aldermen largely supported the crown: 'strong financial ties bound the wealthy citizens to the crown ... the court contented itself with the belief that the disturbances involved the meaner sort of people and that the affections of the better and main part of the city favoured the king.'[321] As a result of this belief, the king placed a guard to the approaches of the Commons with soldiers 'who disliked or despised the Londoners and officers who, being Westminster men, were friends and dependents of the Court.'[322]

Clarendon summarized his conclusions about the link between status and affiliation to crown or parliament:

> ... though the people in general [favoured the king], (except in great towns and corporations, where, besides the natural malignity, the factious lecturers, and emissaries from the parliament, had poisoned the affections,) and especially those of quality, were loyally inclined ...[323]

[319] Purkiss, *The English*, p. 99.

[320] Ibid, p. 286.

[321] S. Porter, S. Marsh, *The Battle for London*, 2010, p. 9; see also D. Hirst, *The Representative of the People? Voting in England under the Early Stuarts*, 1975, p. 138; R. Ashton, *The City and the Court, 1603-1643*, 1979, p. 206; Pearl, *London*, p. xi.

[322] Wedgwood, *The King's War*, p. 32.

[323] Hyde, *The History*, Volume 2, p. 226.

Most contemporaries believed that the main support for parliament came from London and other corporate towns, with a strong support from the middle sort.[324]

Lilly writing in 1651 described how the terms Cavalier and Roundhead originated:

> They [the Puritans] had their hair of their heads very few of them longer than their ears, whereupon it came to pass that those who usually with their cries attended at Westminster were by a nickname called *Roundheads*, and all that took part or appeared for his Majesty, *Cavaliers* ... However the present hatred of the citizens was such unto gentlemen, especially courtiers, that few durst come into the city; or if they did they were sure to receive affronts and be abused.[325]

Pepys in his diary frequently distinguished between citizens and gentlemen living in London; for example at the end of December 1662 he wrote 'only not so well pleased with the company at the house today, which was full of Citizens, there hardly being a gentleman or woman in the house ...'[326]

There is evidence however of tensions between the aristocracy and gentry on the one hand and the middle classes during the outbreak of the civil war. The burden of ship money fell disproportionately on yeomanry and tradesmen, something which was highlighted by William Prynne in his attacks on the

---

[324] An indication of where the city's sympathies lay was the return of four members opposed to the court in the election to the Long Parliament in October 1640.

[325] W. Lilly *The True History of King James I and Charles* I, 1715, pp. 55-56 – first published in 1651, p. 246. The association between puritanism and short hair was also found in New England where the rule was 'that none should wear their hair below their ears'. T. Hutchinson, *The History of the Colony and Province of Massachusetts*, Vol.1, 1936, pp. 130, 131. Some Baptists continued to prohibit long hair as late as 1689. See A.C. Underwood, *A History of the English Baptists,* 1947, p.130.

[326] R. Latham, W. Matthews (eds.), *The Diary of Samuel Pepys,* Volume 3, 1995, p. 295.

crown.[327] These tensions were exacerbated by the attitudes of the aristocracy and gentry towards the new middle classes.

> The pretensions of yeomen to quality with gentry caused resentment amongst some gentlemen. 'The yeomanry' wrote Edward Chamberlayne ...'grow rich, and thereby so proud, insolent, and careless, that they neither give that humble respect and awful reverence which in other Kingdoms is usually given to nobility, gentry, and clergy' ... which has 'rendered them so distasteful ... even to their own gentry' that the latter sometimes wished that the yeomen's activities were less profitable or they were taxed more heavily.[328]

This is consistent with the patterns of wealth depicted in Shepard's analysis of church court depositions, whereby the yeomanry achieved parity with the gentry by the middle of the seventeenth century.

A number of scholars have noted the breaking of the alliance between the gentry and the middle classes, as the demands for political and religious reforms began to emerge.[329] However, this reflected some long-term tensions between these socio-economic groups. For example, as early as 1576, a clause was inserted in an Act of Parliament prohibiting West Country clothiers from buying more than 20 acres of land.[330]

In Somerset it was alleged that

> ... a great part of the estate of every farmer or substantial yeoman should be taken from them; alleging that some lords had said that £20 by the year was enough for any peasant to live by ... persuading the substantial yeomen and freeholders that at least two parts of their states would by that commission taken from them ... For though the gentlemen of ancient families estates in that county were for the most part well affected to the King ... yet there were people of inferior

---

[327] See Manning, *The English People*, pp. 10, 231.
[328] E. Chamberlayne, *Anglia Notitia*, 1672, pp. 61-63.
[329] Manning, *The English People*, p. 46
[330] L. Stone, *The Crisis of the Aristocracy*, 1965, p. 28.

degree, who, by good husbandry, clothing, and other thriving arts, had gotten very great fortunes, and, by degrees getting themselves into the gentlemen's estates, were angry that they found not themselves in the same esteem and reputation with those whose estates they had ... These from the beginning were fast friends to the Parliament, and many of them were now entrusted by them as deputy-lieutenants in their new ordinance of the militia ... [331]

Likewise in Yorkshire when the king summoned the gentry of the county to York in May 1642, he omitted to summon the freeholders, who responded by claiming 'ourselves equally interested in the common good of the county', and as a result 'did take boldness to come in person to York ... thereupon the doors of the meeting house were shut, we utterly excluded ...' [332] Elsewhere 'Lord Paulet in opposition to the Militia at a combustion in *Wells* ... declared that it was not fit for any Yeomen to have allowed more than the poor Moitie of ten pounds a year ... when the power should be totally on their [the royalists'] side, they shall be compelled to live at that low allowance ... the people did not take the speech as only directed to the Yeomen, but to all men under the degree of a Gentleman ... the Tradesmen and Merchants ....' [333]

One Parliamentarian tract published in 1643 claimed

that this was proof that the royalists intended 'a government at discretion' after the French fashion, because 'the middle sort of people of England, and yeomanry' were the chief obstacles to such a change, and as they composed the main part of the militia, 'then by policy, or even plain force' they must be disarmed ... [334]

This can be seen indirectly as a consequence of 'the rise of the yeomanry', creating increasing demands by yeomen for equal

---

[331] Hyde, *History,* Volume 2, p, 296.
[332] Hill and Dell, *The Good Old*, pp. 244, 245.
[333] *A Memento for Yeomen, Merchants, Citizens and All the Commons in England,* August 23, 1642, B.M. E 113 (13), pp. 4, 5.
[334] Manning, *Aristocrats,* p. 69.

status with their aristocratic and gentry neighbours. This resulted in tension between these groups, leading on occasions to violence. For example, 'the cavaliers in Somersetshire have used violence on the yeomanry, and have turned them out of doors, and take their arms from them, the people seeing it could not suffer it, for if they prevail now they think they shall be slaves forever.'[335]

Fear was a leading component of the civil war. As we have seen, in London the king and many Members of Parliament and the House of Lords had left London in early 1642 as a result of the fear of the population threatening them with violence and intimidation. Many of these members had originally supported parliament on constitutional grounds, but fear had driven them into the support of the king. Many Protestants feared Catholics, particularly after Spain's attempt to invade England during the late sixteenth century. In the provinces many of the aristocracy and gentry feared the threats from the poor and the increasing radicalism of the middle classes. And at a later stage of the war, the Presbyterians feared the increasing power of the radicals in the New Model Army.

A similar process occurred in France in the eighteenth century when the middle classes were not allowed to access higher social statuses, which according to Eleanor Barber was one of the factors behind the French Revolution.[336] There is ample evidence that the middle classes played a significant role in political developments in the English civil war, although the claim that the middle sort were the main supporters of parliament has been contested by a number of historians.[337] There is however plenty of contemporary literary evidence to indicate that

---

[335] Manning, *The English People*, p. 328.

[336] E. Barber, *The Bourgeoisie in 18th Century France*, 1957, p. 142.

[337] The main proponent of the middle sort hypothesis is Manning in his *The English People*. The critics of this thesis have pointed out that many of the middle classes supported royalism or remained neutral. See J. Barry and C, Brooks (eds.), *The Middling Sort of People: Culture, Society and Politics in England, 1550-1800*, 1994, p. 22; Morrill (ed.), *Reactions*, p. 71.

the middle classes played an important role in the support of parliament. Keith Wrightson has summarised this evidence:

London demonstrators against episcopacy in 1641 were characterized as being 'men of mean or a middle quality', as distinct from both 'aldermen, merchants or common councilmen' on the one hand, and the 'vulgar' on the other. In Worcester 'the middle sort of people' supported the parliamentarian cause. 'The middle and inferior sort of people' of Birmingham resisted Prince Rupert's advance in 1643 despite the defeatist fears of the 'better sort'. At Bristol 'the King's cause and party were favoured by two extremes in that city; the one the wealthy and powerful men, the other of the basest and lowest sort, but disgusted by the middle rank, the true and best citizens'. Such activism and the terms in which it was described were not confined to urban centres. In Somerset the royalists were said to consist of most of the gentry and their tenants, while parliament had the support of 'yeomen, farmers, petty freeholders, and such as use manufacturers that enrich the country', under the leadership of some gentlemen and others of lesser degree, who 'by good husbandry, clothing and other thriving arts, had gotten very great fortunes' In Gloucestershire the king was supported by both the rich and 'the needy multitude' who depended upon them. Parliament allegedly had the hearts of 'the yeomen, farmers, clothiers, and the whole middle rank of the people'. According to Lucy Hutchinson, 'most of the gentry' of Nottinghamshire 'were disaffected to the parliament', but 'most of the middle sort, the able substantial freeholders, and the other commons, who had not their dependence upon the malignant nobility and gentry, adhered to the parliament.' Again, Richard Baxter saw the king as finding support among most lords, knights and gentlemen of England, together with their tenants and 'most of the poorest people', while parliament had a minority of the gentry 'and the greatest part of the tradesmen and freeholders and the middle sort of men, especially in those corporations and countries which depend on clothing and such manufactures'.[338]

---

[338] K. Wrightson, 'Sorts of people in Tudor and Stuart England' in Barry and Brooks, *The Middling Sort*, p. 46.

The critique of the thesis that the 'middle sort' were the chief supporters of parliament, has not allowed for the major support for parliament of the middle classes in London, who were the prime movers at the beginning of the civil war and were the mainstay of the New Model Army who shaped its outcome.

The turning point in the support of London for parliament occurred in elections held on December 21 1641 to the Common Council brought in men with active parliamentary Puritan sympathies. These elections transformed the politics of London, and Clarendon attributed to them the king's departure from Whitehall early in January 1642.[339]

The take-over by radical elements of the Common Council in December 1641, 'when that body was effectively captured by the radical party ... Now (wrote one later royalist sympathizer) outgoe all the grave, discreet, well-affected Citizens ... and in their Stead are chosen *Fowke* the Traytor, *Ryley* the Squeeking bodyes-maker, *Perkins* the Taylor, *Norminton* the Cutler, young beardless *Coulson* the Dyer, *Gill* the Wine-Cooper, and *Jupe* the Laten-man in *Crooked-Lane, Beadle* of the Ward ...'[340]

This was a time of revolutionary fervour:

when Alderman *Pennington* and Captain *Venne* brought down their Myrmidons to assault and terrrifie the Members of both Houses, whose faces or opinion they liked not ... when these rude multitudes published the names of Members of both Houses, as enemies of the Commonwealth, who would not agree to their frantic propositions; when the names of those were given by Members of the House, that they might be proscribed, and torn in pieces by those Multitudes, when many were driven away for fear of their lives from being present at those consultations?[341]

---

[339] Pearl, *London*, p. 132.
[340] Ashton, *The City*, pp. 205, 206.
[341] Ibid, p. 215. See also Stone, *Causes*, p.145.

This resulted in 236 MPs leaving parliament in June 1642, mostly to join the King at York.[342] Class hostility grew during the civil war, often associated with religious radicalism. Positions in local and other authorities were increasingly held by wealthy members of the middle classes. The nobility and gentry who had supported parliament against the king found that they were neglected, and people of lower status were preferred for places of authority. Clarendon noted that

> The nobility and gentry who had advance the credit and reputation of the Parliament by concurring with it against the King found themselves totally neglected, and the most inferior people preferred at all places of trust and profit ... most of those persons of condition, who ... had been seduced to do them [parliament] service throughout the kingdom, decline to appear longer in so detestable employment; and now a more inferior sort of the common people succeeded in those employments, who thereby exercised so great an insolence over those were in quality above them, and who always had a power over them, that was very grievous ... all distinction of quality being renounced. And they who were not above the condition of ordinary inferior constables six or seven years before, were now the justices of peace, sequestrators, and commissioners; who executed the commands of Parliament in all the counties of the kingdom with such rigour and tyranny as was natural for such persons to use over and towards those upon whom they had formerly looked at such a distance.[343]

Lucy the wife of Thomas Hutchinson tells 'how her husband, the parliamentary officer, found that his allies in Nottinghamshire distrusted civility, thinking it scarce possible for anyone to continue to be both a gentleman and a supporter of the godly interest.'[344]

In 1646 the Presbyterian Thomas Edwards declared that in the previous two years, and especially since parliament's

---

[342] Stone, *Causes*, p.141.
[343] Hyde, *The History*, Volume 4, pp. 287, 315.
[344] L. Hutchinson, *Memoirs of the Life of Colonel* Hutchinson, 1972, p.132.

victory at Naseby, the sectaries had in the most insolent and unheard-of manner abused 'all sorts and ranks of men even to the highest.'[345] Clarenden complained that the sects had 'discountenanced all forms of reverence and respect, as relics and marks of superstition.' In 1663 the Lord Mayor of London issued an order forbidding and repetition of the 'rudeness, affronts, and insolent behaviour' displayed by 'the unruly and meaner sort of people' during the Interregnum towards noblemen, gentlemen and persons of quality passing in their coaches or walking through the streets of the City. This 'undutifulness and contempt of their superiors', he claimed, had been encouraged by the 'late usurped powers.' In fact, similar orders had been issued in 1621, for hostility to strangers and jeering at the coaches of the aristocracy, and were endemic in pre-civil war London.[346]

However, the civil war increased this hostility:

> ... the fury and license of the common people, who were in all places grown to that barbarity and rage against the nobility and gentry, (under the style of *cavaliers*,) that it was not safe for any to live at their houses who were taken notice of as no votaries to the Parliament.[347]

The City authorities complained to the king that most of the disorders came not from them but 'from the unregulated and disorderly suburbs', located in 'the skirts of the city where the Lord Mayor and magistrates of London have neither power ... [and which were] fuller of the meaner sort of people.'[348] The reaction by wealthy merchants in London after 1643 accounted for the development of political presbyterianism in the City.[349] Presbyterianism attracted both aristocrats and the gentry not only in London but elsewhere in the country, and contemporaries saw

---

[345] Manning, *1649: The Crisis*, p. 321.

[346] K. Thomas, *In Pursuit of Civility: Manners and Civilization in Early Modern England*, 2018, p. 322.

[347] Ibid, p. 318. See also Hill and Dell, *The Good Old*, p. 246.

[348] Pearl, *London*, p. 129.

[349] Ibid, p.284.

the Independents, Baptists and Quakers as the main source of the extreme and radical opposition to the crown.[350] The Quakers turned out to be the most radical of the sects, including a refusal to pay tithes or to doth hats to superiors and recognize titles, which appeared extremely threatening to established authority.[351] They also criticised the aristocracy and gentry, claiming that the latter owed their position to the 'Norman Yoke', seizing land and property by forceful dispossession.[352]

Although the Quakers had relatively humble origins – many of them had come from a Baptist background[353] – they were very literate and established their own libraries with printed books and tracts.[354] Although they eventually espoused pacifism, during the civil war period they were active in the parliamentary army.[355] All Puritan denominations appear to have had high levels of literacy, particularly the Presbyterians, many of whose ministers had university degrees.[356]

Socio-Economic Status and the Royalist and New Model Armies.

There is a difficulty in analyzing the social status of the parliamentary army during the civil war because of its changing composition and numbers. 'In March 1649, the Commonwealth had in England 44,373 soldiers ... in July 1652 had nearly 70,000, whereas in February 1660, its numbers were fixed at

---

[350] Jennings, *The Gathering*, pp. 174, 175, 187; G. Yule, *The Independents in the English Civil War*, 1958, p. 57.
[351] Jennings, *The Gathering*, p, 187.
[352] B. Reay, *The Quakers and the English Revolution*, 1985, p. 39.
[353] Jennings, *The Gathering*, p.269; Reay, *The Quakers*, p. 20.
[354] Jennings, *The Gathering*, pp. 260, 261.
[355] Reay, *The Quakers*, pp. 41, 42, 50.
[356] Jennings, *The Gathering,* p. 244.

28,342.'[357] This is less of a difficulty with the royalist army as it was in existence for only a relatively short period.

This essay will focus on the New Model Army, for which there is relatively full information. It was also the most radical of all of parliament's armies, playing the major role in the outcome of the war. According to Ian Gentiles, 'while the number of horse [in the New Model] remained fairly stable between roughly 5,000 and 6,500, the foot and the dragoons underwent violent fluctuations in numbers, from 18,000 to 7,000, owing to massive desertions. The men who stamped the New Model with a distinctive character were therefore a tight group numbering about 5,000 horse and 7,000 foot.'[358] It is these fluctuations which make statistical analysis so difficult, and it is therefore necessary to rely mainly on literary evidence.

The origin of the social status of the New Model Army lies in the recruitment of officers to the Eastern Association. One of the officers of the army, Dodson a native of the Isle of Ely, had served with Cromwell from the outbreak of the war, and described how Cromwell had packed the army with officers sympathetic to the sectaries – that in choosing officers for his own regiment, he had dismissed 'honest gentlemen and souldiers that ware stout in the cause', and replaced them 'with common men, pore and of meane parentage, onely – he would give them the title of godly pretious men'.[359] Whitelocke, another contemporary, described Cromwell's men 'as being mostly freeholders and freeholders' sons, who had engaged in this quarrel upon a matter of conscience.'[360]

However there is some evidence that in the early years the aristocracy and gentry played a significant role in the parliamentary army. Baxter claimed that when 'the *Earl of Essex* came to *Worcester*, with many Lords and Knights, and in a

---

[357] C.H. Firth, *Cromwell's Army*, 1902, pp. 34, 35.
[358] I. Gentiles, *The New Model Army in England, Ireland and Scotland, 1645-1653*, 1992, p. 40.
[359] Holmes, *The Eastern*, p. 199.
[360] A. Fraser, *Cromwell Our Chief of Men*, 1974, p. 100.

flourishing [parliamentary] army, [they were] gallantly cloathed ...'[361] This was confirmed by another source which claimed that in the parliamentary army 'only seven of the new colonels were not gentlemen, and of nine of them were from noble families.'[362] This was in the early stages of the civil war when constitutional concerns were the dominant issue. In June 1647 there was a purge of conservative presbyterian officers from the army, including 'some of the most socially distinguished of the army's founders.'[363]

The discipline for which the New Model was famous for originated in the way Cromwell treated his troops. 'At Huntingdon, two troopers who tried to desert were whipped in the market place ... Colonel Cromwell had 2,000 brave men, well disciplined; no man swears but he pays his twelve pence; if he be drunk he is set in the stocks, or worse, if one call the other "Roundhead" he is cashiered ...'[364] This religious zeal was partly responsible for the discipline that the New Model Army showed in battle, allowing them to defeat royalist armies. However, this was also the result of harsh discipline 'including penalties for drunkenness and fornication; blasphemers [who] had their tongues pierced with a hot iron.'[365] In 1654, two soldiers 'were nailed by their ears to the whipping post at Charing Cross for taking bribes.'[366]

The army also had a reputation for being 'the praying army'[367], and their religious faith along with their discipline 'explained why small handfuls of New Model soldiers were able to put much larger numbers of royalists to flight.'[368] As the Venetian ambassador observed of the New Model, 'This much is

---

[361] Baxter, *Reliquiare Baxterianae*, Part 1, p. 42.
[362] Purkiss, *The English*, p. 421.
[363] I. Gentiles, 'The New Model Officer Corps in 1647: a collective portrait', *Social History*, 22:2 (1997), p. 130.
[364] Ibid, p. 101.
[365] R. Tombs, *The English and their History*, 2015, p. 230.
[366] Lincoln, *London*, p. 137.
[367] Gentles, *The New Model Army, 1645-53*, p. 94.
[368] Ibid, p. 95.

certain that the troops live as precisely as if they were a brotherhood of monks ... It was observed in the late wars that when the royal forces gained a victory they abandoned themselves to wine and debauchery, while those commanded by Cromwell, after their greatest successes were obliged to pray and fast.'[369]

According to Anthony Fletcher, 'the instructions sent to [royalist] commissioners of array made it quite clear ... that the officers were all 'persons of quality' with considerable local estates.'[370] Cromwell largely concurred with this analysis, claiming that he had confronted Hampden about parliamentary soldiers in the early period of the civil war, stating that 'your troopers ... are most of them old decayed serving men and tapsters, and such kind of fellows, and, said I, their troopers are gentlemen's sons, younger sons, persons of quality: do you think that the spirits of such base and mean fellows will ever be able to encounter gentlemen that have honour, courage and resolution in them?'[371]

There is other evidence to confirm this statement. According to one source 'the King's forces in the windy summer morning looked magnificent, with bright fluttering banners of every colour and fantasy, as the light flashed from polished breastplates, glowed on damask banners, taffeta scarves and velvet cloaks.'[372] Cromwell was moved to prayer: 'When I saw the enemy draw up and march in gallant order towards us, and we a company of poor ignorant men ...'[373] According to Gentiles

All Charles's officers at Oxford from the rank of captain upwards, were of gentry or more exalted status. His regimental commanders early in the war were all noblemen or higher gentry. Throughout the

---

[369] Relatzione of England by Giovanni Sagredo, 1656, Razzell, *The English Revolution*, p. 19.
[370] Fletcher, *The Outbreak*, p. 356.
[371] I. Roots (ed.), *Speeches of Oliver Cromwell*, 1989, p 134. See also Ibid, p. 10; Yule, *The Independents*, p. 60.
[372] Wedgwood, *The King's War*, p. 452.
[373] Ibid, p.452.

whole royalist army fully 90 per cent of the regimental commanders were gentlemen or peers ... the practice of promoting men from the ranks, which was so common in the New Model, was wholly absent in the Oxford army.[374]

The difficulty in analysing the New Model's composition is that 'of the total officer corps in 1648, half came from backgrounds so obscure that no information can be recovered about them.'[375] However, Gentles who has made the most detailed study of them concluded that of the officers in 1647 'twenty-two – about 9 per cent of the total – are known to have had some form of higher education ... Thirty-seven men or about one-sixth ... are known to have risen from non-commissioned rank ... [and] a high proportion ... even at the rank of colonel, were men of relatively low social status ... it is the strongly urban character of the officer corps that is most striking.'[376]

These conclusions are confirmed by literary accounts by both royalists and parliamentarians. The royalist Denzil Holles, believed that the officers 'from the general ... to the meanest sentinel, are not able to make a thousand a year lands; most of the colonels are tradesmen, brewers, tailors, goldsmiths, shoemakers and the like.'[377] According to another hostile contemporary account it claimed that if you 'Deduct the weavers, tailors, brewers, cobblers, tinkers, carmen, draymen, broom-men, and then give me a list of the gentlemen. Their names may be writ in text, within the compass of a single halfpenny.'[378] The Earl of Manchester wrote in 1645, that Cromwell had chosen for his army 'not such as were soldiers or men of estates, but such as were common men, poor and of mean parentage, only he would

---

[374] Gentiles, 'The New Model Officer Corps in 1647', p. 143.
[375] Hutton, *The British Republic*, p. 6.
[376] Gentiles, 'The New Model Officer Corps in 1647', pp. 135, 137, 140, 143.
[377] F. Maseres, 'Memoirs of Denzil Lord Holles', *Select Tract Relating to the Civil Wars in England in the Reign of Charles the First*, 1815, p. 277.
[378] *Mercurius Elencticus*, 7-14 June 1648.

give them the title of godly, precious men.'[379]' In August 1643 Cromwell justified his mode of selection in a famous speech.

> It may be it provoked some spirits to see such plain men made captains of horse. It had been well that men of honour and birth had entered into these employments, but why do they not appear? Who would have hindered them? But since it was necessary the work must go on, better plain men than none. ... I had rather have a plain russet-coated captain that knows what he fights for and loves what he knows than what you call a gentleman and is nothing else.[380]

In a vindication of the New Model from the charge of intending to sack London, published in the summer of 1647, it is asserted: 'There are verie few of us, but have most of this world's interest in the Citie of London, being chiefly and principally raised thence, and verie many, especially of our officers, being citizens themselves having their wives and children therein.'[381]

Samuel Pepys in his diary for the ninth December 1663 confirmed the role of London artisans and tradesmen in the New Model Army:

> of all the old army now, you cannot see a man begging about the street. But what? You shall have this Captain turned a shoemaker, the lieutenant, a Baker; this, a brewer; that, a haberdasher; this common soldier, a porter; and every man in his apron and frock, etc, as if they had never done anything else – whereas the other [cavaliers] go with their belts and swords, swearing and cursing and stealing – running into people's houses, by force oftentimes, to carry away something. And this is the difference between the temper of one and the other ... [382]

---

[379] C. Hill, *God's Englishman: Oliver Cromwell and the English Revolution*, 1970, pp. 65, 66.
[380] Ibid, pp. 66, 67.
[381] C.H. Firth, *Cromwell's Army: a History of the English Soldier during the Civil War*, 1912, p. 47.
[382] Latham and Matthews, *The Diary*, Volume 4, 1995, pp. 373, 374.

Previously on the 4th July 1663 while watching the royal army parade through London, he had observed that 'all these gay men [royalist horse and foot] are not the soldiers that must do the King's business, it being such as these that lost the old King all he had and were beat by the most ordinary fellows that could be.'[383]

It was the junior officers of the New Model who frequently undertook independent political action, such as Cornet Joyce's seizing of the king at Holdenbury and placing pressure on Cromwell and the senior officers to bring the king to trial and eventual execution.[384] The wealthy Presbyterians who dominated London's government at this time, attempted to block the New Model's access to parliament in 1647, but this was thwarted by the army sweeping away the resistance of the trained bands.[385] The New Model was reinforced by volunteers raised by Skippon in the suburbs, who were 'predominantly servants and apprentices'.[386] It is no accident that the New Model had been able to gain access to London Bridge through Southwark, which had long been a support of the radicals both in parliament and the army. This culminated in the purging of parliament led by Colonel Pride, leaving a rump of about 70 Independent MPs.[387]

In order to confirm the low social status of the New Model, an analysis has been carried out to compare the socio-economic status through university attendance of Royalist and New Model officers during the civil war period. The essence of the analysis is to make a comparison using an identical methodology for both armies. It indicates that the Royalist officers were of significantly higher social status than those of

---

[383] Ibid, p. 217.
[384] B. Coward, *Cromwell: Profiles in Power,* 1991, p. 50.
[385] J.T. Schroeder, 'London and the New Model Army, 1647', *The Historian,* Volume 19, No. 3, May 1957, p. 249.
[386] L.C. Nagel, *The Militia of London, 1641-1642,* D.Phil.Thesis, Kings College, University of London, p. 303.
[387] Flintham, *Civil War,* p. 41.

the New Model, confirming the literary evidence reviewed above.

Table 5: Proportions of Royalist and New Model Army Officers Graduating from Oxford and Cambridge Universities.[388]

	Total In Sample	Number Graduating from Oxford	Number Graduating from Cambridge	Total Proportion Graduating
Royalist Officers, 1642-60	100	27	25	52%
New Model Officers, 1645-49	100	9	6	15%
New Model Officers, 1649-63	100	7	10	17%

There are probably too many false positives in all samples, as suggested by Gentles' finding that only nine per cent of New Model Army officers had received a higher education in 1648, including at the Inns of Court. This suggests that most of these officers were from non-gentry backgrounds.

---

[388] The above figures are based on a hundred cases selecting the first five names in each alphabetical letter in the relevant biographical dictionaries, covering most alphabetical letters. Only names not appearing in C. Webb's *London Bawdy Court, Consistory Court of London,* Volume 1, 1703-13, 1999 were selected for analysis, in order to avoid common names. The royalist figures are taken from P.R. Newman, *Royalist Officers in England and Wales, 1642-1660: A Biographical Dictionary,* 1981; the New Model Army ones are derived from M. Waklyn, *The New Model Army, Volume 1, 1645-49,* 2015 and M. Waklyn, *The New Model Army, Volume 2, 1649-1663,* 2016. The search for university membership was made through the online alumni listings for both universities.

Conclusion

The revolutionary nature of Cromwell's regime is indicated by a speech he made to the army in 1651 when Charles II threatened to invade England with a Scottish army:

> Cromwell announced to the Army that, if he should fall, England would witness a universal crisis and change the numerous colonels, in all their splendour, who were once tailors, goldsmiths and carpenters [and] would have to make way for the nobility and courtiers.[389]

Aristocrats replaced by tradesmen and artisans in the army – indicating the only social revolution ever to occur in England. The New Model Army was a reflection of a social class which had been influenced by the Leveller movement, holding radical ideas about 'the fundamental rights and liberties ... against all arbitrary power, violence and oppression.'[390] This was an extension of the principles that had led parliament originally to object to Charles I's attempt to impose arbitrary government, a reflection of a culture of individualism. This was a culture particularly associated with literate socio-economic groups, a rebellious culture which could not be suppressed because of the absence of a national army in England.

It was a culture originating in London and other trading towns of England, as well as the pastoral and woodland areas free of manorial control, which in the sixteenth and seventeenth centuries was often associated with puritanism. London's role was expressed most eloquently by the poet John Milton, who described in 1644 his fellow Londoners 'sitting by their studious lamps, musing, searching, revolving new notions and ideas ...

---

[389] Relatzione of England by Giovanni Sagredo, 1656, Razzell, *The English Revolution*, p. 19.
[390] Morrill (ed.), *Reactions*, p. 183.

reading trying all things, assenting to the force of reason ...'[391] This quote indicates not only the basis of puritanism – the rational scrutiny of all ritual and belief – but also the foundation for the process of rationalization analysed by Weber in his discussion of the protest ethic.

Religion became more radical over time, with lesser socio-economic groups coming to dominate the religious and political agenda. It ultimately led to a revolution which involved the trial and killing of the king, the abolition of the House of Lords and the establishment of a republic. This never had the support of the majority of the population, which objected to the control of a standing army and a culture of puritanism. Cromwell had attempted to establish a regime of military control through the Major-Generals, which was unsuccessful. He along with the army officers had also attempted to introduce various forms of parliament, including Barebones Parliament with an emphasis on M.Ps sympathetic to the Puritan cause. All these regimes unravelled partly on libertarian grounds – with the soldiers of the New Model insisting on a 'liberty of conscience'. According to Baxter

> many honest men [in the New Model Army] ... made it ... their religion to talk for this Opinion and for that; sometimes for State Democracy, and sometimes for Church Democracy; sometimes against Forms of Prayer, and sometimes against Infant baptism, (which yet some of them did maintain); sometimes against Set-times of Prayer, and against the tying of ourselves to any Duty before the Spirit move us ... and sometimes about Free-grace and free-will, and all the Points of Antinomianism and Arminianism ... But their most frequent and vehement Disputes were for Liberty of Conscience as they called it ... [392]

This range of views anticipated the growth of nearly all the dissenting congregations in England and Wales during the

---

[391] Worden, *The English Civil Wars*, p. 79.
[392] Baxter, *Reliquiare Baxterianae*, Part 1, p. 53.

eighteenth and nineteenth centuries. This radical diversity of opinion made it difficult to find a religious and political settlement. The Presbyterians had attempted to impose a Puritan settlement along Scottish lines, but with the overall control of parliament, but this was opposed by the New Model with its insistence on liberty of conscience, again reflecting an individualistic culture.[393]

It was perhaps because of these difficulties that led Crowell to eventually advocate a return to a conservative society. In a speech to parliament in 1654 he claimed that 'a nobleman, a gentleman, and a yeoman ... That is a good interest of the nation and a great one.'[394] It was because of this conservatism that he had suppressed the Leveller movement, including the imprisonment and execution of three soldiers at Burford in 1649.[395] Towards the end of his life Cromwell attempted to purge the army of radicals and introduce aristocrats into his personal circle. According to Lucy Hutchinson

> He weeded, in a few months' time, above a hundred and fifty godly officers out of the army, with whom many of the religious soldiers went off, and in their room abundance of the king's dissolute soldiers were entertained; and the army was almost changed from that godly religious army, whose valour God had crowned with triumph, into the dissolute army they had beaten, bearing yet a better name ... Claypole, who married his daughter, and his son Henry, were two debauched cavaliers ... His court was full of sin and vanity, and the more abominable, because they had not yet quite cast away the name of God ... hypocrisy became an epidemical disease ... At last he took upon himself to make lords and knights ... Then the Earl of Warwick's grandchild and the Lord Falconbridge married his two daughters ...[396]

---

[393] Razzell, *English Civil War,* Volume 3, p. 287; Underdown, *Revel,* pp. 208, 247.
[394] Coward, *Cromwell,* p. 102.
[395] See also Purkiss, *The English,* p. 499.
[396] Hutchinson, *Memoirs,* pp. 294, 295.

However on the 15th March 1658 the Venetian ambassador reported that

> ... the Army took very badly the cashiering of the officers, reported, and has made a vigorous remonstrance to the Protector, pointing out that officers cannot be dismissed from an army without a Council of War, and so, as they do not know for what reasons he sent away many of their colleagues, they ask him to restore them to their posts and, by order of His Highness, they have been reinstated in them a few days since ... [397]

Cromwell's attempted changes laid the foundation for the restoration of the crown and a traditional parliament, although many of the provincial members of the New Model Army continued to be attached to 'the Good Old Cause' and political radicalism. For example

> Even in Deal, (after the Restoration a great centre of Nonconformity) maypoles were set up on May Day 1660, and the people set the King's flag on one of them to the fury of the soldiers in the castle who 'threatened, but durst not oppose.'[398]

Something similar occurred in Nottingham in 1660, when a confrontation occurred 'between the young men of the town who were demonstrating for the return of the king, and soldiers of Colonel Hacker's regiment. The Memoirs [of Lucy Hutchinson] tell us that 'the soldiers, provoked to rage, shot again and killed in the scuffle two Presbyterians ...'[399] By 1660 the general population had turned against the Cromwellian regime and the soldiers in Deal Castle were powerless to prevent this popular revolt.

Cromwell concluded before this period that a new constitutional settlement was necessary, and declared to an

---

[397] Razzell, *English Civil War*, Volume 5, p. 83.
[398] M.V. Jones, *The Political History of the Parliamentary Boroughs of Kent, 1642-1662* (London University Ph.D. Thesis, 1967), pp. 467, 468.
[399] Jennings, *The Gathering*, p. 160.

audience of army officers deeply opposed to change: 'It is the time to come to a settlement and lay aside arbitrary proceedings, so unacceptable to the nation.'[400]

However, puritanism and a culture of individualism did not disappear, but was reflected in the rise of religious dissent and a more extensive development of capitalism. Both individualism and capitalism have come to shape modern England, which has dominated economic, social and political life in the twenty-first century.

---

[400] Coward, *Cromwell*, p. 146.

Chapter 5: Malthus: Mortality or Marriage? English Population Growth in the Eighteenth Century.[401]

Introduction

Malthus is the most important influence on thinking about the relationship between economic and demographic development. In his theoretical work, he emphasized the impact of economic factors on fertility and population levels, through shifts in the incidence of marriage. He had been influenced by Adam Smith, who had argued that 'the demand for men, like that for any other commodity, necessarily regulates the production of men; quickens it when it goes on too slowly, and stops it when it advances too fast.'[402] Malthus's work in turn influenced Ricardo, Marx, Marshall and other classical economists, who all assumed the primacy of economics over demography. The exception was Keynes, who accepted that population affected levels of aggregate demand – he was a strong admirer of Malthus – but had little or nothing to say about the impact of population growth on the supply side, in particular the supply of labour.[403]

Malthus's writings reflected the anxieties of his contemporaries in their concern to prevent a decline in their standard of living and economic privileges. His 'preventative' method applied particularly to the middle and upper classes, whereas the 'positive' checks were mainly applicable to the poor. Malthus's theory of population stressed the economic basis of marriage and fertility, with a growth in income leading to earlier marriage and a rise in fertility. However, there was a

---

[401] Unpublished paper.

[402] A. Smith, *An Inquiry into the Nature and Causes of the Wealth of Nations*, Volume 1, p. 98.

[403] J.M. Keynes, *Essays in Biography (ed.) G. Keynes*, 2010; J.M. Keynes, *The Collected Writings of John Maynard Keynes, Volume 7*, 2012.

contradiction between his theoretical conclusions and his analysis of England's population history. Malthus attempted to engage with empirical evidence from parish registers and censuses, but given the unknown reliability of the raw data was forced to make arbitrary assumptions about correction ratios.[404] He also made theoretical statements which may have been correct for the time of writing, but were not accurate for an earlier period. For example, he wrote that 'the higher classes ... often want the inclination to marry, from the facility which they can indulge themselves in an illicit intercourse with the sex. And others are deterred from marrying by the idea of the expenses that they must retrench ...'[405] However, in the seventeenth century the aristocracy and other wealthy groups in England married almost universally and at a very young age.[406]

It is possible to construct from his writings on England an account similar to that in a demographic transition model. In this he emphasized the role of mortality rather than fertility in shaping changes in population levels:

It would appear, by the present proportion of marriages, that the more rapid increase of population, supposed to have taken place since the year 1780, has arisen more from the diminution of deaths than the increase of the births.[407]

He elsewhere amplified this summary statement:

... there is good reason to believe that not only in London, but the other towns in England, and probably also country villages, were at the time [the 1760s] ... less healthy than at present. Dr William Heberden remarks that the registers of the ten years from 1759 to 1768, from which Dr Price calculated the probabilities of life in

---

[404] T.R. Malthus, *An Essay on the Principle of Population*, 1826, pp. 404, 421, 427, 431.
[405] Ibid, p. 397.
[406] See T.H. Hollingsworth, 'The demography of the British peerage', *Population Studies*, Supplement Volume 18, 1965, and data later in this paper.
[407] T.R. Malthus, *An Essay on the Principle of Population*, 1803, p. 311.

London, indicate a much greater degree of unhealthiness than the registers of late years. And the returns pursuant to the Population Act [of 1801], even after allowing for great omissions in the burials, exhibit in all our provincial towns, and in the country, a degree of healthiness much greater than had before been calculated ... The returns of the Population Act in 1811 ... showed ... a greatly improved healthiness of the people, notwithstanding the increase of the towns and the increased proportion of the population engaged in manufacturing employments.[408]

He concluded that disease environment played a critical role in shaping mortality levels: 'A married pair with the best constitutions, who lead the most regular and quiet life, seldom find that their children enjoy the same health in towns as in the country.'[409]

Malthus in his writings gave a sociological rather than an economic analysis of marriage: 'It is not ... among the higher ranks of society, that we have most reason to apprehend the too great frequency of marriage ... [it is] squalid poverty ... [which] prompt universally to early marriages ...'[410] He argued that the 'carelessness and want of frugality observable among the poor, so contrary to the disposition generally to be remarked among petty tradesmen and small farmers,'[411] and that

poverty itself, which appears to be the great spur to industry, when it has once passed certain limits, almost ceases to operate. The indigence which is hopeless destroys all vigorous exertion ... It is the hope of bettering our condition, and the fear of want, rather than want itself, that is the best stimulus to industry, and its' most constant and best directed efforts will almost invariably be found among a class of people above the class of the wretchedly poor.[412]

---

[408] T.R. Malthus, *An Essay on the Principle of Population*, 1989, Volume 1, pp. 256, 267.
[409] Ibid, p. 257.
[410] Ibid, p. 438; Volume 2, pp. 114, 150.
[411] Ibid, Volume 1, p. 359.
[412] Ibid, p. 439.

It was this emphasis on 'bettering our condition' that led Malthus to stress education as the best way of encouraging the postponement of marriage:

.... to better the condition of the lower classes of society, our object should be to ... [cultivate] a spirit of independence, a decent pride, and a taste for cleanliness and comfort among the poor. These habits would be best inculcated by a system of general education and, when strongly fixed, would be the most powerful means of preventing their marrying ... [and] consequently raise them nearer to the middle classes of society.[413]

Malthus is expressing here the insight which has informed much of the literature on modern birth control practices: that education – particularly of women – combined with economic opportunity, is the most powerful way of encouraging fertility reduction.

His conclusion was that falling mortality had led to a reduction in the incidence of marriage:

... the gradual diminution and almost total extinction of the plagues which so frequently visited Europe, in the seventeenth and the beginning of the eighteenth centuries, produced a change [in the incidence of marriage] ... in this country [England] it is not to be doubted that the proportion of marriages has become smaller since the improvement of our towns, the less frequent returns of epidemics, and the adoption of habits of greater cleanliness.[414]

This was an early form of demographic transition theory, and in order to evaluate this argument, it is necessary to examine in detail England's demographic history in the eighteenth century.

---

[413] Ibid, Volume 2, p. 155.
[414] Ibid, Volume 2, p. 198. See also Ibid, Volume. 1, p.193 and Volume 2, p. 115.

The Reliability of Parish Registers

There is an element of uncertainty in all historical demographic measures, including local and regional variations. In the absence of reliable national data, it is necessary to adopt a methodology of the triangulation of data. This allows independent checking of all findings, important where these findings are unexpected and potentially controversial. An example of this is the finding that virtually all women were married in England during the seventeenth century, contradicting the theoretical notion of a European marriage pattern.[415] This conclusion was reached by using five different sources – censuses, church court depositions, burial registers, wills and family genealogies.[416] Likewise, the finding of the halving of adult mortality in the eighteenth century is based on the analysis of apprenticeship indentures, marriage registers, family genealogies, and data on elite groups such as Members of Parliament.[417]

The same methodological principle applies to the measurement of parish register reliability. Central to all discussion of population history before the introduction of civil registration in 1837 is the reliability of parish registers. Nine objective methods measuring burial register reliability are available, involving the triangulation of data.[418] The most important two methods are: (i) the same-name technique and (ii) the comparison of individual entries in probate and burial registers.

The same-name technique is based on a custom in England which gave the name of a dead child to a subsequent child of the same sex. Evidence from local censuses and other

---

[415] J. Hajnal, 'European marriage patterns in perspective' in D.V. Glass, D.E.C. Eversley (eds.), *Population in History: Essays in Historical Demography,* 1965, p. 101.

[416] P. Razzell, *Mortality, Marriage and Population Growth in England, 1550-1850,* 2016, pp. 60-70,

[417] Ibid, pp. 45-60.

[418] Ibid, pp. 15, 16.

listings suggests that there were no living children with the same names in individual families in the period 1676-1849.[419] However, according to probate data for different parts of England during the period 1600-1649 there were thirteen living same-name children out of a total of 2,144 – 0.6 per cent – although some of these children may have been step-siblings.[420]

Where two children of the same family were baptised with an identical name, it is therefore possible to measure the completeness of burial registration by searching for the first same-name child in the burial register. The technique can only be applied to families with at least two recorded baptisms of children of the same sex, but it is a valuable method of assessing the quality of burial registration.

The most important work on England's demographic history using parish registers is that carried out by E.A. Wrigley and colleagues of the Cambridge Group. Their main findings were that after a period of stagnation in the second half of the seventeenth and first half of the eighteenth century, population began to grow rapidly after the middle of the eighteenth century, with about two-thirds of the population increase due to a rise in

---

[419] Galley, Garrett, Davies and Reid initially argued that there were some living same-name English children enumerated in the 1695 Marriage Duty Census, but subsequently conceded that these same-name siblings were a consequence of transcription errors. C. Galley, E. Garrett, R. Davies, A. Reid, 'Living same-name siblings and English historical demography: a final comment', *Local Population Studies*, Number 88, 2012, p.82. See also C. Galley, E. Garrett, R. Davies, A. Reid, 'Living same-name siblings and English historical demography: a reply to Peter Razzell', *Local Population Studies*, Number 87, 2011; P. Razzell, 'Living same-name siblings in England, 1439-1851, *Local Population* Studies, Number 87, 2011; P. Razzell, 'Living same-name siblings in England, 1439-1851: a commentary', *Local Population* Studies, Number 88, 2012. Galley et.al successfully established that there were some living same-name children in Highland Scotland at this time, but all the research reviewed in this paper relates to English demographic experience.

[420] See P. Razzell, 'Living same-name siblings in England, 1439-1851, *Local Population Studies*, Number 87, 2011, p. 67 for a list of the places and dates involved.

fertility, and one third to decreasing mortality.[421] They have argued that the growth of population was mainly the result of the increase in fertility associated with a fall in the age of marriage, which in turn was due to growing real incomes lagged over time, a conclusion largely confirming the theoretical work of Malthus.

Because of deficiencies in parish registration, it was necessary to inflate the number of burials, baptisms, and marriages in order to establish reliable measures of deaths, births, and marriages. During the period in which the Cambridge Group's research was carried out there were no methods available to independently measure the reliability of inflation ratios. This was recognized by Wrigley et.al when they concluded that 'the lack of a reliable alternative data source makes it impossible ... to test effectively the completeness of Anglican registration', resulting in 'arbitrary' inflation ratios which can only be based on 'internal plausibility and internal consistency of the results obtained.'[422]

However there are now available new objective methods of measuring parish register reliability. The following table summarises a same-name analysis of 15 Cambridge Group reconstitution parishes during the period 1650-1837.

Table 1: Proportion of Untraced Same-Name Cases in 15 Cambridge Group Reconstitution Parishes, 1650-1837.[423]

Period	Total Number of Same-Name Cases	Number of Same-Name Cases Traced in Burial Registers	Proportion Of Untraced Cases
1650-99	1,160	873	24.7%
1700-49	1,533	1,246	18.7%
1750-99	1,227	903	26.4%
1800-37	907	705	22.3%

---

[421] E.A. Wrigley, R.S. Davies, J.E. Oeppen, R.S. Schofield, *English Population History from Family Reconstitution, 1580-1837*, 1997, p. 126.

[422] E.A. Wrigley, R.S. Schofield, *The Population History of England, 1541-1871*, 1989, p. 137; Wrigley, Davies, Oeppen, Schofield, *English Population*, pp. 91, 92.

[423] Source: Reconstitution data in Cambridge Group archive.

There appears to have been a slight improvement in burial registration reliability in the first half of the eighteenth century, although other data suggests no significant change in the period between 1650 and 1837.[424]

Research comparing probate with burial register data covering 147 parishes indicates that there were no significant changes in burial registration reliability in the parish register period.[425] The most detailed research available is on the county of Bedfordshire, where a study of all 124 parishes has been carried out.

Table 2: Proportion of Probate Cases Traced in 124 Bedfordshire Burial Registers, 1543-1849.[426]

Period of Probate	Total Number of Probate Cases	Proportion of Burials Untraced
1543-00	611	26%
1600-49	3731	21%
1650-99	4626	26%
1700-49	6030	23%
1750-99	3744	22%
1800-49	3303	27%
Total	22044	24%

Wrigley and Schofield had assumed in their aggregative research that other than defective periods, burial registration was perfect in the period leading up to the middle of the seventeenth century and only deteriorated significantly at the end of the eighteenth century.[427] This is reflected in the inflation ratios they used to

---

[424] Razzell, *Mortality*, pp. 18-23.

[425] Probate data tends to exclude the poorest members of a community, but data for Bedfordshire suggests that the poorest occupational group – labourers – experienced similar levels of burial under-registration as the rest of the population. P. Razzell, C. Spence, M. Woollard, 'The evaluation of Bedfordshire burial registration', *Local Population* Studies, Number 84, 2010, p.45.

[426] Source, Razzell, *Mortality*, p. 18.

[427] Wrigley, Schofield, *The Population*, p. 561.

153

translate burials into deaths which were as follows: 1540-99: 0%; 1600-49: 0%; 1650-99: 1.9%; 1700-49: 4.6%; 1750-99: 10.0%: 1800-39: 25.8%.[428] Data on same-name and probate/burial register research, indicates that approximately 25% of all burials were missing from parish registers in the period 1600-1837, with no clear linear trends in register reliability over time.

The absence of significant changes in burial register reliability is similar to the findings of research on baptism register accuracy. This involved research comparing information in censuses and baptism registers, including an evaluation of the quality of the census data through cross-matching censuses at different dates.[429] There was no linear trend found in the eighteenth century, with about 29 per cent of all births missing from the baptisms registers.[430]

Wrigley and Schofield's inflation ratios for baptisms in the period 1710-1836 are as follows: 1710-42: 11.5%; 1743-62: 13.9%; 1763-80: 16.4%; 1781-1800: 26.0%; 1801-20: 42.9%; 1821-36: 39.1%.[431] They assumed that birth under-registration was relatively low in the period 1710-80, but deteriorated sharply from the 1780s onwards, particularly after 1801. This assumed pattern is at variance with the findings outlined above, which essentially show no major changes in the eighteenth and early nineteenth century.

There is also evidence of a high level of marriage under-registration which is confirmed by Baker in his study of eighteenth century Cardington in Bedfordshire. He with colleagues attempted to trace both native and other adults who had migrated from all parts of the county, and found that 40.1% of baptisms, 31.5% of marriages and 24.9% of burials could not be traced in parish registers.[432] According to a range of evidence, this non-registration

---

[428] Ibid.
[429] P. Razzell, *Essays in English Population History*, 1994, pp. 84-89.
[430] Razzell, *Mortality*, pp. 22, 23.
[431] Wrigley, Schofield, *The Population*, pp. 541-44.
[432] D. Baker, *The Inhabitants of Cardington*, 1973, p. 18.

of births, marriages and deaths was mainly due to the negligence of clergyman and clerks in compiling parish registers.[433]

Wrigley and colleagues attempted to address the problems of parish register reliability by constructing a complex mathematical back projection model. The model suffers from a range of arbitrary assumptions, including the sharp inflation of baptisms and burials at the end of the eighteenth and beginning of the nineteenth century. Additionally, these models are very sensitive to changes in assumption. For example, as a part of their back projection programme, Wrigley and Schofield reduced the size of the age group 90-94 enumerated in the 1871 Census by 44%; if they had chosen instead to reduce this by 40%, their estimate of the English population in 1541 would have been 9% larger.[434]

Estimates of Population Growth

Given that there were no major changes in parish register unreliability in the parish register period, the most valuable data created by the Cambridge Group are the raw uncorrected national figures of baptisms, marriages and burials. These raw national figures provide the basis for the calculation of population changes in the eighteenth century, but with the assumption of zero net migration. For the purposes of this analysis, it is assumed that 29% of births and 28% of deaths went unregistered in the eighteenth century.[435] These figures are used as correction factors because

---

[433] Razzell, *Essays*, pp. 108-11.

[434] R. Lee, D. Lam, 'Age distribution adjustments for English censuses, 1821 to 1931', *Population Studies*, Volume 37, 1983, p. 446.

[435] These proportions are based on figures discussed previously, with about twenty-nine per cent of births missing from baptism registers in the eighteenth century. Approximately twenty-five per cent of deaths in same-name and probate parish samples were untraced in the period 1650-1837, but the number of untraced cases in urban areas appears to have been higher. For example the proportion of untraced cases in London and Liverpool in the period 1700-49 was significantly higher than elsewhere in the parish register period. P.

they yield appropriate population growth figures in the eighteenth century between the 1695 marriage duty census and the first national census of 1801. Applying these correction ratios to the raw national data yields the following population figures.

Table 3: Estimated Population Sizes of England, 1695-1801.[436]

Period	Births Baptisms x 100/71	Deaths Burials x 100/72	Births Minus Deaths	Population Date	Population Size
				1695	4632000
1695-99	1029677	951322	78355	1700	4710355
1700-09	2100998	1840774	260224	1710	4970579
1710-19	2079920	1922863	157057	1720	5127636
1720-29	2225579	2349728	-124149	1730	5003487
1730-39	2402912	2094161	308751	1740	5312238
1740-49	2306889	215421	155468	1750	5467706
1750-59	2437382	1999636	437746	1760	5905452
1760-69	260794	2280840	327064	1770	6232516
1770-79	2903273	2247785	655488	1780	6839889
1780-89	3085997	24788624	607373	1790	7447262
1790-99	3414119	2466510	947609	1800	8394871
1800-01	631897	528639	103258	1801	8498129

The estimated population figure for 1801 – 8,498,129 – is slightly smaller than the figure that Rickman calculated for 1801 – 8.561 million.[437] Given that the above estimates do not make any allowance for changes in migration levels, and that the population figure for 1695 is somewhat arbitrary, the data in Table 3 represent a plausible pattern of population growth in the eighteenth century.

Razzell, *Population and Disease: Transforming English Society, 1550-1850,* 2007, pp.134, 138.
[436] Source: Wrigley and Schofield, *The Population*, pp. 517-52, 577, 588. The population in the start date in 1695 is based on David Glass's reworking of Gregory King's estimate of population at that date.
[437] Ibid, p. 577.

The Table indicates that population diminished in the 1720s but increased gradually after that period, accelerating rapidly at the end of the eighteenth and beginning of the nineteenth century. The raw data suggests that it was a fall in mortality rather than a rise in fertility that was responsible for the increase in population.

Table 4: English Baptism and Burial Rates (Per 1000) in England Calculated from Cambridge Group Data.[438]

Period	Estimated Population	Baptism Rate	Burial Rate
1701-40	5160000 (1721)	30.4	28.7
1741-80	6054000 (1761)	30.3	25.9
1781-1820	8667000 (1801)	29.4	20.6

It is only because Wrigley and Schofield disproportionately inflated the number of baptisms in the period 1781-1820 that they concluded that there was a rise in the crude baptism rate in this period, and yet as we have seen the direct evidence on baptism registration reliability suggests that there were no significant changes in this period. Gregory King's work on the age structure of the English population in 1695 indicates it was very similar to that in 1821 based on national enumeration returns,[439] suggesting that there was no long-term change in age-specific fertility during this period.

Table 4 indicates that it was falling mortality that fuelled population growth, but in order to further clarify the exact demographic changes in the eighteenth century, it is necessary to consider in detail the empirical evidence on mortality, nuptiality and fertility in the parish register period.

---

[438] Source: Baptism and burial totals Wrigley, Schofield, *The Population*, pp. 541-44, 549-52; population figures taken from Table 3.
[439] D.V. Glass, D.E.C. Eversley (eds.), *Population in History: Essays in Historical Demography*, 1965, pp. 212-13.

The History of Infant and Child Mortality

Most studies of infant and child mortality have suffered from the lack of an objective method of measuring burial registration reliability.[440] The same-name method allows objective measurement, stating its procedures in advance and not making adjustments to resulting findings. I have used the technique for the analysis of 10 Cambridge reconstitution parishes, as well as in 15 rural parishes from other areas of England.[441]

---

[440]There are a number of historical studies of infant and child mortality which suffer from this difficulty. See R.E. Jones, 'Further evidence on the decline of infant mortality in pre-industrial England: north Shropshire, 1561-1810', *Population* Studies, Volume 34, 1980, pp. 239-50; J. Landers, 'London mortality in the long eighteenth century', *Medical History, Supplement Number 7*, 1991; R. Houston, 'Mortality in early modern Scotland: the life expectancy of advocates', *Continuity and Change*, Volume 7, 1992; P. Huck, 'Infant mortality in nine industrial parishes in northern England, 1813-36', *Population* Studies, Volume 48, 1994; M. Dobson, *Contours of Death and Disease in Early Modern England*, 1997; C. Galley, *The Demography of Early Modern Towns; York in the Sixteenth and Seventeenth Centuries*, 1998.
[441] Source: Reconstitution data in the Cambridge Group archive; parish registers in the Society of Genealogists library. Same-name correction ratios have been applied to raw IMR and CMR figures. The 10 Cambridge Group parishes are: Alcester; Aldenham; Austrey; Banbury; Bottesford; Colyton; Dawlish; Great Oakley; Ippleden; Morchard Bishop. The 16 rural parishes are: Ackworth; Ampthill; Arrington; Barton-in-the-Clay; Beeley; Breamore; Canewden; Cusop; Eaton Hastings; Kemerton; Sandy; Stow Maries; Truro; Weston Colville; Woodchurch; Youlgreave.

Table 5: Infant and Child (1-4) Mortality per 1000 in 10 Cambridge Group and 15 Rural Parishes, 1700-1837.

Period	Number of Infants at Risk	Number of Children at Risk	IMR	CMR
10 Cambridge Group Parishes				
1700-49	11933	8842	174	110
1750-99	12591	9897	148	97
1800-37	15462	9230	110	99
16 Rural Parishes				
1700-49	8332	5603	182	128
1750-99	9629	6950	150	126
1800-37	9375	6183	94	81

The pattern of mortality in the two samples is similar, although the reductions in mortality between 1700-49 and 1800-37 are greater in the rural areas than in the Cambridge Group sample. This may be partly a function of population size, as the mean population in 1801 of the Cambridge Group parishes was 1,349 and that of the rural sample 589. The average national mean size of the English population in 1801 was about 860,[442] and so the rural parishes are slightly more representative than the Cambridge Group ones.

From research on birth-baptism intervals and infant mortality, it is estimated that a maximum of 5% of children died before baptism in the period 1761-1834. However, many 'sickly' children were privately baptised, reducing mortality before baptism.[443] The infant mortality rates in both samples in 1800-37 were relatively low – 110/1000 and 94/1000 – and this may be partly a function of the exclusion of infants dying before

---

[442] Wrigley, Davies, Oeppen, Schofield, *English Population*, p. 20
[443] Razzell, *Essays*, pp. 106-07.

baptism. Woods estimated that the infant mortality rate in rural areas during the Victorian period was 97 per 1,000 as against 218 per 1,000 in urban areas, with a national average of 150 per 1,000.[444] He calculated the rural rate from data for Dorset, Hertfordshire and Wiltshire, southern counties like those forming the basis of the samples in Table 5. Similar consideration are likely to apply to child mortality rates, for although the child mortality rate for the age group 1-4 nationally in 1838-54 was 134 per 1,000,[445] it is likely to have been significantly less of that in rural areas, similar to that depicted in Table 5.

However, the sample sizes are small and are not necessarily representative of the whole country. They do not include any northern parishes or large towns, and under-represent industrial villages.[446] Infant and child mortality was much higher in large towns than in rural and provincial parishes in the seventeenth and eighteenth centuries. The infant and child mortality rates in 18 rural reconstitution parishes in 1650-1699 were 151/1000 and 106/1000 respectively; the equivalent rates in London, Norwich, Ipswich and Canterbury in a similar period were 304/1000 and 237/1000.[447] Urban infant and child mortality was twice of that in rural and provincial parishes in the late seventeenth century, but by the nineteenth century the average infant mortality rate in these urban areas had reduced to 179 per 1000.[448] However, there is some evidence to indicate that infant mortality grew in some urban and industrial parishes in the first half of the nineteenth century,[449] although the scale of

---

[444] Woods, 'Mortality', pp. 260-61.

[445] Register General Supplement, *45th Annual Report*, p. v

[446] A reconstitution study of Ackworth in Yorkshire for the period 1687-1812 indicates that the pattern of infant and child mortality was similar to that in Table 5, although at a somewhat lower level. The figures are as follows: 1687-1749: IMR: 166, CMR: 114; 1750-1812: IMR: 82, CMR: 77. Razzell, *Mortality*, p.34.

[447] Ibid.

[448] Ibid.

[449] W.A. Armstrong, 'The end of mortality in Carlisle between the 1780s and the 1840s: a demographic contribution to the standard of living debate',

reductions during the eighteenth century in the four urban parishes greatly outweighed the relatively modest increases in urban areas in the nineteenth century.

The pattern of infant and child mortality in the most important urban area – London – is indicated by the results of a reconstitution study of 16 City of London parishes in the period 1539-1849.

Table 6: Infant and Child (1-4) Mortality (Per 1000) in 16 London Parishes, 1650-1849.[450]

Period	IMR	CMR
1650-99	256	282
1700-49	409	176
1750-99	263	270
1800-49	141	118

Infant mortality increased significantly between 1650-99 and 1700-49, before falling very sharply after the middle of the eighteenth century. There was a similar pattern in child mortality, except for the rise in mortality in the second half of the eighteenth century.

Socio-Economic Status and Infant and Child Mortality

One further way of exploring the factors shaping infant and child mortality is to analyse the relationship between socio-economic status and mortality.

Economic History Review, Volume 34, 1981; P. Huck, 'Infant mortality in nine industrial parishes in northern England, 1813-36', *Population Studies,* Volume 48, 1994; S. Szreter, G. Mooney, 'Urbanization, mortality and the standard of living debate: new estimates of the expectation of life at birth in nineteenth century British cities', *Economic History Review*, Volume 51, 1998.
[450] Source: Razzell, *Population*, pp, 13, 134.

Table 7: Infant and Child (1-4) Mortality (Per 1,000) Amongst Elite and Control Families in 17 Cambridge Group Parishes, 1650-1799.[451]

Period	Elite Families		Control Families	
	IMR	CMR	IMR	CMR
1650-99	158	143	180	132
1700-49	177	106	223	146
1750-99	113	69	159	134

An elite family – gentlemen, professionals and merchants – was matched with the next control family in the baptism register, most of whom were artisans and labourers. There was little difference between the two groups in the late seventeenth century, but a sharp divergence thereafter, particularly in child mortality. Other sources indicate a variation in findings, although overall it would appear that these forms of early mortality reduced first amongst wealthy families and only later amongst the general population in the eighteenth century.[452]

Lower infant and child mortality levels amongst the wealthy continued throughout the nineteenth century,[453] although at significantly reduced levels than in the seventeenth century. However, areas with different socio-economic profiles showed if everything a reverse pattern. This can be illustrated with reference to London, where the Registrar-General provided data on mortality by registration sub-district. He classified districts by poverty levels as measured by average rateable value.

---

[451] Source: Razzell, *Mortality*, p. 37.
[452] Razzell, *Population,* pp. 91, 103-05, 111-12; 133; Razzell, *Mortality,* pp. 37-41.
[453] Razzell, *Population,* pp. 112-14.

Table 8: Infant, Child and Adult Mortality in London by Rateable Value of Registration District, 1839-44.[454]

Registration Districts	Mean Annual Value of Property	IMR	CMR	Adult (25-44) Male Mortality per 1000
10 Districts with Lowest Rateable Value	£15	153	52	13
10 Districts with Medium Rateable Value	£26	168	59	15
10 Districts with Highest Rateable Value	£58	167	58	13

Most of the poor districts were in the East End of London, and the wealthy ones in the West End.[455] The lack of an association between socio-economic status and infant mortality is supported by evidence on Quakers, who by the nineteenth century were mainly wealthy merchants and professionals. The infant mortality rate amongst Quakers in London in 1825-49 was 150 per 1000, similar to the rate amongst the total population in equivalent registration districts in 1838-44.[456]

These surprising findings are replicated in other districts of England. In the period 1851-60, mortality levels in the wealthy towns of Bath, Cheltenham, Richmond and Brighton were

---

[454] Source: Ibid, p. 136.
[455] Source: Ibid, p. 136.
[456] Razzell, *Population*, p. 137; Landers, 'London's mortality'.

significantly higher than in poorer districts in the same county.[457] The wealthy areas were towns, and the poorer areas rural districts, indicating that disease environment was more important in these instances than poverty in shaping mortality levels.[458]

To summarise, in rural and provincial areas infant mortally fell sharply between the first half of the eighteenth and nineteenth centuries, nearly halving in some areas. Child mortality in these districts was more stable, although there appears to have been a significant fall in some rural areas at the beginning of the nineteenth century. In London and in other urban districts there were marked falls in both infant and child mortality. Child mortality amongst the wealthy reduced in rural and provincial areas at an earlier period – from the beginning of the eighteenth century onwards – than it did among the general population.

It is less clear what the influence of socio-economic status was on urban infant and child mortality, and in London by the mid-nineteenth century there appears to have been little or no association between poverty and these forms of mortality. Also, as we have seen, in a number of provincial districts mortality was significantly lower in poor than in wealthy areas in the 1850s.

The general timing and extent of reductions in early childhood mortality cannot fully explain the scale of population increase in the eighteenth century. For a full explanation of this surge in population growth we must look elsewhere.

The History of Adult Mortality

There are a number of problems with the reconstitution study of adult mortality, in particular the unreliability of raw burial registration data. Only about ten per cent of the original sample can be included in the analysis, which is not likely to be socially

---

[457] Razzell, *Mortality*, p. 41

[458] See Woods *The Demography*, pp. 170-202 for an analysis of the mortality differences between urban and rural districts in this period.

or demographically representative of the total population.[459] There is also the difficulty of establishing accurate nominal record linkages between baptisms/marriages and subsequent burials, as most parish registers only list the names of people buried without further identifying information. There are however a number of sources which allow the direct measurement of adult mortality, the most important of which are: i. apprenticeship indenture records, and ii. marriage licences.

In the year 1710 the government introduced a national tax on apprenticeship indentures – the Inland Revenue Register (INR Register) – which was in existence until the early nineteenth century. Details of these indentures have survived and are currently being digitised by the Society of Genealogists.[460] The indentures in the early period provide the following information on fathers: name, place of residence, occupation, and whether or not they were alive or dead. Additionally the name of the apprentice was recorded along with the amount paid for the indenture.

A sample of 1,578 cases was selected from the national register, and data on the mortality status of fathers was established. It is estimated that a minimal annual mortality rate for England in 1710-13 was 20.9 per 1,000, which can be compared to figures published by the Registrar-General for a similar age group – 25-44 – in the period 1838-42 – 11 per 1000.[461] This indicates that male adult mortality approximately halved in the period between the early eighteenth and middle of the nineteenth century, a conclusion borne out by a number of other sources.[462]

Marriage licences are one of the most informative sources, covering between 30 and 90 per cent of the

---

[459] Razzell, *Mortality,* p. 43
[460] I would like to thank the Society of Genealogists for making available the digital version of the INR Register, covering the surnames beginning with the letters A to M.
[461] Mitchell and Deane, *Abstract*, p. 38
[462] Razzell, *Mortality,* pp. 45-56.

population.[463] For children under the age of 21, they required parental permission, and where a father was dead, permission of a widowed mother or guardian was required. The licences are available from the beginning of the seventeenth to the end of the eighteenth century, and an analysis of available licences yields the following results:

Table 9: Fathers of Spinsters under Twenty-One: Proportions Dead in English Regions, 1600-1799.[464]

Period of Marriage	London	South of England	East Kent Diocese	Durham Diocese
1600-46	46%	40%	47%	-
1661-99	47%	44%	43%	-
1700-09	46%	47%	50%	-
1710-19	47%	44%	48%	-
1720-29	45%	39%	48%	-
1730-39	46%	39%	34%	-
1740-49	55%	45%	37%	42%
1750-59	40%	41%	27%	28%
1760-69	35%	35%	22%	27%
1770-79	39%	31%	24%	29%
1780-89	31%	32%	28%	25%
1790-99	31%	27%	22%	-

According to this table, male adult mortality nearly halved in all regions in the eighteenth century.[465] As the figures relate to fathers who were alive on average nineteen years before the marriage of their daughters, mortality first began to fall in East Kent between 1710 and 1730, and in London, the South of England and Durham between 1730 and 1750.

According to Table 9 there were gains in life expectancy throughout the whole of the eighteenth century, although in East

---

[463] Razzell, *Population,* pp. 62, 63
[464] Source: Razzell, *Mortality,* p. 48.
[465] Ibid.

Kent most of this took place in the first half of the century. Other evidence indicates that reductions of mortality in Nottinghamshire also appear to have occurred mainly in this period, with the estimated paternal death rate falling from 22 per 1,000 in 1661-63 to 14 per 1,000 in 1754-58 and 10 per 1,000 in 1791-93.[466]

However data on the fathers of masons' apprentices who lived in all areas of the country suggests paternal mortality fell equally in the first and second halves of the century.

Table 10: Mortality amongst Fathers of London Indentured Masons' Apprentices.[467]

Date of Indenture	Number of Fathers Dead	Total Number of Fathers	Proportion of Fathers Dead
1663-99	94	223	42%
1700-49	124	375	33%
1750-1805	43	202	21%

Approximately four-fifths of these fathers lived outside London, residing in every county and country of Great Britain.

Evidence from the marriage licences and apprenticeship indentures suggest that adult mortality was higher amongst the wealthy than the poor, and this may have been the case until the end of the nineteenth century.[468] This was probably due to the 'hazards of wealth' – the consumption of very rich food and alcoholic drinks, and a relative lack of exercise – as well as the result of avoiding childhood infections such as smallpox, which took their toll in adulthood.[469]

However, this reverse socio-economic gradient appears to have been established in the eighteenth century, as revealed by the association between occupation and mortality in East Kent during the period between 1619-46 and 1751-1809.

---

[466] Ibid, p. 49.
[467] Source: C. Webb, *London Bawdy Courts, 1703-13,* 1999.
[468] Razzell, *Population,* pp. 197-226.
[469] J.C. Riley, *The Eighteenth Century Campaign to Avoid Disease,* 1987.

Table 11: Proportion of Deceased Fathers of Spinsters under 21 by Occupation of Husband in East Kent, 1619-1809 (Numbers in Cohort in Brackets).[470]

Occupation	Period		
	1619-1646	1661-1700	1751-1809
Gentlemen, Merchants, Professional	39% (205)	38% (131)	28% (159)
Yeomen, Farmers	41% (274)	42% (169)	15% (207)
Traders, Artisans	46% (491)	49% (326)	26% (397)
Husbandmen	50% (213)	39% (122)	19% (108)
Mariners, Fishermen	42% (144)	45% (103)	24% (158)

Mortality declined significantly during the eighteenth century, approximately halving in most occupational groups. In the seventeenth century gentlemen, merchants and professionals appear to have lower mortality than other groups, but by 1751-1809 the position had been reversed, with this elite group having the smallest reduction in mortality.

However, there is very detailed evidence of the gains in adult life expectancy amongst wealthy Members of Parliament and the aristocracy. The former data allows a very detailed breakdown of men of different ages living in all areas of England.

---

[470] P. Razzell, *Essays in English Population History*, 1994, p. 197.

Table 12: Mean Number of Years Lived by Members of Parliament, 1660-1820 (Number of Cases in Brackets). [471]

Period of First Entry	Age at First Entry - Mean Number of Years Lived		
	Under 29 Years	30-39 Years	40 Years Plus
1660-1690	25.7 (429)	22.5 (458)	17.9 (633)
1715-1754	30.1 (541)	28.2 (422)	18.5 (347)
1755-1789	37.1 (480)	29.9(354)	21.2 (431)
1790-1820	38.1 (571)	32.0 (432)	22.4 (572)

All age groups experienced mortality reductions, but the greatest mortality gains were amongst the youngest age cohort under the age of 29. There was an increase in life expectancy of over 12 years in this group, distributed evenly in the entry period between 1660 and 1789. There were also substantial gains in the 30-39 age cohort – of about 10 years – but these were mainly confined to the entry period between 1660 and 1754. There was a modest increase in life expectancy of nearly 5 years in the oldest 40+ group, which was fairly evenly spread between 1660 and 1820. The above pattern of adult mortality is similar to that found by Hollingsworth in his study of the aristocracy.[472] Although all the evidence considered on adult mortality is for males, his study of the aristocracy suggests that females experienced even more mortality reductions in the eighteenth century.[473]

The timing of the reduction in adult mortality was different from the falls in infant and child mortality which appear to have occurred mainly in the second half of the eighteenth century, and given that life table models assume that infant/child and adult mortality move in the same direction, this suggests that these models are not a reliable basis for understanding eighteenth century mortality trends. The Cambridge Group have used such models in calculating figures of adult mortality, but different assumptions may have been one of the reasons why their figures

---

[471] Source: Razzell, *Essays,* p. 199.
[472] Hollingsworth, *The Demography*, p. 56
[473] Ibid, p. 57.

have changed significantly in recent years. In 1997 Wrigley et.al published life expectancy figures for men aged twenty-five as follows: 1640-89: 30.4 years; 1750-1809: 35.4 years.[474] More recently in 2004, Wrigley has claimed that 'reconstitution data suggest that adult mortality moved from the equivalent of level 5 in model North in the period 1640-89 to the equivalent of level 9 in 1750-1809, or a rise of 10 years.'[475] The latter figure represents a very significant increase over earlier estimates, and is now compatible with the marriage licence and other data reviewed earlier.[476] Wrigley concluded that 'there seems little reason to suppose that the evidence relating to male adult mortality drawn from marriage licences and that drawn from reconstitution are at odds'[477], representing a welcome new consensus.

Explaining Mortality Reductions

The factors responsible for mortality levels are complex. For example, smallpox became much more virulent between the sixteenth and nineteenth century: case fatality rates amongst unprotected children in London rose from about 5% to 45% in this three hundred year period. It is possible that the increasing fatality of smallpox was the result of the importation of more virulent strains with the growth of world trade. It was only the practice of inoculation and vaccination that prevented the disease from destroying a large part of the population.[478] Smallpox also varied in its age incidence between different areas of the country: in the South of England it was a disease of both adults and

---

[474] Wrigley, Davies, Oeppen, Schofield, *English Population*, p. 291.

[475] E.A. Wrigley, *Poverty, Progress and Population*, 2004, pp. 427, 428

[476] According to calculations prepared by Jim Oeppen using the East Kent marriage licence data, there was an increase of 9 years in life expectancy at age 25 between 1650-99 and 1750-1800. Razzell, *Essays*, p. 201.

[477] Wrigley, *Poverty*, p. 431.

[478] P. Razzell, *The Conquest of Smallpox*, 2003.

children, whereas in the North and elsewhere it affected mainly young children. This is important as case-fatality rates differed markedly between different age groups.[479]

To some extent, disease had its own internal logic, so that for example the disappearance of the plague in England in the 1660s does not appear to be the result of any environmental or other improvements. However, it is known that environmental factors did influence the incidence of disease. Mortality was higher in marshland areas, in industrial and urban districts, in certain coastal and estuarine regions, and lower in isolated rural areas with the right geographical and ecological characteristics.[480]

It is possible that the lower levels of infant mortality amongst the wealthier socio-economic groups in Table 7 are partly a function of wealth, although falling elite mortality in the second half of the eighteenth century suggests that non-economic factors were responsible.[481] The rapid fall in child mortality in elite families in the eighteenth century, at a time when it was stable amongst the control population, indicates that this reduction of mortality was exogenous to economic development. Also, the lack of an association between socio-economic status and child mortality in the mid-nineteenth century depicted in Table 8 and found elsewhere, suggests that disease environment rather than poverty was the most important factor in shaping the level of mortality.

The explanations of these trends are complex: the wealthy are known to have fled London and other towns during the plague, to have escaped childhood diseases such as smallpox by moving away from areas known to be affected by the disease, and to have avoided marsh areas known to suffer from endemic malaria.[482] It is possible among other factors that by the mid-

---

[479] Ibid, pp. xi-xix.
[480] Dobson, *Contours*; Razzell, *Population,* pp. 98, 99.
[481] Also, the level of infant mortality in Bedfordshire was higher amongst the elite than the control population in 1700-49. See Razzell, *Population*, p. 133.
[482] Riley, *The Eighteenth Century*; Dobson, *Contours*.

nineteenth century the avoidance of disease was no longer important in protecting wealthy groups from infection, particularly when they lived in urban areas. The falls in infant mortality in rural and provincial parishes from the middle of the eighteenth century may have been in part due to an autonomous reduction in disease incidence,[483] as well as the result of a variety of health improvements. These included better breastfeeding practices, inoculation/vaccination against smallpox, and improved personal and domestic hygiene,[484] linked to growing literacy amongst women.

The dramatic reduction of infant mortality in London was also probably a result of major improvements in public health – increased water supplies, better drainage, and rebuilding of the urban landscape – as well as much better maternal and neo-natal care.[485]

Although most of these measures were not the result of economic developments, clearly economic change did have an indirect influence on mortality. Agricultural improvements led to the drainage of marshland which may have contributed to the elimination of malaria,[486] and the production of cheap cotton cloth enabled working class families to improve their standard of personal hygiene. There was also an economic element in some of the other factors responsible for mortality decline: for example, the rebuilding of houses and house floors in brick and stone. The increasing use of coal enabled water to be boiled more

---

[483] J.D. Chambers, *Population, Economy and Society in Pre-Industrial England*, 1972.

[484] E.L. Jones, M.E. Falkus, 'Urban improvement and the English economy in the seventeenth and eighteenth centuries' in P. Borsay 'Cleaning up the Great Wen: public health in eighteenth century London', in W.F. Bynum, R. Porter (eds.), *Living and Dying in London: Medical History Supplement*, Number 11, 1991; Razzell *Essays*, pp. 224-29; Razzell, *The Conquest*.

[485] M.D. George, *London Life in the Eighteenth Century*, 1966, p. 61; I. Loudon, *Death in Childbirth: an International Study of Maternal Care and Maternal Mortality, 1800-1950*, 1992; I. Loudon, *The Tragedy of Childbed Fever*, 2000, p.61.

[486] Dobson, *Contours*.

easily, important for personal and domestic hygiene.[487] However, elite social groups had always had the economic resources necessary for these improvements, and the majority of them probably resulted from new attitudes towards disease, personal hygiene and the environment.[488] These changes in attitude and belief appear to have first influenced the educated and wealthy, and gradually spread to the general population later in the eighteenth and nineteenth centuries.

However, the reduction in adult mortality occurred more-or-less equally amongst all areas of the country and in all socio-economic groups, suggesting that there was an 'autonomous' fall in the adult death rate from the early eighteenth century onwards.[489]

The History of Nuptiality and Fertility

The Cambridge Group data in Table 5 suggest that there was no long-term rise in fertility in the eighteenth century, as there were no significant changes in baptism registration reliability or changes in the age structure of the national population. However, the factors shaping fertility are complex and need to be examined in some detail. The Cambridge Group found from their reconstitution research that there was a decline of about two-and-a-half years in the average age of marriage of spinsters during

---

[487] I would like to thank Tony Wrigley for pointing out the potential importance of coal in boiling water for improving personal hygiene. For the use of boiling water and milk in preventing infant diseases see I. Marks and M. Worboys, *Migrants, Minorities and Health,* 1997, p. 192.

[488] This shift in attitudes was partly associated with the eighteenth century enlightenment movement. The Royal Society's statistical investigation in the 1720s into the effectiveness of inoculation – comparing natural smallpox mortality with that amongst the inoculated – is perhaps the first historical example of a scientific assessment of a medical treatment. Razzell, *The Conquest,* pp. 172-74.

[489] Chambers, *Population.*

this period.[490] This finding is somewhat contradicted by data from marriage licences – which indicate that average age of marriage rose by about a year in the eighteenth century – but these licences tended to exclude the poorest socio-economic groups.[491]

There is a difficulty with reconstitution calculation of marriage ages. Marriage registers in the early period rarely give information on the marital status of grooms or brides, and there was a major shift in marital status during the eighteenth century. Wrigley and Schofield concluded that 'perhaps as many as 30 per cent of all those marrying were widows or widowers in the mid sixteenth century ... By the mid nineteenth century, in contrast, it is clear from civil registration returns that a comparable proportion was much lower at 11.27 per cent.'[492] Marriage Licence data confirm this conclusion, but it represents a problem for reconstitution research on marriage ages. During the late seventeenth century about 26 per cent of spinsters in East Kent married widowers, and on average they married 3.8 years later than spinsters marrying bachelors.[493] A twenty per cent reduction in the number of widower marriages would lead to a fall of 0.76 years – 3.8 x 1/5 – in the overall marriage age of spinsters, and this would be the result of the changing marital status of grooms and brides during this transition period.

Nevertheless, new evidence suggests that the fall in the average marriage age of spinsters found by the Cambridge Group is largely genuine. Although there is a lack of reliable national data, marriage licences indicate that there was a radical shift in the relative ages at which the wealthy and the poor married in the seventeenth and eighteenth centuries. In Nottinghamshire and Gloucestershire during the seventeenth century the average age of spinsters marrying labourers and husbandmen was over 26

---

[490] Wrigley, Davies, Oeppen, Schofield, *English Population*, p. 149.
[491] Chambers, *Population*.
[491] Razzell, *Mortality,* p. 71.
[492] Wrigley and Schofield, *The Population*, pp. 258, 259.
[493] Razzell, *Population,* p. 131.

years, whereas the average for yeomen, gentlemen and professionals was between 22 and 24 years.[494] These figures include spinsters marrying both bachelors and widowers, but an analysis of the 100 first cases of spinsters marrying bachelors reveals a similar pattern:

Table 13: Marriage Ages of Spinsters Marrying Bachelors in the Diocese of Nottinghamshire, 1672-1685.[495]

Gentlemen & Professionals	Yeomen	Artisans & Tradesmen	Labourers
Mean = 23.0 Years	Mean = 23.5 Years	Mean = 24.1 Years	Mean = 25.2 Years
Proportion Under 21 = 29%	Proportion Under 21 = 23%	Proportion Under 21 = 9%	Proportion Under 21 = 5%

The high marriage age of spinsters marrying labourers is confirmed by a reconstitution study of their marriages occurring in Bedfordshire in the period 1650-1749. It was possible to trace 77 marriages in the baptism register, yielding a mean age at marriage of 26.7 years with 18 per cent marrying under the age of 21.[496] The mean age is higher than that listed in Table 13 for labourers, and this may be because it included marriages to widowers as well as bachelors.

A transition in this pattern occurred in the eighteenth century and was very marked in the Archdeaconary of Chichester, as revealed by the proportions of spinsters marrying under the age of 21:

---

[494] Ibid, pp. 242-43.

[495] Source: T.M. Blagg, F.A. Wadsworth (eds.), *Abstracts of Nottinghamshire Marriage Licences 1577-1700,* 1930.

[496] The analysis was carried out on data in the Bedfordshire Family History Database covering 124 parishes in the county, selecting all marriages where the groom was listed as a labourer and the bride as a spinster.

Table 14: Proportion of Spinsters Marrying Under 21 in the
Archdeaconary of Chichester, Sussex, 1754-1799.[497]

Period	Labourers		Yeomen, Gentlemen & Professionals	
	Number	% Under 21	Number	% Under 21
1754-69	142	9%	142	22%
1770-99	163	25%	163	14%

By the nineteenth century there were significant differences in marriage ages between these socio-economic groups. Marriage ages were sometimes included in civil registration returns, and an analysis of Surrey and Bedfordshire parishes where such information was recorded, yielded the following differences.

Table 15: Marriages of Brides Marrying Bachelors in Surrey and
Bedfordshire, 1837-71.[498]

Occupation	Brides Signing The Marriage Register	Mean Age At Marriage (Years)	Proportion Marrying Under 21
Surrey			
Labourers	68.0%	23.0	31.4%
Artisans &Tradesmen	90.0%	24.4	17.2%
Farmers	96.0%	26.1	12.9%
Elite Occupations	99.4%	25.3	17.8%
Bedfordshire			
Labourers	34.2%	22.2	37.6%
Artisans &Tradesmen	67.0%	23.0	26.4%
Farmers	83.3%	25.1	10.5%
Elite Occupations	100%	27.8	15.8%

---

[497] Source: Razzell, *Population*, p. 244.

[498] Source: Marriage civil registers in the Surrey and Bedfordshire Record Offices. The marriages were selected from parishes in alphabetical sequence up to the parish of Ham in Surrey and Potsgrove in Bedfordshire for the period 1837-71. The numbers of marriages in the calculation of marriage ages were as follows: Surrey: labourers: 1,759; artisans & tradesmen: 2,039; farmers: 102; elite occupations (gentlemen, professionals & merchants): 102. Bedfordshire: labourers: 1,955; artisans & tradesmen: 1,268; farmers: 102; elite occupations: 38.

There was approximately a three year difference in the mean age of marriage between labourers and farmers/elite occupations, with artisans and tradesmen occupying an intermediate position. There were similar differences in marriage ages of spinsters in England & Wales in 1884-85. The mean age of brides marrying bachelor labourers was 23.7 years, farmers 28.9 years, and professionals 26.4 years.[499] This is the reverse to what was found in the seventeenth century, as a result of labourers' marriage ages falling significantly and those of elite occupations rising during the eighteenth and early nineteenth centuries.

This was the socio-economic pattern of marriage described by Malthus, with the poor marrying at a much earlier age than the wealthy. He was born in the parish of Wotton, Surrey, where in later life he became curate, and his family home was in the neighbouring village of Albury.[500] He was very familiar with the marriages of the poor of these parishes, as well as the marriage habits of his wealthier contemporaries. It is probable that reduced adult mortality led to the rich to marrying much later, contrasted with the poor marrying much earlier as a result of pauperisation.[501] The artisan and tradesmen class appear to

---

[499] Woods *The Demography*, p. 86.

[500] P. James, *Population Malthus: His Life and Times*, 1979, pp. 13, 34, 40.

[501] As we saw earlier, Malthus stressed the link in England between poverty and early marriage. There is no consensus on patterns of real income and economic inequality in the eighteenth and early nineteenth century. For example, see G. Clark, 'The long march of history: farm wages, population, and economic growth, England 1209-1869' *Economic History Review*, Volume 6, 2007; G. Clark, 'The consumer revolution: turning point in human history, or statistical artifact', *Department of Economics, University of California, Davis, Working Paper*, 2010; S. Broadberry, B.M.S. Campbell, A. Klein, M. Overton, B. Van Leewen, *British Economic Growth, 1270-1870*, 2015. However, the increasing pauperisation of labourers at the end of the eighteenth and beginning of the nineteenth century was described by nearly all contemporaries, including Horatio Nelson. See N.H. Nicolas, *The Dispatches and Letters of Vice Admiral Lord Viscount Nelson, Volume 1, 1777-94*, 1845, p. 295. See also J. Howlett, *Examination of Mr Pitt's Speech in the House of Commons ... February 12th, Relative to the Condition of the Poor*, 1796; D.

have occupied an intermediate position, with little change in their marriage ages. However, the frequency of marriage was also a major determinant of fertility, and as Wrigley and colleagues have concluded 'until the middle of the eighteenth century the substantial swings in nuptiality were produced almost exclusively by wide variations in the proportion of women never marrying.'[502]

There is now evidence that marriage was nearly universal in the seventeenth century. Shepard and Spicksley have compiled data from church court depositions covering nearly all areas of England, showing that only about 3 per cent of women aged above 45 were single at the beginning of the seventeenth century.[503] Information from a range of other sources – censuses, church court deposition, burial registers, wills and family genealogies – confirm this conclusion.[504] This changed during the eighteenth century as illustrated by data for the London Consistory Court.

Davies, *The Case of Labourers in Husbandry*, 1796; W. Cobbett, *Rural Rides*, 2001; J. and B. Hammond, *The Village Labourer*, 1911; J. and B. Hammond, *The Town Labourer*, 1917; J. and B. Hammond, *The Skilled Labourer*, 1919; G. Taylor, *The Problem of Poverty*, 1969; B. Inglis, *Poverty and the Industrial Revolution*, 1972; E.P. Thompson, *The Making of the English Working Class*, 1980; D. Vincent, *Bread, Knowledge and Freedom: a Study of Nineteenth Century Working Class Autobiography*, 1981; J. Humphries, 'The lure of aggregates and the pitfalls of the patriarchal perspective: a critique of the high wage interpretation of the British industrial revolution', *Economic History Review*, Volume 66, 2013.
[502] Wrigley and Schofield, *The Population*, p. xix.
[503] Razzell, *Mortality*, p. 65.
[504] Ibid, pp. 60-70.

Table 16: Proportion of Female Deponents Single in the London Consistory Court, 1583-1817.[505]

Period	Age Group – Proportion Single			
	15-24	25-34	35-44	45+
1586-1611	62%	15%	1%	0%
1703-1713	72%	25%	7%	4%
1752-1783	77%	43%	14%	5%
1792-1817	76%	53%	13%	15%

There were significant reductions in the frequency of marriage in all age groups during the eighteenth century, and this was also the case in Yorkshire and other areas of England.[506] The explanations for this trend are complex but it appears that it occurred particularly amongst the wealthy and the well-educated.[507] There were major changes in literacy levels amongst wealthy women in the eighteenth century, as illustrated by the proportion of women signing wills in London.

Table 17: Proportion of Women Signing London Wills, 1599-1851.[508]

Period	Proportion Signing Wills	Number Of Cases
1599-1601	2%	100
1639-1641	15%	100
1699-1701	38%	100
1749-1751	64%	100
1799-1801	77%	100
1849-1851	86%	100

---

[505] Source: Ibid, p. 67.

[506] Ibid, pp. 60-70. Recently Szreter and Garrett have argued that there was a decline in the frequency of marriage from the middle of the eighteenth century onwards. S. Szreter, E. Garrett, 'Reproduction, compositional demography, and economic growth: family planning in England before the fertility decline', *Population and Development Review,* 2000, p. 67.

[507] Razzell, *Mortality,* pp. 74-77.

[508] Source: Ibid, p. 86. The figures are based on the first 100 women leaving wills selected alphabetically in the periods in question.

However, literacy was not a sufficient condition to sustain a single marital status, as in the late eighteenth century many of the poor were literate but with very high levels of marriage frequency.[509] It was important to have the economic resources to be able to sustain a single marital status, although these are complex issues requiring further clarification.

The socio-economic patterns of marriage age and the frequency of marriage had a direct impact on fertility levels. The general relationship between status and fertility was widely recognised by contemporaries in the nineteenth century, summarized by Wrong as follows:

> In England most of the writers who took part in the Malthusian controversy in the early part of the nineteenth century were full aware of the existence of a negative relationship between fertility and socio-economic status. It was referred to by Malthus himself, by William Godwin, John Stuart Mill, Harriet Martineau, and Nassau Senior, to mention only a few of the better know intellectual figures of the day.[510]

Glass was the first to analyse the relationship between socio-economic status and fertility which occurred in the middle of the nineteenth century. He found a strong correlation between the social status of a London registration district and its gross reproduction rate in the period 1849-51, even allowing for the presence of servants.[511] There were similar associations in other wealthy and poor districts, with the wealthy areas having higher literacy and lower fertility rates.[512] Data for Bedfordshire indicates that fertility was particularly high amongst labourers compared to other occupational groups:

---

[509] Ibid, pp. 75-77.

[510] J. Wrong, 'Class fertility differentials before 1850', *Social Research*, Volume 25, 1958, p. 67.

[511] D.V. Glass, 'Fertility and economic status in London', *Eugenics Review*, Volume 30, 1938, p. 118.

[512] Razzell, *Mortality*, pp. 81-83.

Table 18: Bedfordshire Baptism Fertility Rates, 1849-51.[513]

Occupation	Number Of Baptisms	Number Of Men Living Aged 20-50 In 1851	Annual Fertility Rate Per 1000 Living
Labourers	5280	10887	16.2
Artisans, Tradesmen & Others	3008	11120	9.0
Farmers	294	1148	8.5

The findings on status and fertility are consistent with the evidence on the relationship between status and marriage previously discussed. The overall impact of marriage patterns and fertility levels is more difficult to assess. The falling mean age of marriage amongst labourers – and they formed a large part of the total population – has to be contrasted with the declining frequency of marriage amongst other groups. The best evidence on changing fertility levels in the eighteenth century is provided by Table 4, which indicates that there was no significant change during this period, suggesting that the decline in mean marriage age was balanced by an overall reduction in the frequency of marriage.

Conclusion

Contrary to his well-known theory, Malthus presented evidence to show that population growth in eighteenth century England was largely caused by falling mortality rather than rising fertility, and that the frequency of marriage diminished as a result of this reduced mortality. This was an early form of the demographic transition theory, and data is produced in this paper to confirm

---

[513] Source: Ibid, p. 84.

this conclusion. Adult mortality approximately halved from the beginning to the end of the century, with reductions occurring amongst all socio-economic groups and in all areas of the country. Infant and child mortality fell at a later date from the middle of the eighteenth century onwards, reducing first amongst the wealthy.

New evidence suggests that nearly all women were married in the seventeenth century, contradicting Hajnal's theoretical notion of a European marriage pattern. As predicted by Malthus, the reduction in mortality led to a fall in the incidence of marriage. The proportion of married women diminished during the eighteenth century in all age groups, particularly amongst the wealthy and literate, linked to a major increase in female literacy. This was counter-balanced by a decrease in the mean age at marriage amongst the poor, compared to an increasing age of marriage amongst the wealthy. The net effect of these developments was the stabilisation of fertility.

It is argued that the reduction in mortality was largely independent of economic growth. The fall in mortality probably resulted from an autonomous reduction in disease virulence, along with a number of medical innovations and an improvement in personal and public hygiene.

A detailed review of the evidence on England's population growth in the eighteenth century indicates that it was Malthus's more empirical analysis rather than his theoretical arguments that were valid for this period. It was a time in which a demographic transition was taking place, with mortality falling largely as a result of changes in the disease environment. Adult mortality approximately halved amongst all socio-economic groups and in all areas of the country from the early eighteenth century onwards, confirming Malthus's analysis. However, infant and child mortality reduced from the middle of the eighteenth century which is not consistent with Malthus's prediction of a decline of infectious diseases at the beginning of the century. These forms of mortality first reduced amongst the wealthy,

suggesting that economic factors were not primary in shaping these mortality patterns.

Also as predicted by Malthus, there was a significant reduction in the incidence of marriage. There were also changes in the age of marriage, with the wealthy and middle classes marrying at a significantly later date, and the poor marrying at an increasingly earlier age. It appears that labourers and the poor suffered increasing pauperisation resulting from growing life expectancy and population numbers, leading to demoralization and early marriage. The later marriage of the wealthy and middle classes was probably largely the result of reduced mortality, although there is evidence that the growing education and literacy of women may have also played a role. This is similar to findings about the influence of women's education on fertility levels in developing countries in the twentieth century.

New research indicates that nearly all women were married in the seventeenth century, contradicting Hajnal's notion of a European marriage pattern. This changed in the eighteenth century particularly amongst the elite, and combined with shifts in class based marriage ages, this resulted in a significant socio-economic gradient in fertility levels in the first half of the nineteenth century. As with marriage ages the incidence of marriage was probably linked to the growing literacy of women.

This is consistent with demographic transition theory, different from Malthus's theoretical arguments about the relationship between economic development and population growth for which he is famous. The transformation of mortality levels without significant economic development is similar to the twentieth century experience of poor countries such as Sri Lanka, Cuba, Kerala, Costa Rica and Albania.[514] Although the

---

[514] S.B. Halstead, J.A. Walsh, K. S. Warren, *Good Health at Low Cost*, 1985; J. Caldwell, 'Routes to low mortality in poor countries', *Population and Development Review*, Volume 12, 1986; A. Gjonca, *The Paradox of Mortality Transition in Albania, 1950-90*, 1991; R.A. Easterlin, 'How beneficent is the market? A look at the modern history of mortality', *European Review of Economic History*, Volume 3, 1999; D.M. Cutler, A.S. Deaton, A. Llera-

183

Cambridge Group has argued that Malthus's theoretical arguments are largely valid for England in the eighteenth century, the evidence reviewed in this paper indicates that it was diminishing mortality rather than increasing fertility that was the prime reason for population growth in this period.

Demography has been seen traditionally by economists and other social scientists as a function of economics, but the evidence presented in this paper shows that population has acted in England during the eighteenth century largely through changes in disease patterns as an independent force in helping to shape England's economic and social history.

Muney, 'The determinants of mortality', *Journal of Economic Perspectives*, Volume 20, 2006; R.A. Easterlin, 'Cross sections are history' *Population and Development Review*, Volume 38, 2012.

Chapter 6: The History of Infant, Child and Adult Mortality in London, 1538-1850.[515]

Introduction

It is widely accepted that London's population growth since the sixteenth century has had a significant impact on its economic and social development, influencing not only the supply of labour but also the demand for a range of goods and services, including housing and the urban infrastructure.[516] It has also been generally assumed that because of its high level of mortality before the nineteenth century, most of London's growth was brought about by migration rather than endogenous population increase.[517] Furthermore, it has been widely believed that there was a close association between poverty and all forms of mortality from at least the sixteenth century onwards.[518] However, many of these assumptions remain untested due to the lack of reliable evidence as a result of inadequate source material.

Most previous research on London's demographic history has been based on the Bills of Mortality,[519] although

---

[515] Written jointly with Christine Spence and published in *The London Journal,* Volume 32, Issue 3, 2007.

[516] V. Harding, 'Early modern London 1550-1750', *London Journal*, Volume 20, 1995, p. 36; L. Schwarz, 'London, 1700-1850', *London Journal*, Volume 20, 1995; L. Schwarz, *London in the Age of Industrialisation: Entrepreneurs, Labour Force and Living Conditions*, 1992.

[517] Harding, 'Early modern London', p. 36

[518] R. Finlay, *Population and the Metropolis, the Demography of London, 1580-1640*, 1981; Harding, 'Early modern London', p. 39; B. Luckin 'Perspectives on the mortality decline in London, 1860-1920', *London Journal*, Volume 22, 1997; R. Woods, 'Mortality, poverty and environment' in R. Woods, J. Woodward (eds.), *Urban Disease and Mortality*, 1984, p. 24.

[519] See for example J. Brownlee, 'The health of London in the eighteenth century', *Proceedings of the Royal British Medical Society*, Volume 18, 1925; A.B. Appleby, 'Nutrition and disease: the case of London, 1550-1750',

186

the reliability of this source has been subject to much criticism.[520] There is also the problem that the Bills only allow an aggregative study of London's population history, whereas much modern demographic research focuses on individual families enabling a more detailed study of a range of variables.[521] We have attempted to address these issues by creating family-level data, and assessing the quality of these data through detailed methodological analysis.

The present paper concentrates on the history of mortality, seeking to establish changing levels of mortality in the period between the middle of the sixteenth and nineteenth centuries. Parish registers, guild records, wills, census listings and the Bills of Mortality have been used as a basis for creating family reconstitution and other data. The focus in this paper has been on samples of individual families from a variety of different parishes and districts in London. Given the nature of the data, the conclusions reached are necessarily provisional. However, we have attempted to construct a picture of mortality change over this long period, in the belief that this creates fruitful hypotheses about long-term patterns of mortality. Only minimal interpretation of suggested trends has been carried out, mainly because of the absence of studies of disease patterns during the period covered.

An analysis of the relationship between wealth/poverty and mortality has been included. Virtually all writers on the

---

Journal of Interdisciplinary History, Volume 6, 1975; P.R. Galloway, 'Annual variations in deaths by cause, prices and weather in London 1670-1830', *Population Studies*, Volume 39, 1986.
[520] W. Heberden, *Observations on the Increase and Decrease of Different Diseases*, 1801; W. Ogle, 'An Inquiry into the trustworthiness of the old Bills of Mortality', *Journal of the Statistical Society*, Volume 55, 1892; A. Hardy, 'Diagnosis, death and diet: the case of London, 1750-1909', *Journal of Interdisciplinary History*, Volume 18, 1988.
[521] For this type of individually based research see Finlay, *Population and Metropolis*; J. Landers, *Death and the Metropolis: Studies in the Demographic History of London*, 1993.

subject – including Chadwick, Marx, Engels and Mayhew[522] – have assumed that poverty was strongly associated with ill-health and high mortality, and yet we have found in our research that this was not the case in London before the mid-nineteenth century. For example, as we will see later, the healthiest areas with the lowest mortality in 1838-44 were not the wealthy districts of the West End, but the poor areas of the East End of London. We will argue in this paper that mortality was not primarily shaped by wealth and poverty, but mainly by exogenous disease patterns largely independent of economic factors.[523]

Likewise it has been widely assumed that London until the nineteenth century was a 'mortality sink', sucking in England's surplus population because of its inordinately high mortality.[524] One of the main findings of the paper is that in the period between 1550 and 1650, London's infant and child mortality was relatively low, and that this helped generate the rapid population growth of the city during this period.

Additional work will be required to evaluate these radical conclusions, but we hope the paper will stimulate further research on London's population history in the belief that this will significantly illuminate the history of the city over a three hundred year period.

---

[522] E. Chadwick, *The Sanitary Conditions of the Labouring Population*, 1842. For Marx's and Engels' views on the relationship between poverty and health see F. Engels, *The Condition of the Working Class in England*, 1845; for Mayhew's discussion of the effects of poverty see H. Mayhew, *The Morning Chronicle Survey of Labour and the Poor: the Metropolitan Districts*, 6 Volumes, 1980.

[523] For a discussion of these issues see P. Razzell, C. Spence, 'Poverty or disease environment? The history of mortality in Britain, 1500-1950', in M. Breschi and L. Pozzi (eds.), *The Determinants of Infant and Child Mortality in Past European Populations*, 2004; P. Razzell, C. Spence, The hazards of wealth; the history of adult mortality in pre-twentieth century England', *Social History of Medicine*, Volume 19, 2006.

[524] See Harding, 'Early modern London, 1550-1700', p. 36.

Infant and Child Mortality

Evidence on infant and child mortality is available in the London Bills of Mortality for the period from 1728 onwards, and is summarized as follows:

Table 1: Infant and Child Mortality from the London Bills of Mortality, 1728-1829.[525]

Period	Number of Baptisms	Burials Under 2 as a % of the Number of Baptisms	Burials Aged 2-5 as a % of the Number of Baptisms	Burials Under 5 as a % of the Number of Baptisms
1728-29	33712	61.1%	14.6%	75.7%
1730-39	170196	59.8%	13.7%	73.5%
1740-49	145260	60.8%	14.9%	75.7%
1750-59	147792	50.8%	12.7%	63.5%
1760-69	159603	49.4%	13.2%	62.5%
1770-79	173178	44.6%	12.1%	56.7%
1780-89	176299	36.1%	10.3%	46.4%
1790-99	187345	33.0%	11.1%	44.1%
1800-09	199443	27.8%	10.9%	38.6%
1810-19	221334	24.4%	8.7%	33.1%
1820-29	256576	22.6%	8.0%	30.6%

Table 1 indicates that infant and child mortality was more or less constant between 1728 and 1749, but fell steadily and progressively from 1750 to 1829. There has, however, been controversy about the reliability of the Bills of Mortality and there is no consensus about the quality of either birth or death registration.[526]

---

[525] Source: J. Marshall, *The Mortality of the Metropolis*, 1832.

[526] The uncertain quality of the Bills of Mortality has led scholars to adopt significantly different correction ratios for inflating baptism and burials into estimated births and deaths. For two very different estimates of mortality based on the Bills of Mortality see J. Landers, 'Mortality and metropolis: the case of London 1675-1825', *Population Studies*, Volume 41, 1987, p. 63; R.

Attempts have been made to address this problem by applying family reconstitution techniques to parish register and other data. Finlay has analysed a number of London parish registers for the period 1580-1650,[527] and Landers and Vann & Eversley have used London Quaker records for reconstitution research.[528] None of these studies has been able to completely resolve the problem of burial register reliability. Finlay found very low rates of infant mortality for most of the parishes studied — in one case as low as 55 per 1,000[529] — and assumed that much of this was due to burial under registration. The findings of the separate studies carried out by Landers and Vann & Eversley on Quaker infant mortality were contradictory,[530] and this may have been because of the different nature of the samples involving variations in data quality.

We have conducted reconstitution research on a number of parishes in the City of London, linked to the published and indexed London 1695 Marriage Duty Act Listing, which provides not only details of living family members, but also levels of taxable wealth.[531] The creation of reconstitution data was facilitated by the genealogical work of Percival Boyd, who in the late 1930s and 1940s compiled 238 volumes of family histories for London inhabitants, covering a

---

Woods, 'Mortality in eighteenth century London: a new look at the Bills', *Local Population Studies*, Number 77, 2006.

[527] Finlay, *Population and Metropolis*.

[528] Landers, *Death and the Metropolis*; R.T. Vann, D. Eversley, *Friends in Life and Death: the British and Irish Quakers in the Demographic Transition*, 2002.

[529] R.A.P. Finlay, 'The accuracy of the London parish registers, 1580-1653', *Population Studies*, Volume 32, 1978, p. 99.

[530] See J. Landers, 'Mortality in eighteenth century London: a note', *Continuity and Change*, Volume 11, 1996.

[531] See D.V. Glass (ed.), *London Inhabitants within the Walls*, 1965.

total of 59,389 family groups.[532] Boyd used parish registers, guild records, marriage licences, wills and a whole miscellany of sources, to create individual family histories mainly for the sixteenth, seventeenth and eighteenth centuries, enabling the tracking of children from baptism through to the date of last independent observation of the family.

The individual family sheets are not in standard format but usually include information on names of parents and children, as well as date of baptism and burial of children. Boyd sometimes estimated the year of birth of a child from wills and other documentary sources, and the lack of standardization means that his family histories have to be treated with some care. However, as we are concerned here with mortality and not fertility, it is the quality of burial registration which is most important. Given the uncertain quality of burial register data, it is important to evaluate its reliability before embarking on detailed research on mortality.

There was a custom in England of giving the name of a dead child to a subsequent child of the same sex. Evidence from local censuses and other listings suggests that there were a minimal number of living children with the same name in individual families in the period up to the middle of the seventeenth century, and none after that period.[533] Where two children of the same family were baptized with an identical name, it is therefore possible to measure the completeness of burial registration by searching for the first same-name child

---

[532] This material is deposited in the library of the Society of Genealogists. For details of this source see A. Camp, 'Boyd's London burials and citizens of London', *Family Tree*, Volume 1, 1985, p. 12; J. Beach Whitmore, 'London citizens', *Genealogists Magazine*, 1944.

[533] We have examined the 1695 census listing of the city of London carried out under the Marriage Duty Act, and have been unable to find any living same-name children in any of the families enumerated. See D.V. Glass (ed.), *London Inhabitants Within the Walls*, 1965. For an examination of other census and a discussion of the same-name method see P. Razzell, 'Evaluating the same-name technique as a way of measuring burial register reliability' *Local Population Studies*, Number 64, 2008.

in the burial register. (It is the first of a pair of children with identical names that is designated as a same-name child.) The technique can only be applied to families with at least two recorded baptisms of children of the same sex, but it is a valuable method of assessing the quality of burial registration.

This can be illustrated by the example of one family listed by Boyd and traced in the 1695 Marriage Duty Listing (see Table 2).

Table 2: The Family of Samuel and Sarah Fowler, Tyler and Bricklayer, of St. Antholin's, London.[534]

Name of Child	Date of Baptism	Date of Burial
Thomas	05/07/1677	04/01/1721
Samuel	**04/05/1679**	**29/04/1681**
William	08/01/1683	03/06/1708
Samuel	10/05/1685	15/02/1688
John	**07/08/1687**	--
John	**12/05/1689**	**09/10/1692**
Sarah	22/04/1691	06/02/1748
Mary	18/07/1693	12/11/1694
John	21/11/1695	--

Of the three same-name cases, highlighted in bold, two of them were traced in the burial register. The second same-name case John baptised on the 7th August 1687 was found neither in the burial register nor in the 1695 Marriage Duty Listing, indicating that he probably died without being registered. (The last John was baptised in late 1695 and

---

[534] Source: 1695 Marriage Duty Listing: Samuel Fowler, wife Sarah, son James, son Thomas, son William, daughter Sarah. Of St. Antholin's Parish.

therefore did not appear in the Marriage Duty Listing made before that date.)

The same-name method allows for the correction of burial under-registration by multiplying the number of recorded burials by the total number of same-name cases and dividing by the number of same-name cases found in the burial register. In the case of the Fowler family, the correction ratio is 3/2. This inflation ratio corrects both for non-registration due to omission from the burial register, as well as burial in neighbouring parishes and elsewhere, accounting for all forms of under-registration.

A sample was constructed from the Boyd volumes by selecting, in sequence, families from the first eight parishes in volumes 1-28, and this sample has been used in all tables analysing Boyd family listings. The eight parishes included in the sample were: St. Christopher le Stocks, St. Edmund Lombard Street, St. Martin Outwich, St. Antholin, St. John Baptist, All Hallows Bread Street, St. John Evangelist, and St. Mary Woolnoth. These eight parishes are not necessarily representative of over 100 parishes that existed in the City of London, although independent evidence to be considered later suggests that mortality levels in the eight parishes were probably fairly typical of London as a whole.

We can compare the burial registration experiences of wealth holders with those not owning the form of wealth eligible for extra taxation indicated in the 1695 Marriage Duty Act returns.[535] Of 64 same-name children from wealth-holding families included in Boyd's sample and traced in the Marriage Duty Listings, 18 (28 per cent) could not be found in the burial register, compared to 30 of 81 (37 per cent) from non-wealth holding families.

Of 37 eligible same-name children [536] not found in the burial register, none could be found in the Marriage Duty

---

[535] The main form of wealth listed was the ownership of real estate worth £600 or more, although other categories of wealth-owners were also included.
[536] These 37 same-name children were those born before 1695.

Listing, providing some support for the assumption that a missing same-name case is equivalent to an unregistered burial. Overall, 33 per cent of same-name cases could not be traced in the burial register, suggesting that about a third of all infant and child deaths were not registered. Applying the overall same-name correction ratio to all baptisms and infant burials in the sample generates a corrected infant mortality rate of 334 per 1,000 for the period 1681-1709. John Landers has independently estimated that infant mortality in London at the end of the seventeenth century was at least 360 per 1,000.[537] Given that mortality before baptism is excluded from the figure of 334 per 1,000, it is very similar to that estimated by Landers.

Child mortality can be calculated by establishing the children at risk — children surviving the first year and remaining in independent observation (through a recorded event of another family member in the Boyd and marriage duty records) until their fifth year — and dividing the number of corrected child burials (burials multiplied by the same-name ratio) by the number of children at risk. We can estimate infant and child mortality rates amongst those listed as owning and not owning taxable wealth in the Marriage Duty Act listing as summarised in Tables 3 and 4.[538]

---

[537] Personal communication from John Landers. According to the London Bills of Mortality child burials under the age of two represented about 60 per cent of baptisms in the period 1728-1739, suggesting that the same-name ratios in Table 2 do not overstate the levels of under-registration of burials. See Marshall, *Mortality*, p. 63.

[538] Boyd's data probably includes more wealth-holders than was typical for London as a whole. Glass estimated that about 27 per cent of the population were wealth-holders paying the higher level of taxation, lower than the proportion of wealth-holders in Table 3 and 4.

Table 3: Corrected Infant Mortality Rates (per 1000) among London Wealth and Non-Wealth Holders, 1681-1709.[539]

Wealth Holders				Non-Wealth holders			
Number Baptisms	Number Infant Burials	Same Name Ratio	IMR	Number Baptisms	Number Infant Burials	Same Name Ratio	IMR
611	131	61/46	284	642	155	81/51	383

Table 4: Corrected Child (1-4) Mortality Rates (per 1000) among London Wealth and Non-Wealth Holders, 1681-1709.[540]

Wealth Holders				Non-wealth holders			
Number Children (1-4) at Risk	Number Child Burials	Same Name Ratio	CMR	Number Children (1-4) at Risk	Number Child Burials	Same Name Ratio	CMR
448	62	61/46	184	424	62	81/51	232

Both infant and child mortality were highest among non-wealth holders, although these forms of mortality were still high amongst wealthy families, with nearly half of their children dying under the age of five.

It is possible to extend research on the Boyd data both backward and forward in time. Tables 5 and 6 contrast data for the total sample with that for members of the 12 great livery companies, designated as elite families.[541]

---

[539] Source. *Boyd's London Inhabitants.*
[540] Source. *Boyd's London Inhabitants*; Glass, *London Inhabitants.*
[541] B. Weinreb, C. Hibbert, *The London Encyclopedia*, 1993, pp. 167-77.

Table 5: Infant Mortality (per 1000) in the City of London, 1539-1849.[542]

Total Sample			Elite Families	
Period	Number Baptisms	IMR	Number Baptisms	IMR
1539-99	839	155	485	121
1600-49	1073	238	610	222
1650-99	1020	256	465	261
1700-49	704	409	194	422
1750-99	720	263	-	-
1800-49	199	141	-	-

Table 6: Child (1-4) Mortality (per 1000) in the City of London, 1539-1849.[543]

Total Sample			Elite Families	
Period	Number Children At Risk	CMR	Number Children At Risk	CMR
1539-99	616	168	404	134
1600-49	770	224	485	190
1650-99	686	282	340	291
1700-49	387	176	131	240
1750-99	435	270	-	-
1800-49	102	118	-	-

After 1750 there is insufficient information on elite families for a breakdown of these data. The proportion of same-name cases untraced in the burial register for the whole period

---

[542] Source: Boyd's *London Inhabitants*; Glass, *London Inhabitants*. Full details of Tables 5 and 6 are to be found in P. Razzell, *Population and Disease: Transforming English Society. 1550-1950*, 2007, p. 134.
[543] Source: Ibid.

1539-1849 is identical in both the total and elite samples – 112/320 and 51/146 – 35 percent. The proportion of untraced cases for the complete sample over time was as follows: 1539-1599: 17/48 (35 per cent); 1600-1649: 31/83 (37 per cent); 1650-1699: 32/99 (32 per cent); 1700-1749: 29/68 (43 per cent); 1750-1849: 6/22 (27 per cent). The numbers are too small to analyse differences between elite families and the total sample, or variations over time in the period 1750-1849.

Mortality was lower amongst the elite group than in the total sample population during the period 1539-1649, but this differential was reversed in the period 1650-1749 when mortality was higher among wealthier families. However, the most striking feature of Tables 5 and 6 is the very significant increase in infant and child mortality between the periods 1539-1599 and 1700-1749 in both groups. Infant mortality increased by about two-and-a-half times in the total sample, and more than tripled among elite families during this period. Child mortality approximately doubled in both groups between the sixteenth and the middle of the eighteenth century. There was also a marked drop in infant mortality among the total sample after the middle of the eighteenth century, similar to that depicted in the Bills of Mortality, although child mortality fluctuated during the eighteenth century before falling sharply in the early nineteenth.

The low infant mortality rate in the sixteenth and early seventeenth century is confirmed by Finlay's research on four parishes: the uncorrected rate for this period was as follows: All Hallows Bread Street, 1538-1653: 83/1,000; St Peter Cornhill, 1580-1650: 107/1,000; St Christopher le Stocks, 1580-1650: 55/1,000; St Michael Cornhill, 1580-1650: 109/1,000.[544] The equivalent uncorrected rate for the total Boyd sample for 1539-1649 is 131/1,000, indicating that the latter is not an understatement of London's infant mortality in this period.

---

[544] Finlay, *Population and Metropolis*.

Given the unexpected finding of a marked increase in infant and child mortality from the sixteenth to the middle of the eighteenth century, a special reconstitution study was carried out for the parish of St Bartholomew's for the period 1618-1849 (Table 7).

Table 7: Infant and Child Mortality (per 1000) in St. Bartholomew's the Less, London, 1618-1849.[545]

Period	Number of Infant Baptisms	Number of Children (1-4) at Risk	IMR	CMR
1618-49	328	143	191	282
1650-99	592	224	260	254
1700-49	564	202	342	278
1750-99	371	148	129	91

There was no overall change in child mortality between 1618 and 1749, but a sharp increase in infant mortality – from 191/1,000 to 342/1,000 – confirming at least in part the findings from the analysis of the Boyd data. There were also marked falls in infant and child mortality after 1750, similar to those found in Tables 1, 5 and 6. However, the proportion of infants traced through to the age of five was significantly less in the St. Bartholomew's than in the Boyd sample, and this is probably because the latter included a large proportion of permanent householders.

There is also the problem of increasing birth-baptism intervals which occurred in the eighteenth and early nineteenth century. The St. Bartholomew's the Less baptism register contains information on dates of birth and baptism for the period 1650-1812

---

[545] The figures are derived from the St. Bartholomew's parish register in the Society of Genealogists' Library. Full details of Tables 5 and 6 are to be found in the article published in *The London Journal*, Volume 32, 2007.

Table 8: Birth-Baptism Intervals in St. Bartholomew's the Less,
1650-1812.[546]

Period	Proportion Under Two Weeks	Proportion Above Two and Below Six Weeks	Proportion Above Six Weeks	Number Information on Birth-Baptism Intervals
1650-99	89%	10%	1%	583
1700-49	57%	43%	1%	753
1750-99	22%	70%	8%	457
1800-12	1%	65%	34%	71

The proportion of infants baptised within two weeks of birth fell steadily throughout the eighteenth century. This creates a problem of measuring neonatal mortality as many infants would have died before baptism without being registered in the burial register (under canon law unbaptized children were not members of the Anglican Church and were therefore not formally allowed to be buried by it). This is a form of burial under-registration which cannot be measured by the same-name method. However, it has been estimated that nationally approximately five per cent of infants died before baptism in the period 1838-1844,[547] which in London would represent about a third of all infants dying in the first year. Some clergymen baptised infants known to be at risk of dying, and so perhaps the lower proportion is a more accurate representation of unregistered infants. Table 8 indicates that the measurement of infant mortality using baptism and burial registers becomes progressively more difficult towards the end

---

[546] Full details of the Table are to be found in the article published in *The London Journal*, Volume 32, 2007.
[547] P. Razzell, *Essays in English Population History*, 1994, p. 147.

of the eighteenth and the beginning of the nineteenth century because of the increasing interval between birth and baptism.

It is possible to analyse infant and child mortality in St. Bartholomew's by socio-economic status. The parish register designates elite status by describing fathers as 'esquire', 'gentlemen' or 'Mr',[548] and the following table compares the mortality of this elite group with that of the non-elite population.

Table 9: Infant and Child (1-4) Mortality in St. Bartholomew's the Less by Socio-Economic Status, 1619-1848.[549]

	Elite Group		Non-Elite Population	
	1619-1749	1750-1848	1619-1749	1750-1848
Number of Infant Baptisms	371	119	1152	256
Number of Children (1-4) at Risk	200	48	384	101
IMR	307	160	260	93
CMR	300	83	277	91

---

[548] Full details of the Table are to be found in the article published in *The London Journal*, Volume 32, 2007. Additional research confirms the elite status of fathers given the titles of esquire, gentlemen or Mr. In the two periods 1655-70 and 1751-1812, information is given on whether people were buried inside or outside the church: 75 of 92 (83 per cent) members of elite families were buried inside the church, compared to 4 of 29 (14 per cent) of servants. Of 55 people buried inside the church and located in the 1695 Marriage Duty listing, 33 (65 per cent) were in families with £600+ fixed wealth or £50 p.a., whereas none of the 26 people buried outside and traced in the 1695 Listing were in the higher wealth category.

[549] For the source of this data see the St. Bartholomew's Parish register in the Society of Genealogists' Library.

The sample sizes are small for the post-1750 period, but the figures in Table 9 indicate that infant mortality was slightly higher in the elite than the non-elite group in both 1619-1750 and 1750-1848, and child mortality was higher in 1619-1749. This is similar to the finding on socio-economic status and mortality in Tables 5 and 6 for the period 1650-1749, but different from the conclusions in Tables 3 and 4 for 1681-1709. However, the periods and nature of the samples are different in each of the separate studies, and the mortality differences between wealthy/elite and other families are not greatly significant in any of the samples covered by the above tables.

These findings on infant and child mortality are very similar to those of John Landers on London Quakers for the period 1650-1849. The Quakers were a relatively prosperous group and perhaps occupied an intermediate socio-economic position between the wealthy and non-wealthy groups analysed in the present article. Table 10 only covers the period 1650-1849, but the overall level and pattern of mortality change is similar to that discussed earlier in this paper

Table 10: Age-Specific Mortality Rates per Thousand among London Quakers, 1650-1849.[550]

Cohort	Age (Years)		
	0-1	1-2	2-4
1650-74	251	103	190
1675-99	263	113	132
1700-24	342	145	177
1725-49	341	143	186
1750-74	327	150	159
1775-99	231	101	141
1800-24	194	93	85
1825-49	151	77	93

[550] Source: J. Landers, 'London's mortality in the long eighteenth: family reconstitution Study', *Medical History*, Supplement No. 11, 1991, p.7.

Mortality under the age of two increased up to the middle of the eighteenth century, and fell in the last half of the eighteenth and first half of the nineteenth century, while later child mortality decreased mainly in the first half of the nineteenth century. Landers' study mainly covers the area south of the river, and the evidence discussed in this article has focused on the City of London. However, both appear to have been fairly representative of London in the eighteenth and first half of the nineteenth century. There was relatively little variation in infant and child mortality between different districts in London at the beginning of civil registration, even between those with different socio-economic characteristics.

The Registrar General published details of the mean rateable value of housing in all registration districts, allowing an analysis of the relationship between poverty and mortality at the district level. Table 11 summarises mortality by district, arranged by level of mean rateable value, in the period immediately after the introduction of civil registration.

Table 11: Infant, Child (1-4) and Adult (25-44) Mortality in London, 1838-44.[551]

Registration District	Mean Annual Value of House Property (£)	IMR	CMR	Adult Mortality
Bethnal Green	8.1	159	54	11
Camberwell	12.3	141	34	14
Shoreditch	13.4	149	55	14
Bermondsey	13.5	140	59	11
Newington	14.1	160	47	10
Stepney	14.8	159	50	12
St. George,	15.4	182	63	13

[551] Source: Register General, *5th Annual Report,* 1843, p. 446; Register General, *8th Annual Report,* 1848, pp. 192-93; Register General, *9th Annual Report, Folio Edition,* 1848, pp. 236-38.

Southwark				
Greenwich	15.8	149	46	20
Rotherhithe	19.9	146	59	15
Lambeth	21.5	149	51	10
Mean Average of 10 Above Districts	14.9	153	52	13
Hackney	22.4	144	33	11
Whitechapel	22.4	194	75	20
St. George in the East	23.6	168	66	14
Islington	24.9	148	38	10
East & West London	25.3	186	82	21
Clerkenwell	25.4	155	47	11
St. Saviour & St. Olave	27.1	188	76	35
St. Luke	27.9	132	64	10
Kensington & Chelsea	29.1	163	47	12
Holborn	29.7	200	65	10
Mean Average of 10 Above Districts	25.8	168	59	15
Poplar	31.7	134	42	15
Westminster	32.4	180	65	17
Pancras	33.1	166	52	15
St. Giles	47.8	188	38	12
Strand	48.8	173	67	11
Marylebone	57.5	167	60	14
St. James Westminster	69	169	68	10
City of London	77.5	151	61	11
St. George Hanover Square	79.2	166	52	16
St.Martin's in the Fields	101.8	177	73	15
Mean Average of 10 Above Districts	57.9	167	58	14

The ten districts with the lowest rateable values – mainly in the East End of London – had the lowest infant and child mortality rates. In interpreting these findings, there is the problem of institutional mortality where deaths in hospitals and workhouses sometimes occurred outside the district of birth.[552] There appears to have been greater fluctuations in adult rather than infant or child mortality in the period 1838-44, although Farr made mathematical adjustments to allow for institutional mortality in this period.[553]

Robert Woods found a link between poverty and infant mortality in London during the 1880s,[554] using Booth's estimates of poverty by district. The poor districts at this time were more or less the same as those in the 1840s – most being in the East End of London – so it is possible that the social class gradient in infant mortality only began to establish itself in London during the latter part of the nineteenth century. However, the evidence in this paper indicates little or no association between poverty and infant/child mortality in the period 1550-1850, suggesting that disease played a largely exogenous role in shaping London's mortality patterns. This is an important and unexpected finding which will be discussed later in the paper.

Adult Mortality

Adult mortality is difficult to measure through reconstitution research because only a small proportion – usually about 10 per cent – can be traced from birth to the date of adult death. There are also formidable difficulties in establishing correct

---

[552] B. Luckin, G. Mooney, 'Urban history and historical epidemiology: the case of London, 1860-1920', *Urban History*, Volume 24, 1997, p. 47.
[553] Ibid.
[554] R. Woods, 'Mortality, poverty and environment' in R. Woods, J. Woodward (eds.), *Urban Disease and Mortality*, 1984, p. 24.

individual identity in baptism and burial registers. Special techniques are required to assess adult mortality levels, and there are two main sources available for this purpose in London during the period 1580-1849, marriage licences and apprenticeship records. According to an analysis of a sample of 14 London parish registers, 65 per cent of marriages were by licence in the first half of the seventeenth century, a proportion which had increased to 91 per cent by 1651-1750, before declining to 31 per cent at the beginning of the nineteenth century.[555] For women marrying under the age of twenty-one, parental consent was required, usually by written affidavit. The majority of marriage licence allegations have survived for London, and they usually contain the following relevant information: 1. Whether father alive or dead at date of marriage. 2. If father alive, his name and place of residence. 3. If father dead, name of mother or where relevant, guardian.

Because of uncertainty about father's place of residence – many young women who were married in London were migrants from the country – it is difficult to carry out an exact analysis of London's paternal mortality. Also, there is no reliable information on fathers' ages, although this is likely to be strongly influenced by age at marriage. The limited amount of evidence available indicates that there were no long- term changes in the mean age of male marriage during the seventeenth, eighteenth and early nineteenth centuries, suggesting that fathers' ages did not change significantly during this period.[556]

---

[555] P. Razzell, 'The conundrum of eighteenth century English population growth', *Social History of Medicine*, Volume 11, 1998, p. 484.

[556] According to marriage licence data, the mean age of marriage of London bachelors was 27.6 in 1630-36 and 27.2 in 1693-95. The figures for 1630-36 are based on the first 200 marriages selected from the Bishop of London marriage licences. See G.J. Armytage (ed.), *Allegations for Marriage Licences Issued by the Bishop of London 1611-1828,* Volume 26, 1887 The figures for 1693-95 are derived from the first 200 marriages selected from the Vicar Generals' marriage allegations in the Society of Genealogists' library. The

Table 12: Spinsters Marrying Under 21: Fathers Listed as Dead, London Marriage Licences.[557]

Period	Total Number of Cases	Number of Fathers Dead	Proportion of Fathers Dead
1600-41	696	303	44%
1661-99	1950	901	46%
1700-49	2500	1171	47%
1750-89	1937	694	36%
1840-49	500	143	29%

Table 12 indicates a slight rise in paternal mortality between 1600-1641 and 1700-1749, although there were fluctuations of mortality in this period, such as a rise to 55 per cent in the 1660s. This rise was probably partly due to the effect of the plague, although Table 10 includes data on fathers living and dying outside of London, who were presumably less vulnerable to plague mortality.

Overall paternal mortality was high and relatively stable during the period 1600-1749, but declined significantly and steadily from the middle of the eighteenth century onwards, falling from 47 per cent in 1700-49 to 29 per cent in 1840-49. The chronology of the fall in paternal mortality is similar to that found for infant and child mortality, although

---

mean age of marriage of bachelors in England & Wales in 1867-82 was 25.8 years, but the London average was probably higher than this in the early nineteenth century. 4.3 per cent of bachelors married under 21 nationally, compared to 1.6 per cent in the metropolis in 1843-44. See the Register General, *7th Annual Report,* 1843-44, pp xxx, xxxi; Registrar General, *45th Annual Report,* 1882, p. viii.

[557] For the period 1600-41, the data are based on the analysis of the Bishop of London's marriage licences in Armytage, *Allegations.* For the periods after 1661, the figures are based on an analysis of cases selected in sequence from the start of the dates of the Vicar-General's marriage licence allegations deposited in the Society of Genealogists' Library.

the latter more than halved between 1725-1749 and 1825-1849, whereas paternal mortality declined by about 38 per cent.

The long-term trend in paternal mortality is confirmed by independent evidence from apprenticeship records, although there is some uncertainty about the quality of data because of the potential problem of self-selection.[558]

The high paternal mortality in London at the beginning of the eighteenth century is confirmed by data from the national apprenticeship register compiled for taxation purposes. Of 373 cases listed in London and Middlesex for the period 1710-1713, 37 per cent of fathers were dead at the date of the indenture of their son, significantly higher than the percentage found in the same period for the northern rural counties of Northumberland, Rutland, Westmoreland and Yorkshire – 27 per cent (91 of 336 cases) – and in Scotland – 22 per cent (33 of 151 cases).[559]

An analysis of the socio-economic status of fathers and levels of paternal mortality indicates that mortality was higher amongst wealthy fathers. This was true both nationally and also in London, the latter indicated in Table 13.

Table 13: Mortality Among London Fathers Listed in the British Apprenticeship Register, 1710-13,[560] by Amount of Premium Paid.

Premium Paid	Number of Cases	Proportion of Fathers Dead
£9 And Under	110	32%
£10-£19	93	41%
£20+	99	42%

Fathers paying the higher premiums were gentlemen, merchants and others with high socio-economic status occupations, whereas those paying lower premiums were

---

[558] It is possible that poor widows had no incentive to place their sons into apprenticeships, although there is no direct evidence on this and any possible distortions are unlikely to have varied greatly over time.

[559] The data are based on the analysis of the British apprenticeship register lodged in the Society of Genealogists' Library.

[560] Ibid.

labourers, porters and others with manual occupations.[561] Higher paternal mortality in wealthier groups is an unexpected finding, although the sample sizes are small and there are data to indicate that boys from different socio-economic groups were apprenticed at slightly different ages, affecting the period in which fathers were at risk of dying.[562]

However, there is evidence that fathers' ages were probably very similar between the different occupational groups.[563] Larger samples are required before confident conclusions can be reached about the relationship between premium levels and paternal mortality.

A review of actuarial evidence from insurance companies and friendly societies found that adult mortality was higher amongst middle class than working class groups in the first half of the nineteenth century, a finding that was confirmed for some occupational groups by early census and civil registration data.[564] It is possible that the families of socio-economic elites were more vulnerable to infection through geographical mobility and contact with a greater number of disease environments, e.g. merchants travelling and trading with foreign countries. Additionally, elite families probably escaped some childhood diseases – such as smallpox – through avoidance practices, which made them vulnerable to the diseases as adults. There is also evidence that life-style factors – the excessive consumption of food, alcohol and tobacco, accompanied by the lack of physical activity – damaged the health of the wealthy, both in London and elsewhere.[565]

---

[561] See Razzell and Spence, 'Poverty', p. 63.

[562] Samples taken from the national apprenticeship register for the period of 1710-13 indicate that the average ages of apprentices in the different premium categories were as follows: £1-5: 14.4 years; £6-14: 14.9 years: £15+: 15.9 years. See Razzell and Spence, 'Poverty', p. 63. These figures are based on an analysis of Vicar General's marriage allegations in the Society of Genealogists' Library.

[563] The mean age at marriage in London does not appear to have varied greatly by social status at this time. In 1687, the mean age of marriage of London bachelors according to marriage licences was as follows: merchants, gentlemen and professionals: 26.8 years (N = 200); tradesmen and artisans: 26.4 (N = 360); mariners, servants and labourers (1687-94): 27.5 (N = 135).

[564] Razzell and Spence, 'The hazards of wealth', pp. 59, 60. See also Table 9.

[565] Ibid.

The Impact of Mortality on London's Population

Table 14 summarises estimates of London's population during the period 1520-1851, estimates which are very approximate because of the uncertain reliability of the source material.[566]

---

[566] Finlay and Shearer have put forward a set of alternative population figures, but these are partly based on inflation ratios applied to parish register data. These ratios are significantly different from those used in the present paper, highlighting the uncertain nature of all population estimates before the advent of national census registration in 1801. See R. Finlay, B. Shearer, 'Population growth and suburban expansion', in A.L Beier, R. Finlay (eds.), *London 1500-1700: The Making of the Metropolis*, 1986. The figures for London are taken from E.A. Wrigley, 'A simple model of London's importance in changing English society and e conomy 1650-1750', *Past and Present,* Volume 7, 1967, p. 44; E.A. Wrigley, *People, Cities and Wealth*, 1987, p. 162. For Greater London, see B.R. Mitchell, P. Deane, *Abstract of British Historical Statistics*, 1971, p. 19. Estimates of England's population for 1600-1801 are based on Rickman's returns of national baptisms, assuming a constant baptism rate. See Mitchell and Deane, *Abstract*, p. 5; E.A. Wrigley, R.S. Schofield, *The Population History of England, 1541-1871*, 1981,

Table 14: Estimated Population Size of London, 1520-1851.[567]

Date	Estimated Population of London	Period	Annual % Increase	Estimated Population of England	London's population as a % of England's Population
1520	55000			2600000	2.1%
1600	200000	1520-1600	3.3%	4300000	4.7%
1650	400000	1600 1650	2.0%	5250000	7.6%
1700	575000	1650-1700	0.9%	5100000	11.3%
1750	675000	1700-1750	0.3%	6000000	11.2%
1801	960000	1750-1801	0.8%	8600000	11.2%
	Greater London			England & Wales	
1801	1117000			8900000	12.6%
1851	2685000	1801-1851	2.8%	17900000	15.0%

The inverted U-pattern of growth – rapid during the sixteenth and the first half of the seventeenth century, slowing during 1650-1750, and beginning to grow more rapidly after 1750 – is similar to the pattern of infant and child mortality depicted in Tables 5 and 6. This suggests that for the period before 1650,

---

[567] The figures for London are taken from Wrigley, 'A simple model', p. 44; E.A. Wrigley, *People, Cities and Wealth*, 1987, p. 162. For Greater London, see Mitchell and Deane, *Abstract*, p. 19. Estimates of England's population for 1600-1801 are based on Rickman's returns of national baptisms, assuming a constant baptism rate. See Mitchell and Deane, *Abstract*, p. 5; Wrigley and Schofield, *The Population*, p. 574. The estimate of English 1520 population is derived from Wrigley and Schofield, *The Population*, p. 575.

mortality did not prevent rapid population growth as it did after the middle of the seventeenth century.[568]

The exact role of mortality in shaping London's population is complex, as there are a number of other factors, including fertility and migration, which were important for population growth. Before the widespread practice of birth control in the second half of the nineteenth century, fertility was largely shaped by marriage patterns. Although full and accurate information on marriage age in London is not available for the whole period 1550-1850, marriage licences do indicate the numbers of women marrying under the age of 21 due to the legal requirement of parental consent.

According to figures in Table 15, nearly half of single women living in London were married under the age of 21 in the early seventeenth century, and this was one of the factors associated with rapid population growth during the period.

---

[568] For a discussion of the role of mortality in shaping population growth in the period 1650-1750 see E.A. Wrigley, 'A simple model'.

Table 15: Proportion of Single Women Resident in London Marrying Under the Age of Twenty-One, Marriage Licences, 1600-1849.[569]

Period	Number of Single Women Marrying Under 21	Total Number of Marriages of Single Women	Proportion of Single Women Marrying Under 21
1600-39	188	400	47.0%
1661-99	162	400	40.5%
1700-49	138	500	27.6%
1750-99	50	500	10.0%
1800-49	28	500	5.6%

The proportion of women marrying under 21 fell significantly during the eighteenth and early nineteenth centuries, and this may have been partly the result of the reduction in adult mortality, which allowed women to achieve desired fertility at a later age of marriage.

Also as we saw earlier, the proportion of women ever marrying in London also fell significantly during the eighteenth

---

[569] S o u r c e : The first hundred consecutive marriages were selected at the beginning of each decade for the periods covered by Table 16. For 1600-39, the marriages were taken from Armytage, *Allegations*. For all subsequent periods, the marriages were selected from the copies of the Vicar General's marriage allegations in the Society of Genealogists' Library. The early age of marriage at the beginning of the seventeenth century is confirmed by V.B. Elliott, 'Single women in the London marriage market: age, status and mobility, 1598-1619', in R.B. Outhwaite (ed.), *Marriage and Society: Studies in the Social History of Marriage,* 1981. The proportion of single women marrying in London during the first half of the nineteenth century is similar to that found by the Registrar General in 1843-44: 7.7%. See the Registrar General, *Seventh Annual Report,* 1843-44, 1846, pp. xxx, xxxi.

and early nineteenth century,[570] and along with the decline in early marriage contributed to the slowing of London's population growth. However in the long run it did not prevent a resumption of a very rapid increase in London's population during the first half of the nineteenth century, which was largely the result of the reduction in mortality.

Table 14 indicates that long-term population increased much more rapidly in London than it did in the rest of England and Wales. It grew from an estimated 2.1 per cent of the national total in 1520 to 15.0 per cent in 1851, and some of this growth was fuelled by migration. Table 16 summarises data on the geographical origin of plumbers' and masons' apprentices.

Table 16: Geographical Residence of Fathers of Plumbers' and Masons' Apprentices Indentured, 1570-1799.[571]

Period	Number of Plumbers' Apprentices	Proportion of Fathers Residing Outside London	Number of Masons' Apprentices	Proportion of Fathers Residing Outside London
1570-99	21	86%	--	
1600-49	67	85%	--	
1650-99	140	71%	994	68%
1700-49	129	57%	884	37%
1750-99	56	39%	347	32%

Migration patterns revealed by Table 16 are confirmed by additional evidence based on apprenticeship records,[572] although

[570] See p. 185.?

[571] For the source material on which these figures are based see C. Webb (ed.), *London Apprentices, Volume 33: Plumbers' Company, 1571-1800*, 2000; C. Webb (ed.), *London Apprentices, Volume 27: Masons' Company, 1663-1805*, 1999. The figures for plumbers in the 1650-99 category are based on the period 1663-99.

[572] For confirmation of the very high proportion of migrants in the early seventeenth century, see Elliott, 'Single women', p. 84. An analysis of the

213

data derived from marriage licences suggest a lower level of in-migration in the early seventeenth century. Bishop of London licences indicate that 61 per cent of single women in London were migrants in 1583-86, a proportion that had fallen to 53 per cent in 1601-05, and 38 per cent by 1630-40.[573] Although lower than the proportions for apprentices, the marriage licence data confirm that in-migration was very important in London during the late sixteenth and early seventeenth century.

The decline in the percentage of migrants among apprentices in the eighteenth century was probably linked to the slow-down in population growth in the country at large, although Table 14 indicates that there was little or no change in London's share of the national population between 1700 and 1801, suggesting that London's increase was hampered by the high infant and child mortality in this period. However, mortality fell sharply after the end of the eighteenth century, engendering a rapid endogenous growth in population with minimal inward migration.

Discussion

The reasons for the patterns of mortality discussed in this paper must be largely speculative, given the absence of detailed work on the history of disease mortality in London during this period. The more than doubling of infant and child mortality between the sixteenth and the middle of the eighteenth century was not mirrored by a similar increase in adult mortality during the same period. Early mortality appears to have increased significantly in

---

records of the apprentices who acquired the freedom of the City of London indicates that the proportion of fathers living outside London fell from 77 per cent in 1673-74 (N = 200) to 14 per cent in 1822-24 (N = 99). See 'City of London Freedom Certificates' Guildhall Library, Corporation Record Office, reference CF1.

[573] The first 200 marriages were selected for analysis in each of the periods 1583-86, 1601-05 and 1630-40 from Armytage, *Allegations*.

all socio-economic groups in the period 1550-1750, suggesting that changes in the standard of living did not play a significant role in shaping mortality patterns, particularly as this was a period when real incomes were rising generally in London and elsewhere.

There is evidence that some diseases became more virulent during the period 1550-1850. Most people dying from smallpox in London during the sixteenth, seventeenth and eighteenth centuries were children, indicating that the disease was endemic, affecting everyone born in the city.[574] The case-fatality rate of smallpox in two London parishes during the sixteenth century was approximately 5 per cent,[575] compared to a case-fatality rate of about 45 per cent amongst unvaccinated children in London in the 1880s.[576] There is considerable evidence that smallpox became more fatal in London throughout the seventeenth, eighteenth and nineteenth centuries[577] – possibly as a result of the importation of more virulent strains with the growth of world trade – and this could explain in part the increase in infant and child mortality up to the middle of the eighteenth century. Inoculation and vaccination were practised in London after that period, although it is doubtful whether they made a major impact,

---

[574] See T.R. Forbes, *Chronicle from Aldgate*, 1971; R. Hoveden, *The Register of Christenings, Marriages and Burials of the Parish of Allhallows London Wall, 1559-1675*, 1878; J. Landers, 'Age patterns of mortality in London during the long eighteenth century: a test of the high potential model of metropolitan mortality' *Social History of Medicine*, Volume 3, 1990, p. 53.

[575] Forbes found in his study of the parish of Aldgate that there were 117 death from smallpox out of a total of 5,309 – 2.2 per cent – during 1583-99. 83 of the 117 deaths – 71 per cent – were under the age of ten, and as there were 3,236 baptisms in the parish during this period, this indicates a case-fatality rate of about 4 per cent. See Forbes, *Chronicle*. There were 12 deaths from smallpox in Allhallows London Wall during 1574-98, 10 of which were under the age of 7, with 442 baptisms in the parish during this period, indicating a case-fatality rate of under 5 per cent. See Hovenden, *The Register*.

[576] P. Razzell, *The Conquest of Smallpox,* 2003, pp. 168, 177.

[577] Ibid, pp. 166-78.

particularly among the poor, until the end of the eighteenth century.[578]

The disappearance of the plague in the 1660s does not appear to have made a significant long-term impact on mortality in London. It is possible that this was because other diseases were replacing plague as a cause of death. We have seen that smallpox was becoming more fatal to children, and this was probably true of certain other diseases. Typhus was probably introduced into England in the sixteenth century,[579] it affected adults more than children,[580] killed rich and poor alike, and became widespread in both town and countryside during the seventeenth century.[581] In London, diseases classified by contemporaries as fevers increased significantly during this period. Fever and ague accounted for about 6 per cent of all deaths in Aldgate during the period 1583-99, most deaths occurring among adolescents and adults.[582] According to the London Bills of Mortality, about 15 per cent of all deaths were due to fever in the first half of the eighteenth century, again most of them adults.[583]

There was a fall in the number of fever deaths among adults in London and elsewhere during the second half of the eighteenth century,[584] and much of this reduction in mortality

---

[578] Ibid, pp. 74, 96, 97.

[579] H. Zinsser, *Lice and History*, 1963, p. 279.

[580] A.J. Saah, 'Rickettsia prowettsia (epidemic louse-borne typhus)', in G.L. Mandell, J.E. Bennett, R. Dolin (eds.), *Principles and Practice of Infectious Diseases*, Volume 2, 2000; C. Creighton, *A History of Epidemics in Britain*, Volume 2, 1965, p. 47.

[581] Creighton, *A History*, Volume 2, pp. 30-33. The environmental conditions favourable to the spread of typhus appear to have been present in England well before the sixteenth century. Body lice continued to be prevalent in both town and countryside into the eighteenth and nineteenth centuries.

[582] Forbes, *Chronicle*.

[583] Vann and Eversley, *Friends*, pp. 212-15, 234.

[584] Ibid, p. 234. Schwarz has noted the decline of mortality from fever, smallpox, and consumption and the diseases of infancy in London during the eighteenth century. See L. Schwarz, 'Review article death in the eighteenth century', *Continuity and Change*, Volume 11, 1996, p. 300.

was probably linked to the gradual elimination of typhus infection. Woollen underwear was replaced by linen and cotton garments during this period, and more effective washing – involving the boiling of clothing – was probably responsible for the progressive elimination of both body lice and typhus.

In addition to inoculation and the introduction of linen and cotton garments, there were a number of other improvements which may have helped reduce mortality, e.g. the use of colostrums in breastfeeding after the middle of the eighteenth century.[585] However, many of these improvements would have been adopted first by the wealthy and then only later by the general population, and the evidence on the fall in mortality is that it affected all socio-economic and all age groups from the middle of the eighteenth century onwards. A study of the Bills of Mortality and parish registers which list cause of death suggests that a range of diseases diminished during the latter half of the eighteenth and first half of the nineteenth century – smallpox, fevers (probably including typhus and typhoid fever) and convulsions (probably including diarrhoea/gastrointestinal diseases).[586] Most of these are dirt diseases and it is possible that there was a transformation of the environment in the middle of the eighteenth century which had a major impact on disease incidence. Roy Porter wrote of the 'cleaning of the Great Wen' during this period, associated with a number of Local Improvement Acts which appeared to have transformed London's overall disease environment.[587]

The economic and social consequences of London's population growth have been well-documented by Fisher,

---

[585] Creighton, *A History*, p. 14

[543] R. Forbes, 'Births and deaths in a London parish: the record from the registers', *Bulletin of the History of Medicine*, Volume 55, 1981, p. 390; Vann and Eversley, *Friends*, p. 218; J. Landers, A. Mouzas, 'Burial seasonality and causes of death in London, 1670-1819' *Population Studies*, Volume 42, 1988, p. 64.

[587] R. Porter, 'Cleaning up the Great Wen: public health in eighteenth century London', *Medical History Supplement Number 11*, 1991.

Wrigley and others.[588] London provided an expanding market for a range of agricultural and industrial commodities, and was a major centre of manufacturing activity.[589] Its national and international trade laid the foundation for subsequent industrialization, and it acted as a focal point for the dissemination of a more cosmopolitan way of life.[590] None of this would have been possible without population growth, and the inverted U-shaped cure of economic and social development – rapid expansion between 1520 and 1700, followed by a long period of stagnation and subsequent rapid growth at the end of the eighteenth century – would not have occurred without a similar cycle of exogenous demographic development, both in London and nationally.[591]

Conclusion

The overall conclusions to be reached on the history of mortality in London from this research are as follows:

1. Infant and child mortality more than doubled between the sixteenth and the middle of the eighteenth century in both

---

[588] See F.J. Fisher, *London and the English Economy, 1500-1700*, 1990; Wrigley, 'A simple model'; Beier and Finlay (eds.), *London.*

[589] See J.A. Chatres, 'Food consumption and internal trade' in Beier, Finlay, *London.*; A.L Beier, 'Engine of manufacture: the trades of London', in Beier and Finlay, *London.*

[590] Wrigley, 'A simple model'; Beier and Finlay, *London.* Not only did the population increase in London during the sixteenth and early seventeenth centuries have economic and social consequences for the country at large, but it probably had a significant influence on political developments in the mid-seventeenth century. The City of London provided critical financial and military support for the Parliamentary cause – the City's trained bands constituted the core of the early Parliamentary army. See S. Porter (ed.), *London and the Civil War*, 1996.

[591] There is evidence that the cyclical fluctuations in mortality in London were also found in the country at large. See P. Razzell. 'Population, poverty and wealth: the history of mortality and fertility in England, 1550-1850', Razzell, *Population and Disease.*

wealthy and non-wealthy families.

2. Mortality peaked in the middle of the eighteenth century at a very high level, with nearly two-thirds of all children – rich and poor – dying by the time of their fifth birthday.

3. Mortality under the age of two fell sharply after the middle of the eighteenth century, and older child mortality decreased mainly during the late eighteenth and early nineteenth century. By the second quarter of the nineteenth century, about thirty per cent of all children had died within the first five years. This latter fall in mortality appears to have occurred equally among both the wealthy and the non-wealthy population.

4. There was little or no change in paternal mortality from 1600 to the first half of the eighteenth century, after which there was a steady fall until the middle of the nineteenth century. The scale of the reduction in paternal mortality was probably less than the fall in infant and child mortality. The latter more than halved between the middle of the eighteenth and nineteenth centuries, whereas paternal mortality fell by above a third in the same period.

5. There appears to have been a minimal social class gradient in infant, child and adult mortality in London during the period 1550-1850. This is an unexpected finding, raising fundamental questions about the role of poverty and social class in shaping mortality in this period.[592]

6 Although migration played a leading role in fostering population increase in London during the sixteenth and early seventeenth centuries, relatively low infant and child mortality made a major contribution to population growth in this period.

The absence of a general link between wealth and mortality has been one of the major findings of this paper. The research has also found an inverted U-shaped pattern of long-term infant and

---

[592] For a discussion of the role of wealth in shaping adult mortality see Razzell and Spence, 'The hazards of wealth'.

child mortality, with mortality more than doubling between the sixteenth and the middle of the eighteenth century, before falling sharply after this period. These findings represent a radical challenge to conventional assumptions about London's mortality history. However, the explanations and implications of these demographic patterns have yet to be fully explored and only detailed further reconstitution research on individual parishes – particularly with those with information on cause of death, age and occupation in the burial register – will answer some of these outstanding questions.

Chapter 7: Population Growth and the Increase of Socio-Economic Inequality in England, 1550-1850.[593]

Introduction

Malthus: 'Farmers and capitalists are growing rich from the real cheapness of labour'.[594]

In 1965, H.J. Habakkuk presented a 'heroically simplified version of English history' elaborating the role of population growth:

> ... long-term movements in prices, in income distribution, in investment, in real wages, and in migration are dominated by changes in the growth of population. Rising population: rising prices, rising agricultural profits, low real incomes for the mass of the population, unfavourable terms of trade for industry – with variations depending on changes in social institutions, this might stand for a description of the thirteenth century, the sixteenth century, and the early seventeenth, and the period 1750-1815. Falling or stationary population with depressed agricultural profits but higher mass incomes might be said to be characteristic of the intervening periods.[595]

It is not possible to test Habakkuk's thesis in any detail because there is no consensus on economic trends and changes in the economy during the early modern period. Attempts have been made by economic historians to resolve these difficulties by adopting mathematical models, but these have resulted in

---

[593] Unpublished paper.
[594] T.R. Malthus, *An Essay on the Principal of Population*, 1989, p. 28.
[595] H.J. Habbakuk 'The economic history of modern Britain', in D.V. Glass, D.E.C. Eversley (eds.), *Population in History: Essays in Historical Demography*, 1965, p. 148.

significantly different conclusions.[596] The differences are the result of disagreements on estimates of population, the impact of technology, employment levels, the incomes of women and children, changing occupational structure, and the effect of enclosures on the demand for labour. The problem is that there is no reliable national evidence to evaluate competing ideas, and attempts to resolve these difficulties have led to the use of models which necessarily require a range of arbitrary assumptions. As E.P. Thompson demonstrated, the lack of reliable national evidence has bedevilled the long standard of living debate, which is unlikely to ever be resolved by econometric analysis.[597]

In his study of income and wealth inequalities, Thomas Piketty has written that:

For far too long economists have sought to define themselves in terms of their supposedly scientific method. In fact, those methods rely on an immoderate use of mathematical methods ... the new methods often lead to a neglect of history and of the fact that historical experience remains our principle source of knowledge.[598]

Piketty has quoted historical evidence for England, including the structure of income and wealth in the early nineteenth century

---

[596] See for example G. Clark 'The long march of history: farm wages, population, and economic growth, England 1209-1869', *Economic History Review*, 60, 2007, pp. 97-135; S. Broadberry, B.M.S. Campbell, A. Klein, M. Overton, B. Van Leewen, *British Economic Growth, 1270-1870*, 2015. There are similar disagreements amongst economic historians about the growth of labour productivity during the period 1759-1831: Crafts and Harley estimate that average labour productivity in British industry grew by 0.26% a year in the period 1759-1801, and 0.21% from 1801 to 1831, whereas the corresponding estimates from Broadberry, Campbell, and van Leeuwen are 0.63% and 0.68%.' M. Kelly, C. O'Grada, 'Adam Smith, watch prices, and the industrial revolution', *The Quarterly Journal of Economics*, 2016, pp. 1728, 1729.
[597] E.P. Thompson, *The Making of the English Working Class*, 1966, pp. 189-349.
[598] T. Piketty, *Capital in the Twenty-First Century*, 2014, pp. 574, 575.

through the works of Jane Austen. This paper seeks to place the debate about socio-economic inequality in a broader historical context, in part by evaluating the relationship between population and socio-economic status in England from the sixteenth century onwards. Given the lack of consensus on national economic trends, it will only be possible to examine whether the historical evidence is consistent with Habakkuk's thesis, without analysing all the other possible factors influencing socio-economic inequality and levels of real income.

There is one fundamental issue largely neglected by the participants in the debate about the standard of living. This was summarized by the historian John Lovell when discussing J.L. and Barbara Hammond's work on the impact of industrialization on the life of labourers in the period 1760-1832:

> ... if population growth was caused by factors independent of the economy – if in other words it was an independent variable – then it becomes possible to regard the industrialization process as one that was vitally necessary for the welfare of the mass of the population, for if there had been no rapid expansion of economic activity, no leap forward in productivity, then the growth of numbers would ultimately have produced a crisis of subsistence. Such a crisis of subsistence did in fact occur in one part of the British Isles where the growth of population was not matched by that of industry. This was in Ireland, where the pressure of population resulted in small famines in 1817-18 and 1822 and a catastrophic famine in 1846.[599]

Lovell's argument has some validity, but it does not entirely resolve the debate between optimists and pessimists. There may have been no famines in England in this period, but this does not resolve the issue of changes in the overall standard of living. Additionally, it does not answer the question of what were the

---

[599] J.L. and B. Hammond, *The Town Labourer 1760-1832*, 1978, p. xii. Connell estimated that the population of Ireland increased from 2,167,000 in 1687 to 4,753,000 in 1791. See K.H. Connell, *The Population of Ireland, 1750-1845*, 1950, p. 25.

consequences of population growth for socio-economic inequality?

The History of English Population Growth.

The population of England had approximately doubled in the first half of the nineteenth century, and existing evidence indicates that population had grown from the middle of the eighteenth century onwards.[600] Most economists have assumed the primacy of economics over demography, reflecting the views of Malthus who in his theoretical work emphasized the impact of economic factors on fertility and population levels, through shifts in the incidence of marriage.[601] Although Malthus's theory of population stressed the economic basis of marriage and fertility – a growth in income leading to earlier marriage and a rise in fertility – in his account of England's experience he reversed his analysis. He concluded that mortality associated with the disease environment was the key driver of population growth, and a review of the evidence for the eighteenth and early nineteenth centuries confirms this conclusion.[602]

Population Change and Levels of Real Income and Socio-Economic Inequality

Although there is no definitive general national data, there is statistical and literary evidence for individual periods that can be used to illuminate the relationship between population change and socio-economic inequality. The second half of the sixteenth

---

[600] E.A. Wrigley, R.S. Schofield, *The Population History of England and Wales*, 1981; P. Razzell, 'Malthus: mortality or fertility: the history of English population in the eighteenth century'.
[601] Malthus, *An Essay*, 1989, Vol. 1, pp. 15, 92, 192, 193.
[602] Malthus, *An Essay*, 1989, p. 311; Razzell, Malthus: Mortality or Marriage?'

century was a period of rapid population growth and an increase in prices. There are some estimates that population grew by over 30 per cent in the period 1570-1609 and prices more than doubled between 1550 and 1600.[603] Lawrence Stone noted the changes that had taken place in English society during the sixteenth century as a result of population growth: 'the excess supply of labour relative to demand not only increased unemployment, but forced down real wages to an alarming degree ... [there was] a polarisation of society into rich and poor: the upper classes became relatively more numerous and their real incomes rose; the poor also became more numerous and their real incomes fell.'[604]

Recent research by Alexandra Shepard using church court depositions indicates that wealth inequality increased markedly during the sixteenth and seventeenth century. In the mid-sixteenth century the median real wealth of the gentry was £16.00, for yeomen £5.34; and for labourers £1.58. By the second quarter of the seventeenth century it had risen for both gentry and yeomen to £50.00, but for labourers it had declined to £1.03.[605]

After a period of stagnation in the second half of the seventeenth and first half of the eighteenth century, population began to grow from the middle of the eighteenth century, accelerating rapidly at the end of the eighteenth and beginning of the nineteenth century.[606] There is no current consensus on the

---

[603] E.A. Wrigley, R.S. Schofield, *The Population History of England and Wales*, 1981; B.R. Mitchell, P. Deane, *Abstract of British Historical Statistics*, 1971, pp. 484-486; J. Thirsk, 'The farming regions of England' in J. Thirsk, (ed.), *The Agrarian History of England and Wales, 1500-1640*, 1967, pp. 857, 858, 1861; E.H. Phelps-Brown, S.V. Hopkins, 'Seven centuries of the prices of consumables compared with builders' wage rates' in E.M. Carus-Wilson (ed.), *Essays in Economic History, Volume 2*, 1962, pp. 193-195.
[604] L. Stone, 'Social mobility in England, 1500-1700', *Past and Present*, Volume 33, 1966, pp. 26-29, 49.
[605] Data from *Perceptions of Worth and Social Status in Early Modern England*, ESRC Reference Number RES-000-23-1111.
[606] Wrigley, R.S. Schofield, *The Population*; Razzell, *Mortality*.

changing pattern of real income and economic inequality during the seventeenth and eighteenth centuries.[607] In the absence of reliable general statistical data, it is necessary to turn to literary evidence. Keith Snell has concluded that 'there was no doubt among contemporaries that real wages fell in the southern (and many Midland counties) [in 1760-1830].'[608] He quoted an extensive bibliography to support this conclusion, and added that 'the list could be considerably extended, and there were virtually no contrary opinions.'[609]

Although not definitive, the increasing poverty of labourers and the poor can be illustrated through autobiographical evidence which has a degree of authenticity by its immediacy and directness. This includes that from Admiral Horatio Nelson, who had no ideological interest in exaggerating the poverty of labourers. In a letter to the Duke of Clarence in 1790 he described the condition of the poor in Norfolk:

> That the poor labourer should have been seduced by promises and hopes of better times, your Royal Highness will not wonder at, when I assure you, that they are really in want of everything to make life comfortable. Hunger is a sharp thorn, and they are not only in want of food sufficient, but of clothes and firing.[610]

Nelson also claimed that labourers could not afford candles, soap or shoes, and for 'drink nothing but water, for beer our poor labourers never taste.'[611]

---

[607] J. Humphries, 'The lure of aggregates and the pitfalls of the patriarchal perspective: a critique of the high wage economy interpretation of the British industrial revolution', *Economic History Review*, 66, 2013, pp. 693-704; P.H. Lindert, 'When did inequality rise in Britain and America?' *Journal of Income Distribution*, 9, 2000.

[608] K.D.M. Snell, *Annals of the Labouring Poor*, 1985, p. 25.

[609] Ibid.

[610] N.H. Nicolas, *The Dispatches and Letters of Vice Admiral Lord Viscount Nelson, Volume 1, 1777-94*, 1845, p. 295.

[611] T. Coleman, *Nelson*, 2002; Nicholas, *The Dispatches*, p. 297.

One of the most detailed and reliable accounts was provided by the Reverend John Howlett, who had been the Vicar of Great Dunmow in Essex for about 50 years. Describing the condition of labourers he wrote in 1796:

> ... for the last forty or fifty years, some peculiarly favoured spots excepted, their condition has been growing worse and worse, and is, at length, become truly deplorable. Those pale famished countenances, those tattered garments, and those naked shivering limbs, we so frequently behold, are striking testimonies of these melancholy truths.[612]

He argued that these developments were the result of 'the rapid increase of population on the one hand and from the introduction of machines and variety of inventions ... [which have led to] more hands than we are disposed or think it advantages to employ; and hence the price of work is become unequal to the wants of the workmen.'[613] He compiled figures of income and expenditure in his parish, using details of wages from farmers' wage books and local knowledge of family incomes and consumption, for the two ten-year periods, 1744-53 and 1778-87. The annual expenditure per family in the first period was £20.11s.2d and earnings £20.12.7d, leaving a surplus of 1s.5d. In the second period the figures were £31.3s.7d and £24.3.5d, leaving a deficit of £7.0s.2d.[614] Howlett concluded that

> Of this deficiency the rates have supplied about forty shillings; the remaining £5 have sunk the labourers into a state of wretched and pitiable destitution. In the former period, the man, his wife, and children, were decently clothed and comfortably warmed and fed: now on the contrary, the father and mother are covered with rags;

---

[612] J. Howlett, *Examination of Mr Pitt's Speech in the House of Commons ... February 12th, Relative to the Condition of the Poor*, 1796, p. 2

[613] Ibid, p. 19. Technology was clearly important in displacing labour during the eighteenth and nineteenth centuries, but this issue is beyond the scope of the present paper.

[614] Ibid.

their children are running about, like little savages, without shoes or stockings to their feet; and, by day and night, they are forced to break down the hedges, lop the trees, and pilfer their fuel, or perish with cold. [615]

Much of the decline in real incomes was the result of increasing prices, and Table 1 suggests that some of the price increases were the result of growing demand resulting from population increase. Bread was a staple food for the poor and 'constituted about 44 per cent of total family expenditure in the 1760s but this had risen to about 60 per cent by 1790.'[616] 'Not wages, but the cost of bread, was the most the most sensitive indicator of popular discontent ... Any sharp rise in prices precipitated riot.'[617] The price of bread was used under the Speenhamland system to subsidise wages. The price of bread is therefore central to the analysis of the relationship between increasing population and changes in prices. Information on the price of bread in London is available for the whole of the eighteenth and first half of the nineteenth century, and the following table summarises data on its association with population growth.

---

[615] Ibid, p. 49. For budgets of labouring families in 1796 which showed an almost universal deficit of expenditure over income, see D. Davies, *The Case of Labourers in Husbandry*, 1796, pp. 7, 176-227; F.M. Eden, *The State of the Poor*, Volume 3, 1797, pp. cccxxxix-cccl. Davies and Eden compiled between them budgets in twenty-three counties of England.
[616] Snell, *Annals*, p. 26.
[617] Thompson, *The Making*, p. 63.

Table 1: The Relationship between Increasing Population and the Price of Bread in London.[618]

Period	Mean Population of London	Mean Price of 4lbs of Bread in London (Pence)
1700-49	625,00	5.1
1750-99	788,000	6.4
1801-51	1,631,000	10.7

Although only one of a number of possible explanatory factors,[619] Table 1 suggests that the increasing demand resulting from the growth of population had a major impact on the price of bread.

Cobbett presented detailed evidence of the pauperisation of labourers at the end of the eighteenth century. By 1805 he came face to face with the poverty of southern agricultural workers:

> The clock was gone, the brass kettle was gone, the pewter dishes were gone; the warming pan was gone ... the feather bed was gone, the Sunday-coat was gone! All was gone! How miserable, how deplorable, how changed the Labourer's dwelling, which I, only twenty years before, had seen so neat and happy.[620]

He linked the pauperisation of labourers with the decline of the living-in system and the increasing wealth of farmers:

> [The] farm-house was formerly the scene of plain manners and plentiful living. Oak clothes-chests, oak chest of drawers, and oak tables to eat on, long, strong, and well supplied with joint stools ... there were, in all probability, from ten to fifteen men, boys and maids ... [but now] a *parlour*! Aye, and a carpet and bell-pull too! ...

---

[618] E.A. Wrigley, 'A simple model', p. 44; B.R. Mitchell, P. Deane *Abstract of British Historical Statistics*, 1971, pp. 497, 498. The population figures are the averages between the population numbers in 1700, 1750, 1801 and 1851.
[619] For the range of possible explanatory factors see J.L. and B. Hammond, *The Town Labourer 1760-1832*, 1995, pp. 102-110.
[620] W. Cobbett, *Rural Rides*, 2001, p. x.

[and a] mahogany table, and the fine chairs, and the fine glass ... And ... decanters, the glasses, the 'dinner set' of crockery ware ... it [is now] *Squire* Charington and the *Miss* Charingtons ... transmuted into a species of mock gentle-folks ... [621].

Although there is no reliable national statistical data to support the local and literary evidence, there is some data for southern and western counties which indicates that there were sharp falls in the real incomes of poor men and women in the late eighteenth and early nineteenth century. Snell has compiled figures of the annual wages of southern and western farm and domestic servants taken from poor law settlement examinations. These figures cover the whole period 1741-1840, and have the advantage of relying on direct witness statements. They focus on unmarried young men and women hired by the year, which conferred poor law settlement. They relate to employment for the whole year, and were paid at the end of the year, addressing the major difficulty of establishing changing unemployment levels. These categories of worker were boarded and lodged during the year, so in that sense were safeguarded from many of the effects of price fluctuations. Frequently their statements were checked by parish authorities, providing some independent surety for their reliability. There is some evidence from other sources which suggests that these trends proximate to weekly wage trends affecting other largely unskilled rural and market-town workers in these southern and western English counties, which covered about sixty per cent of the total population of England.[622]

---

[621] Ibid, pp. x, xviii, 358.
[622] Snell, *Annals*, pp. 23-28; Mitchell and Deane, *Abstract*, p. 20.

Table 2: Mean Real Wages (£) of Farm and Domestic Servants in Southern and Western Counties, 1741-1840.[623]

Period	Mean Real Male Annual Wages (£)	Mean Real Female Annual Wages (£)
1741-50	7.398	4.802
1751-60	5.919	4.546
1761-70	7.994	4.532
1771-80	7.361	4.226
1781-90	7.751	4.007
1791-1800	6.614	3.541
1801-10	5.212	3.319
1811-20	4.9	3.574
1821-30	5.43	4.421
1831-40	4.828	4.086

Male mean wages were more-or-less constant in the period between 1741 and 1790 but fell sharply in the period 1791-1840. Female real wages fell gradually from the 1740s onwards, with a slight recovery in the two decades between 1821 and 1840.

The Captain Swing riots in 1830 occurred widely in southern and eastern counties, and according to Hobsbawm and Rude 'the basic aims of the labourers were singularly consistent: to attain a minimum living wage and to end rural unemployment ... [much of it the result of] a permanent surplus of labour ... due in the first instance to the growth of population.'[624]

There is some evidence that wealth became more unequally distributed in the late seventeenth and eighteenth centuries. Clark has summarized data from wills in Essex, Kent, Buckingham, Surrey and Suffolk in the seventeenth and eighteenth centuries:

---

[623] Snell, *Annals*, pp. 23-28; E.H. Phelps-Brown, S.V. Hopkins 'Seven centuries of the prices of consumables, compared with builders' wage rates' in E.M. Carus-Wilson (ed.), *Essays in Economic History*, Volume 2, 1962.

[624] E.J. Hobsbawm, G. Rude, *Captain Swing*, 1973, pp. 22, 163.

In the farming sector there is an almost complete disappearance of what would be a growing agricultural proletariat from probate records. In the seventeenth century there were only 0.55 yeomen for every husbandman/labourer. This ratio moved dramatically in favour of yeomen: 1600-49: 1.37; 1650-99: 2.7; 1700-69: 4.6.[625]

This suggests that not only labourers and husbandmen were becoming increasingly impoverished, but that yeoman farmers were growing wealthier. This is also indicated by evidence on agricultural occupations in Cambridgeshire and Bedfordshire.

Table 3: Percentage Distribution of Wills in Cambridgeshire and Bedfordshire, 1601-1800.[626]

Period	Farmers & Yeomen	Husbandmen	Labourers & Servants	Number of Wills
1600-1649	42.0%	27.8%	29.8%	2023
1650-1699	65.6%	17.6%	16.9%	2000
1700-1749	64.7%	16.0%	19.3%	2409
17500-1799	82.1%	8.5%	9.5%	1495

[625] G. Clark, 'The consumer revolution: turning point in human history, or statistical artifact', *Department of Economics, University of California, Davis, Working Paper*, 2010.

[626] The data for Cambridgeshire is taken from N. Evans, 'Occupations and status of male testators in Cambridgeshire, 1550-1750', in T. Arkell, N. Evans, N. Goose (eds.), *When Death Do Us Part*, 2000, p. 181; the Bedfordshire material is derived from P. Razzell, C. Spence, M. Woollard, 'The evaluation of Bedfordshire burial registration, 1538-1851', *Local Population Studies*, 84, 2010. Labourers and husbandmen who left wills were much poorer than yeoman and farmers. In 1585-1638 in Essex, Kent, Buckingham, Surrey and Suffolk the average assets bequeathed by yeomen/farmers was £406, whereas that bequeathed by husbandmen was £87 and that by labourers £42. See G. Clark, G. Hamilton, 'Survival of the richest; the Malthusian mechanism in pre-industrial England', *Journal of Economic History*, 66, 2006, p. 11. In a sample of inventories from eight parts of England in 1675-1725, the equivalent figures were: Yeomen/Farmers £165, Husbandmen £32, Labourers £16. L. Weatherrill, *Consumer Behaviour and Material Culture, 1660-1760*, 1988, p. 212.

the changing distribution of occupations is consistent with the increasing pauperisation of labourers and the growing wealth of farmers in the South of England.

There is also evidence that wealthy families came to dominate elite occupations in the late eighteenth and early nineteenth century.[627] For example, the proportion of East Indian Company army officers from the landed gentry rose from six per cent in 1758-1774 to nineteen per cent in 1805-1834; the equivalent figures for the aristocracy were two to five per cent.[628]

Real wages were higher in the North of England as a result of industrialization in the nineteenth century,[629] but there is some evidence that the pauperisation of the working class was not confined to the South of England.[630]. Charles Shaw in his autobiography described the conditions of workers in the Staffordshire Potteries in the 1830s and 1840s:

All the great events of the town took place … [in] the market place. During the severity of winter I have seen one of its sides nearly filled with stacked coals. The other side was stacked with loaves of bread, and such bread. I feel the taste of it even yet, as if made of ground straw, and alum, and Plaster of Paris. These things were stacked there by the parish authorities to relieve the destitution of the poor. Destitution, for the many, was a chronic condition in those days, but when winter came in with its stoppage of work, this destitution became acute, and special measures had to be taken to relieve it. The crowd in the market-place on such a day formed a ghastly sight. Pinched faces of men, with a stern, cold silence of manner. Moaning women, with crying children in their arms, loudly proclaiming their sufferings and wrongs. Men and women with loaves or coals, rapidly

---

[627] P. Razzell, *Population and Disease: Transforming English* Society, 2007, pp, 236-239.
[628] Ibid, p. 236.
[629] J. Caird, *English Agriculture in 1850-51*, 1968; Mitchell and Deane, *Abstract*, pp. 346, 347; E.H. Hunt, 'Industrialization and regional inequality in Britain, 1760-1914', *The Journal of Economic History*, 46, 1986.
[630] P. Razzell, R. Wainwright, *The Victorian Working Class*, 1973, pp. xix-xxiv.

departing on all sides to carry some relief to their wretched homes – homes, well, called such ... This relief, wretched as it was, just kept back the latent desperation in the hearts of these people.[631]

Not all workers were resigned to the poverty they experienced at this time. John Buckmaster described in his autobiography the political turmoil that occurred in Buckinghamshire during the 1830s:

Numbers of men were out of work, bread was dear, and the Chartist agitation was violently active. Copies of the *Northern Star* and other Chartist papers found their way into every workshop. Meetings were held almost every evening and on Sundays. Some of the speeches advocated physical force as the only remedy ... Lectures on Peterloo, the Bristol Riots, the Monmouth Rising, and the Pension List were common. Bad trade, low wages, and dear bread were the stimulating causes of widespread discontentment. Men were driven to their lowest depth of hatred of the governing classes ... the country was passing through the throes of a political convulsion which was fast ripening into a revolution. The mechanics institute gradually degenerated into a violent revolutionary club.[632]

Underlying many of these conditions were the increasing employment of cheap labour.[633] In 1809, the abolition of protective legislation had allowed the increasing employment of children and unskilled workers in the new factories.[634] Over 80 per cent of the labour force in English and Scottish factories in 1833 was women and children, paid about a third of the wages of male workers.[635]

---

[631] C. Shaw, *When I Was a Child*, 1980, pp. 42, 43.
[632] J. Buckmaster, *A Village Politician*, 1982 pp. 98, 99, 124, 153. For a detailed account of the political consequences of the pauperisation of the working class see Thompson, *The Making*.
[633] H. Mayhew, *The Morning Chronicle Survey*, 6 Volumes, 1980.
[634] Thompson, *The Making*, p. 529.
[635] J. Humphries, *Childhood and Child Labour in the British Industrial Revolution*, 2010; Razzell, *Mortality*, p. 106.

Not all the worst conditions were found in the new factories, they were often found in small sweated workshops and among garret masters working from home, described by Mayhew in such detail.[636] Many people were forced to work in these places because of an excess of labour. One of Mayhew's informants told him:

> The speculators find plenty of cheap labour among the country lads. A hand fresh up from the country can't get employment at the best shops, unless he's got some friends, and so, after walking all London, he is generally down to look for a job among the speculators at low wages.[637]

It was not just low wages, but a high incidence of unemployment that was the cause of much poverty. Mayhew stated that 'In almost all occupations there is ... a *superfluity of labourers*, and this alone would tend to render the employment of a vast number of the hands of a casual rather than a regular character. In the generality of trades the calculation is that one-third of the hands are fully employed, one third partially, and one-third unemployed throughout the year.'[638] One boot-maker in Mayhew's survey directly linked demographic trends with its impact on aggregate demand and increasing poverty levels:

> The cause of the trade being so overstocked with hands is, I believe, due in great measure to the increase in population. Every pair of feet there is born, certainly wants a pair of shoes; but unfortunately, as society is at present constituted, they cannot get them. The poor, you see sir, increase at a greater rate than the rich.[639]

A witness before the 1833 House of Commons Select Committee on the State of Agriculture stated that 'it is the surplus of labourers that are suffering, of which there are many in almost

---

[636] Mayhew, *The Morning Chronicle*.
[637] Ibid, Vol. 5, p. 108.
[638] Ibid, Vol. 2, p. 300.
[639] Ibid, Vol. 3, p. 139.

every parish, and these men are very badly off ... It used to be customary to have them [employed] for a whole year and employ them in the winter, but that is not the case now.'[640] A detailed account of the life of agricultural labourers was provided by the *Morning Chronicle Survey* in the middle of the nineteenth century:

Their labour is at the command of anyone who bids for it; and as their employment is precarious, and their wages fluctuating, their lives are spent, in the majority of cases, in constant oscillation between their homes and the workhouse ...[641]

The Growth of Capitalism

Many of the above developments were associated with the growth of capitalism, linked to the creation of labour surpluses resulting from population growth.[642] At the end of the eighteenth century Cobbett described the growth of capitalism, arguing that bankers and city merchants played a significant role in the consolidation of estates and farms:

The small gentry, to about the third rank upwards ... are all gone, nearly to a man, and the small farmers with them. The Barings [merchant bankers] alone have, I should think, swallowed up thirty or forty of these small gentry without perceiving it ... The Barings are adding field to field and tract to tract in Herefordshire; and as to

---

[640] M. Neuman, *The Speenhamland County: Poverty and the Poor Law in Berkshire 1782-1834*, 1982, p. 20.
[641] Razzell and Wainwright, *The Victorian*, pp. 3-5
[642] J. Whittle, *The Development of Agrarian Capitalism: Land and Labour in Norfolk, 1440-1580*, 2000; L. Shaw-Taylor, 'The rise of agrarian capitalism and the decline of family farming', *Economic History Review*, 65, 2012; C.K. Harley, 'British and European industrialisation' in L. Neal, J.G. Williamson (eds.), *Capitalism: Volume 1: The Rise of Capitalism from Ancient Origins to 1848*, 2014; Razzell, *Mortality*, pp. 99-108.

the Ricardos, they seem to be animated with the same laudable spirit
... [acquiring a number of] estates ... [643]

He further described the way the gentry and aristocracy employed urban stock brokers to speculate in stocks and shares, directly linking rural and urban capitalism,[644] which is confirmed by Stone's account of the economic activities of the aristocracy in the eighteenth and nineteenth centuries:

> By 1750 there were few great landlords who did not have some money – often a great deal – in the public funds of the Bank of England. In this sense they were themselves becoming inextricably linked with the monied interest, and their mental attitudes to banking and stock speculation changed accordingly ... Others poured surplus cash into canal companies and turnpike trusts in the eighteenth century, and into railroad companies and dockyards in the nineteenth. From the early seventeenth century onward many were deeply involved in urban development of London.[645]

The poverty of workers in factories was directly linked to the increasing wealth of the factory owners, described by an anonymous cotton spinner in 1818 as follows:

> ... with very few exceptions, they [the employers] are a set of men who have sprung from the cotton-shop without education or address ... but to counterbalance that deficiency, they give you enough of appearances by an ostentatious display of elegant mansions, equipages, liveries, parks, hunters, hounds ... They bring up their families at the most costly schools ... and to support all this, their whole time is occupied in contriving how to get the greatest quantity of work turned off with the least expense ... the greater part of the master spinners are anxious to keep wages low ... for the purpose of taking the surplus to their own pockets.[646]

---

[643] Cobbett, *Rural Rides*, p. 223.
[644] Ibid, pp, 6, 115.
[645] L. Stone, *An Open Elite: England 1540-1880*, 1995, p. 189.
[646] Thompson, *The Making*, pp. 199, 200.

This is essentially an illustration of the influence of capitalism on England's economic life. Harley has recently concluded that 'the emergence of Britain's modern growth depended more on a long history of capitalism than on the industrial revolution.'[647] The development of capitalism depended not only on the existence of a surplus of labourers but also on a number of political, social and economic factors.[648] However, population growth played a critical role in providing one of the necessary conditions – a large surplus of labour – which occurred at various periods in England's history between 1550 and 1850.

Conclusion

Evidence reviewed in this paper is consistent with Habakkuk's thesis about the role of population growth in shaping levels of socio-economic inequality in England during the early modern period. Population growth was not shaped by economic factors but by changes in the disease environment, which resulted in significant falls in adult and child mortality. As a result, population played a major independent role in economic change between 1550 and 1850. Although only one of a number of possible factors, the evidence presented indicates that increasing population resulted in the creation of labour surpluses and a growth in aggregate demand. The consequence of England's growing population was an increase in inequality and poverty for the mass of its labouring population at different times in the early modern period, but particularly in the late eighteenth and the first half of the nineteenth century. This was the period of both rapid population increase and the growth of capitalism, resulting in increasing socio-economic inequality. However, the economic developments associated with capitalism also increased

---

[647] C.K. Harley, 'British and European industrialisation' in L. Neal, J.G. Williamson (eds.), *Capitalism: Volume 1: The Rise of Capitalism from Ancient Origins to 1848*, 2014, p. 492.
[648] Razzell, *Mortality*, pp. 99-122.

productivity, preventing the famine conditions that occurred in Ireland, which also experienced a significant increase in population but without an industrial revolution. In spite of rapid economic growth in England, the development of capitalism was associated with the increasing pauperisation of the poor at the end of the eighteenth and first half of the nineteenth century.

Chapter 8: Socio-Economic Status and Adult Mortality in England: a Historical Study, 1881-1891.[649]

Introduction

Currently, and throughout the twentieth century, there is clear evidence of a social gradient in adult mortality, in England and elsewhere.[650] The Registrar-General of England and Wales published figures for adult mortality ratios for men by occupationally defined social class for the period 1910-1953, which showed a social class gradient amongst men in 1910-12, with particularly large differences between Social Classes I and V. This persisted throughout the first half of the twentieth century, although it had diminished somewhat by 1949-53.[651] Inequalities widened again after 1970, and appear to have worsened even further in the 1990s, contributing to the current major concern over the health effects of social inequality.[652] Although there are various methodological debates about these trends, it seems clear from these reports of the Registrar General, and other sources, that a social gradient in mortality was a feature of twentieth century England.

Evidence for the nineteenth century is, however, less clear. Many contemporary commentators linked poverty with poor health and higher mortality amongst adults. However, much of the data for this conclusion was based on death

---

[649] Unpublished paper, written jointly with Emily Grundy.

[650] G. Davey Smith, D. Dorling, M. Shaw, *Poverty, Inequality and Health in Britain*, 2001; General Register Office, *Fifth Registrar-General's Annual Report, 1841*, pp. xxviii-xxxi; R.G. Wilkinson, K. Pickett, *The Spirit Level: Why Equality is Better for Everyone*, 2010; E. Chadwick, *Report on the Sanitary Condition of the Labouring Population of Great Britain*, 1965.

[651] J. Parker, C. Rollett, K. Jones in A.H. Halsey (ed.) *Trends in British Society since 1900*, 1971.

[652] Davey-Smith, *Poverty*; Wilkinson, *The Spirit Level*.

registers which did not take account of the population at risk, a flaw first pointed out by Farr in his discussion of life tables.[653] This critique is particularly relevant to the work of Chadwick, who used information from death registers on occupation and age at death to estimate mortality ratios, without allowing for the population at risk.[654]

Chadwick's work influenced a number of influential contemporary thinkers, including Engels and Mayhew.[655] Early reports from the Registrar-General which indicate occupational and social class differences in adult mortality during the nineteenth century,[656] also suffered from various difficulties. These include possible numerator-denominator bias as the population at risk is calculated from census information and the number of deaths from civil registration returns (a weakness also of twentieth century estimates), which use different methods of classification of data. Descriptions of occupations are also often ambiguous and difficult to classify, with heterogeneous variations within occupational categories, often locally based. Additionally, analyses of national data does not allow for the role of geographical place, which often had a significant influence on mortality.[657]

For example, clergymen and agricultural labourers both had low adult mortality rates in the late nineteenth and early twentieth century,[658] probably due to their residence in rural areas. Available data also does not cover all occupations, so that labourers – who were one of the most numerous and poorest occupational groups – are excluded from some analyses.[7]

---

[653] General Register Office, *Fifth Registrar-General's Annual Report, 1841*, pp. xxviii-xxxi
[654] Chadwick, *Report*.
[655] P. Razzell, *Population and Disease: Transforming English Society, 1550-1850*, 2007.
[656] R. Woods, *The Demography of Victorian England and Wales*, 2000.
[657] E. Garrett, A. Reid, K. Schurer, S. Szreter, *Changing Family Size in England and Wales: Place, Class and Demography, 1891-1911*, 2001.
[658] Woods, *The Demography*; *Supplement to the Registrar-General's Seventy-Fifth Annual report, Part IV: Mortality of Men in Certain Occupations in the Three Years 1910, 1911 and 1912*.

Farr's own investigation of mortality rates in London indicated no significant difference in mortality between wealthy and poor areas of London in 1838-44.[659] Neison also concluded from Insurance Company and Friendly Society records that there was no link between poverty and adult mortality.[660] However, the latter is subject to the problem of selection as results are based on those who chose, and could afford, to join and remain in Friendly Societies.

One way of partly dealing with these problems is to trace individuals directly through census, civil death register and other source material so avoiding numerator-denominator bias. Additionally, census data provide information on indicators of socio-economic status other than occupation and allow geographical factors to be taken into account. The potential of linked census and registration data has been explored to some extent in two previous small scale studies. In a study of forty-seven Bedfordshire parishes in the 1840s, tracking married couples between the 1841 and 1851 Censuses, results indicated that there was slightly higher mortality amongst professionals, merchants and gentleman than amongst labourers.[661] A similar methodology was employed in research on Ipswich in the 1870s, which suggested that adult mortality was higher in Social Classes I and II than in IV and V, although by the 1890s the position had been slightly reversed.[662]

In the study reported here we have extended this method and applied it to a national sample of married people enumerated in the 1881 Census. The methodological aim of the paper was to investigate tracing rates between census and other sources, principally registration of deaths, and the extent to which using census derived information on transitions from being married to being widowed can be used to extend identification of deaths.

---

[659] Razzell, *Population*, p. 136.
[660] Ibid, p. 220-23.
[661] Ibid, p. 201-02.
[662] Ibid, p. 204.

The substantive aim was to investigate the extent of social inequalities in adult mortality in late nineteenth century England.

Methods: Data.

We compared the mortality of two contrasting groups: 'elite' couples, defined as those with two or more domestic servants, and poor couples defined on the basis of husband's occupation as a labourer. The link between family income and the number of domestic servants has been widely documented for the period 1825-1906.[663] In general terms, the wealthier the family the greater the number and types of servant they employed, although this association is not perfectly linear.[664] The occupations of head of households in two-servant+ families identified in the current research are heavily concentrated in professional, business and landed families, although also including a number of farmers. Eight married couples were chosen from each county of England, four from each rural parish and four from each county town. We selected the first couple in the 1881 Census enumeration list with two or more domestic servants – designated as elite couples – and then the next family headed by a labourer, known to be one of the poorest occupational groups in England at the end of the nineteenth century.[665] This method of selection was repeated four times for each parish in the sample resulting in 156 elite and 156 labourer couples – and was adopted in order to compare

---

[663] B.S. Rowntree, *Poverty: a Study of Town Life*, 1901; J.A. Banks *Prosperity and Parenthood: a Study of Family Planning among the Victorian Middle Classes*, 1954; J. Burnett, *Plenty and Want*, 1968; P. Horn *The Rise and Fall of the Victorian Servant*, 1974; L. Schwartz, 'English servants and their employers during the eighteenth and nineteenth centuries', *Economic History Review*, 1999 Volume 52.

[664] E. Higgs, 'Domestic servants and households in Victorian England', *Social History*, Volume 8, 1983.

[665] Rowntree, *Poverty*; Burnett, *Plenty*.

well-defined groups with significantly different socio-economic profiles but the same geographic location.

Sample members were then traced in the 1891 Census, as well as in the civil register index of deaths. The methodology used involved triangulation between census, civil register, and probate sources. Tracing in the census was undertaken to identify those still alive (present in the census) and those whose death could be inferred by the fact that their spouse was present in 1891 but identified as widowed. Two family history sites were employed for this purpose. A first search was made using *Find My Past* and a second using *Ancestry*. It was necessary to use two sites because of the variable accuracy of the transcripts on which the family history indexes are based; variations in the spelling and presentation of birth places; inaccuracies in age reporting. Eighty-nine per cent of cases were traced through the *Find My Past* website, and a further eleven per cent in *Ancestry*.

In summary the following steps were carried out:

1. A search was made for the 1881 sample in the *Find My Past* 1891 census online index.

2. For unidentified cases, a further tracing exercise was carried out on the *Ancestry* 1891 census index.

3. A search was then carried out in the civil registration death index.

The civil registration death index contains information on the name of the individual, his or her age, the registration district in which the death was registered, and the quarter/ year of death. There is no information on kinship connections, occupation or other details which would facilitate identification and allow classification by socio-economic status.

Probate calendars usually provide information on place of death, address, exact date of death and kinship relationships but are only available for a proportion of the population with wealth to bequeath. These calendars have been digitized and indexed by the *Ancestry* family history site for the period 1861-1941, and this data was used to check assumptions about the identification of deaths. In order to trace husband and wives between censuses the following key information is available in the censuses: 1. Name. 2. Age. 3. Birthplace. 4. Registration District. 5. Occupation. 6. Name, birthplace and age of children. Some of this information is also available in the death indexes – name, age and registration district of death.

There are a number of problems in linking census data for individuals, including the variable accuracy of the transcripts on which the family history indexes are based and the remarriage after widowhood especially for women changing their surname on remarriage. In cross-matching census data, a correct identification was assumed to take place when name, birthplace and age to within plus or minus five years were found to be the same. Other identifying information – such as spouse's and children's names, ages and birthplaces, plus occupational information – was also used where necessary. The research employed manual matching which inevitably employs an element of judgment, although the range of identifying information available is sufficiently great to minimize the impact of observer variation (and would suggest potential for computerised matching).

The major problem in the research however is the relative paucity of identifying information in the death indexes. If a person dies outside the registration district in which they were enumerated, it is very difficult to establish a reliable match from census to death index. It was therefore necessary to make recording of death in a previously identified enumeration district of residence a criteria for judging a link between a census and a death record (this was not a criteria in the census matching because of the wider range of information available in the census). Other matching criteria used were name and age.

Results

Table 1: Information on Tracing of Sample Couples in the 1891 Census.

Tracing in 1891 Census	Elite Couples	Labourer Couples	All Couples
Husband & Wife Both Traced	64.1%	65.4%	64.7%
Husband Traced As A Widower	8.3%	6.4%	8.0%
Wife Traced As A Widow	13.5%	8.3%	10.9%
Neither Traced	14.1%	16.0%	15.1%
Total Number Of Couples	156	156	312

Overall, it was possible to trace 84.9 per cent of all 1881 sample couples in the 1891 census through identification of one or both spouses. The remainder will include couples both of whom died or emigrated and transcription errors and variations in the presentation of matching information. Of 233 elite husbands and wives traced alive in the 1891 Census, 71 – 30.5 per cent – were located in a different registration district, whereas the equivalent figure for labourers' husbands and wives was 43 out of 237 – 18.1 per cent.

Identifying Deaths

Three methods were used to ascertain death of one or both members of a couple:

1. Widows and widowers were identified in the 1891 Census.
2. A search was made of the BMD civil register index of deaths.
3. An attempt was made to trace all identified deaths in the *Ancestry* probate calendar index.

As previously noted, the most difficult part of the research is the quality of the death register index and the limited information in it. Criteria for deciding on a match therefore included registration in the known census district of enumeration in 1881 and/or known enumeration district (of sample member of their surviving spouse) in 1891. In order to examine this assumption, an analysis was made of death entries for the spouses of husbands and wives who were listed as widowers and widows in the 1891 census. Of 61 such cases that occurred in the period 1881-1891, it was possible to trace 49 – 80.3 per cent – in the death register index. These findings illustrate the value of having two methods of measuring the incidence of deaths. Up to 20 per cent of deaths were not located in the death register index, but the data on widowers and widows allows us to correct for this deficiency. The latter information indicates that a death took place within a particular decade, whereas for about 80 per cent of cases it is possible to identify the exact quarter and year of death.

The above figures on the identification of deaths assume that a death that occurs within an appropriate enumerated registration district is correctly identified. In order to test this assumption a search was made in the *Ancestry* probate calendar index for all identified deaths cases, both those of spouses of surviving widows and widowers and those identified independently.

Table 2: Deaths Identified in the Civil Register Index Traced in the Probate Calendar Index, 1881-1891.

	Total Deaths Listed In Civil Register Index	Number Traced In Probate Calendar	Proportion Traced
Elite Males	24	21	87.5%
Elite Females	13	2	15.4%
Male Labourers	22	2	9.1%
Labourers' Wives	15	1	6.7%
Total	74	27	36.5%

As perhaps expected, it was possible to identify a much higher proportion of elite males in the probate calendar than other groups. In every case, the information in the calendar indicated that death register index entries were correct, in most cases listing the names of widows and widowers, along with details of address and other identifying information. The calendar entries include data on the amount of personal estate, which will be of value in classifying socio-economic status in future work.

Table 3: Adult Mortality among Couples in Elite and Labourers' Families, 1881-1891.

	Elite Husbands	Labourer Husbands	Elite Wives	Labourer Wives	Total
Number In 1881	156	156	156	156	624
Number Traced 1881-91	146	142	136	140	564
Number Alive In 1891 Census	115	117	121	121	474
Number Dead Through Census Tracking	23	16	14	15	20
Number Dead Through Civil Register	8	9	1	3	21
Proportion Dead Of Traced Cases	21.2%	17.5%	11.0%	12.9%	15.8%
Mean Age (Years) in 1881	48.0	43.0%	43.2	41.5	44.1

Table 3 summarizes the results discussed above, and shows the estimate of the proportion of each group who died 1881-1891 derived from these various sources. This suggests higher survival among women than men but little difference in the mortality of elite and labourer groups. However the distribution of the samples by age group varied slightly and the mean age of labourers (42.4) was slightly younger than that of the elite (45.6) (although the difference was not statistically significant). Results from a logistic regression model in which the outcome was dichotomised to alive/dead (and those untraced were excluded) and including age (single years), sex, elite/labourer status and rural or urban residence showed that odds of death did not vary significantly by elite/labourer status (or for labourers relative to elite: 1.06, 95% confidence interval 0.66-1.73). (Table 4)

Table 4: Logistic Regression of Adult Mortality among Couples in Elite and Labourers' Families, 1881-1891.[666]

	Odds Ratio	95% CI	P
Labourer (Ref. Elite)	1.068	0.658-1.732	NS
Women (Ref. Men)	0.679	0.416-1.108	NS
Age	1.062	1.043-1.081	<0.00

Table 4 shows, that as would be expected older age was associated with an increased risk of death by 1891, but that there was no significant difference between labourers and the elite.

Discussion

There is a well-established association between social class and adult mortality in England from the early twentieth century onwards. However, this association may not have been evident in earlier periods raising questions about the pathways between

---

[666] Number = 590, excluding those not traced.

social inequality and adult mortality in differing historical contexts.

For the present research, a national sample of 312 married couples was selected from the 1881 English Census comprising four elite and four labourer couples drawn from one urban and one rural parish in each county of England. Mortality 1881-1891 was ascertained through linkage to the 1891 Census and the civil register death index. About ninety per cent families were traced in the census or the death index. Results showed no significant differences between mortality of elite and labourer couples for either husbands or wives

These results illustrate firstly the potential for linking several data sources to provide more information about variations in mortality in the late nineteenth century. Triangulation was used in which transitions from being married to widowed were used to help identify deaths of spouses. However this method does have limitations. Firstly in both contemporary and historical populations it is known that the married have better health and lower mortality than the non married, so the sample is selected to some extent. Secondly, loss to follow up may be associated with death of both spouses. For these reasons and the way the sample was selected, it is not truly random, although the design meant that those included were matched geographically and so avoids problems of the distorting effects of place.

The extent, origin, and evolution of inequalities in health in England and elsewhere is a major topic of current debate in social policy and epidemiology, particularly as such inequalities appear to have widened in the last quarter of the twentieth century.[667] As noted by Wilkinson and Pickett, although social inequality was greater in earlier historical periods, there are some indications that these inequalities were not reflected in health differentials to the same extent as in contemporary

---

[667] Davey-Smith, *Poverty*; Wilkinson et.al., *The Spirit Level.*; J. Spijker, L. Van Wissen, 'Socioeconomic determinants of male mortality in Europe: the absolute and relative income hypothesis revisited', *Genus*, Volume 66, 2010.

populations.[668] Studies which have compared the aristocracy and the total population, for example, suggest that there were minimal associations between socio-economic status and adult mortality prior to and into the nineteenth century.[669] Preston and Haines also concluded from their analysis of child mortality in late nineteenth century America that differentials by level of income were not important.[670] More generally, Preston has argued that before the modern scientific understanding of how life style and personal health behaviour influence disease risks, the disease environment was more important than socio-economic status in shaping changing mortality patterns.[671]

Indeed greater material resources may have had some negative effects in enabling lifestyles including excessive consumption of high fat foods and alcohol and limited physical exercise.[672] There is evidence to suggest that the rural poor were forced to grow their own food, were unable to consume large amounts of alcohol because of their poverty, and were required to engage in intense physical activity as a result of their working conditions. By contrast, the wealthy are known to have consumed large amounts of rich food, alcohol and tobacco, and engaged in only in minimal amounts of physical activity because of the presence of household servants.[673] Thus in the nineteenth century for certain conditions, such as heart disease, there is some evidence of a reverse gradient (with richer people

---

[668] Wilkinson et.al., *The Spirit Level.*

[669] A. Day Bailey Hutchinson, 'On the rate of mortality prevailing amongst families of the peerage during the nineteenth century', *Journal of the Statistical Society*, Volume 24, 1863.

[670] S.H. Preston, M.R. Haines, *Fatal Years: Child Mortality in Late Nineteenth century America,* 1991.

[671] S.H. Preston, 'The changing relationship between mortality and level of economic development' *Population Studies*, Volume 29, 1975.

[672] M. Livi-Bacci, *Population and Nutrition: an Essay on European History,* 1991; P. Razzell, C. Spence, 'The hazards of wealth: adult mortality in pre-twentieth century Britain', *Social History of Medicine*, Volume 19, 2006.

[673] Razzell and Spence, 'The hazards'.

having poorer health).[674] Research in Sweden, Denmark, Holland and Switzerland has supported these conclusions, suggesting that the association between socio-economic status and all-cause adult mortality only emerged at the end of the nineteenth century, and that before the twentieth century 'overall, a causal link between income and mortality is put into question.'[675]

Our results provide some limited evidence to suggest that there were no major socio-economic differences in all-cause adult mortality at the end of the nineteenth century. The above conclusions are however provisional, as there is no large-scale national data at the individual family level on socio-economic status and adult mortality to reliably establish the link between socio-economic status and adult mortality. The present paper can be viewed as a first step in creating such national data and further clarifying the historical relationship between social inequality and adult mortality

---

[674] M. Marmot, R.G. Wilkinson, *Social Determinants of Health*, 1999.
[675] T. Bentsson, F. Van Poppel, 'Socioeconomic inequalities in death from past to present: An introduction' *Explorations in Economic History*, Volume 48, 2011.

Chapter 9: The Hazards of Wealth: Adult Mortality in Pre-Twentieth-Century England.[676]

Socio-Economic Status and Adult Mortality before the Twentieth Century

One of the most reliable studies of socio-economic status and mortality before the twentieth century is that by Hollingsworth on the aristocracy. It is possible to compare his findings with those for England and Wales, in the middle of the nineteenth century, after the introduction of civil registration.

Table 1: Expectation of Life at aged 20 amongst the Aristocracy and the Population of England and Wales (Years).[677]

Cohort Born	Males	Females
Aristocracy, 1825-49	42.0	48.3
England & Wales, 1840-41	39.2	41.7
Aristocracy, 1850-74	42.9	52.1
England & Wales 1860-61	42.7	45.7

Among men, the aristocracy had a slight advantage in life expectancy at age 20 in the first cohort, but this had disappeared by the later period, whereas female aristocrats had higher adult life expectancy in both periods.

There is data on the Royal Family which suggests that they suffered very high infant and child mortality in the sixteenth

---

[676] Written jointly with Christine Spence and published in the *Social History of Medicine*, Volume 19, Issue 3, 2006.
[677] For the source of this data see T.H. Hollingsworth, *The Demography of the British Peerage, Supplement to Population Studies*, Volume 18, Number 2.

and seventeenth century, with about two-thirds of children dying by the fifth birthday.[678] This was probably due to the squalid conditions of royal palaces, as well as the unhygienic practices of midwifery and the 'touching of the King's Evil' (a form of tuberculosis) which was practised by monarchs in this period.[679] Royal child mortality fell dramatically in the eighteenth and nineteenth centuries, probably associated with improvements in hygiene and midwifery, as well the practice of smallpox inoculation and vaccination.

Royal data illustrates the importance of place and the role of disease environment in shaping mortality levels.[680] This can be illustrated through research published by the Victorian actuaries Bailey and Day in 1863. They compared the life expectancy of the peerage with that in the general population of England, as well as those living in healthy districts.

Table 2: Male Life Expectancy, Mid-Nineteenth Century.[681]

Age	Peerage Families	English Life Table Dr Farr	Healthy Districts Dr Farr
20	41.46	39.99	43.40
30	35.51	33.21	36.45
40	28.33	26.46	29.29
50	21.40	19.87	22.03
60	14.56	13.6	15.06
70	8.77	8.55	9.37

[678] P. Razzell, *Population and Disease: Transforming English Society, 1550-1850*, 2007, p. 91.
[679] Ibid, pp. 149-156.
[680] For a discussion of place in shaping mortality see E. Garrett, S. Reid, S. Szreter, K. Schurer, *As Others Do Around Us: Place, Class and Demography in England and Wales, 1891-1911*, 2001; P. Razzell, C. Spence, 'Poverty or disease environment: the history of mortality in Britain, 1500-1950', in M. Breschi, L. Pozzi (eds.), *The Determinants of Infant and Child Mortality in Past European Populations*, 2004.
[681] See A. Hutcheson Bailey, A. Day, 'On the rate of mortality prevailing amongst families of the peerage during the nineteenth century', *Journal of the Statistical Society*, Volume 24, p. 69.

Life expectancy was slightly higher at all ages among the peerage than in the English population, although it was less than in those living in healthy districts. The aristocracy spent long periods living in London, in other towns and rural areas, all with different mortality risks. It is therefore important to present data, wherever possible, within geographical regions and districts, and to attempt to control for the role of place in shaping mortality levels.

The major problem with evidence on adult mortality before the advent of civil registration is the reliability of source material. Creating data through family reconstitution suffers from the problem of high migration, with only about ten per cent of reconstitution populations remaining in observation from birth to death.[682] There is also the difficulty of the unknown reliability of parish burial registers, and the problem of a variation in the reliability of data by socio-economic status, and there is no reliable evidence on the accuracy of adult burial registration by socio-economic status.

One way of addressing this problem is by analysing sources which give information on the mortality status of parents. Marriage licences and apprenticeship indentures were legally required to include information on consent of parents, in some cases by written affidavit, and where a father had died, this was usually indicated in the licence or indenture. However, the problem of self-selection means that these sources are not necessarily representative of the general population, although they do provide valuable evidence when viewed with other independent data. As we saw previously, marriage licences for East Kent yield data on occupation and paternal mortality for 289 parishes in the period 1619-1809. This data indicates that adult mortality was slightly lower among gentlemen, merchants and professionals than in other occupational groups in the first two periods, but higher in the second half of the eighteenth century.

---

[682] P. Razzell, *Mortality, Marriage and Population Growth in England, 1550-1850*, 2016, p. 43.

The latter finding is confirmed by a study of marriage licences in Nottinghamshire and Sussex.

Table 3: Proportion of Fathers of Spinsters and Bachelors under 21 Dead in Nottinghamshire and Sussex, 1754-1800.[683]

Occupational Group	Number Cases	Number Fathers Dead	Proportion Fathers Dead
Labourers, Servants	225	36	16%
Husbandmen	180	34	19%
Artisans, Tradesmen	582	123	21%
Farmers, Yeomen	457	76	17%
Gentlemen, Professionals	92	32	35%

Although the sample sizes are small, the pattern is similar to that revealed for East Kent, but with a higher proportion of gentlemen and professional fathers dead. The higher mortality amongst the wealthy may have been partly a function of greater ages of fathers, but the limited amount of evidence does not support this conclusion. In the absence of birth control, the average age of fathers was probably largely shaped by age of marriage, and data from Nottinghamshire suggest that this did not vary greatly between different socio-economic groups in the first half of the eighteenth century. By the late nineteenth century, men from wealthier socio-economic groups married significantly later than those from the poorer social classes.[684]

---

[683] For the source of data, see T.M. Blagg (ed.), *Abstracts of the Bonds and Allegations for Nottinghamshire Marriage Licences*, 1946-7; L.M. Shaw, *Nottinghamshire Marriage Bonds, 1791-1800*, 1987; D. Macleod, *Calendar of Sussex Marriage Licences*, Volumes 32 and 35, 1926 and 1929; E.W.D. Penfold (ed.), *Calendar of Sussex Marriage Licences for the Archdeaconry of Lewes, 1772-1837*, Volumes 25 and 26, 1917 and 1919.

[684] For other evidence on this topic see Razzell, 'Malthus: mortality or fertility: the history of English population in the eighteenth century'.

Table 4: Median Age of Marriage of Grooms Listed in Nottinghamshire Marriage Licences, 1701-1753 (Number of Cases in Brackets).[685]

Period	1701-20	1721-40	1741-53
Gentlemen	26 (168)	28 (118)	25 (55)
Yeomen, Farmers	26 (141)	27 (186)	25 (412)
Artisans, Tradesmen	25 (57)	25 (133)	24 (119)
Husbandmen	27 (487)	26 (695)	26 (254)
Labourers	26 (138)	27 (89)	25 (85)

There is additional evidence available on paternal mortality by socio-economic status during the early eighteenth century period. Apprenticeship indentures include information on amount of premium paid and the occupation of fathers, and there was a strong association between occupation and premium level, with gentlemen, merchants and professionals paying the highest premiums, and labourers and servants paying the lowest ones.

Table 5: Mortality amongst Fathers listed in the British Apprenticeship Register 1710-13 by Amount of Premium Paid.[686]

Premium Paid	Number of Cases	Proportion Father Dead
£1-£5	541	23%
£6-£19	587	30%
£20+	512	34%

---

[685] J.D. Chambers, 'The course of population change' in D.V. Glass, D.E.C. Eversley (eds.), *Population in History: Essays in Historical Demography*, 1965, p. 332.
[686] Razzell, *Mortality*, p. 51.

Table 5 indicates a positive correlation between wealth and adult mortality among apprentices' fathers. The association between wealth and mortality might be partly explained by the wealthy living more frequently in London and other unhealthy towns and cities, but as Table 6 indicates, even in an unhealthy area like London, there was a link between wealth and mortality.

Table 6: Mortality amongst London Fathers listed in the British Apprenticeship Register 1710-13 by Amount of Premium Paid.[687]

Premium Paid	Number of Cases	Proportion of Fathers Dead
£9 and Under	110	32%
£10-£19	93	41%
£20+	99	42%

Although the number of cases is small, there is still the same gradient between wealth and mortality in London as found nationally.

All the above evidence from marriage licences and apprenticeship indentures is subject to a measure of uncertainty because of the lack of exact information on the ages of fathers and the self-selected nature of the samples. More reliable data become available with the introduction of national censuses and civil registration in the nineteenth century. However, because of the way the data have been processed and interpreted, it is often itself of uncertain reliability. For example, Chadwick and others produced data to show that the wealthy lived longer than the poor, but this material was generated through a faulty methodology, using age at death as a measure of life expectancy, and not allowing for differences in the age structure of the population at risk.[688]

---

[687] Ibid, p. 52.

[688] For Chadwick's data on poverty and mortality, see M.W. Flinn (ed.), E. Chadwick, *Report on the Sanitary Condition of the Labouring Population of Great Britain, 1842*, 1965, pp. 219-27. For a critique of the methodology of

Farr produced evidence on the different registration districts of London, including information on their socio-economic characteristics and associated mortality levels.[689] He classified the mean rateable value of each district and published initial findings on two of the districts, which showed some association between wealth and mortality. He did not pursue this analysis but subsequently provided raw data for all districts which are analysed in Table 7.

Table 7: Adult (25-44) Mortality in London, 1838-44.[690]

Registration Districts	Mean Annual Value of Rated Property on Each House	Adult (25-44) Male Mortality per 1000
10 Districts with Lowest Mean Rateable Value	£15	13
10 Districts with Medium Rateable Value	£26	15
10 Districts with Highest Rateable Value	£58	13

The districts with the lowest rateable values were mostly in the East End and the wealthiest in the West End of London. Table 8 indicates that there was no significant association between the wealth of a district and its adult mortality level.

It is possible to construct reliable statistics of adult mortality for the period after 1841 in individual rural and urban parishes by using censuses and information in burial registers.

---

using age of death, see Registrar General, *Fifth Annual Report*, 1842, pp. 236-38.
[689] General Register Office, *Fifth Annual Report 1842*, p. 446; General Register Office, *Eighth Annual Report 1845*, pp. 192-93; General Register Office, *Ninth Annual Report (Folio Edition) 1846*, pp. 236-38.
[690] Razzell, *Mortality*, p. 40.

This involves tracking married couples in the censuses of 1841 and 1851, and linking this data with that in the parish burial registers for the intervening years. This methodology has the advantage of triangulation, allowing the comparison of information about widows and widowers in the census of 1851 with that in the burial registers. The selection of married couples allows the measurement of independent demographic events for establishing the period at risk – the listing of a spouse in a burial register, the baptism of a child, or the enumeration of the husband or wife in a later census.

To evaluate the impact of socio-economic status on adult mortality, a sample was constructed for 48 Bedfordshire parishes,[691] selecting the first married couple with elite status in the census of 1841. All professional, merchant and independent families with at least one domestic servant were selected for the elite category – there was an average of 3.2 servants per family – and they were matched with the next labourer's family of a similar age in the census schedule. The age of labourers selected was within plus or minus five years of that of elite husbands.

---

[691] The parishes were chosen in sequence from the Registrar-General's list of censuses of 1841 and were as follows: Ampthill, Arsley, Aspley Guise, Bedford St Cuthbert's, Bedford St John's, Bedford St Mary's, Bedford St Paul's, Biggleswade, Blunham, Clifton, Clophill, Colmsworth, Cranfield, Dunstable, Eaton Socon, Flitton, Harrold, Haynes, Henlow, Higham Gobion, Holwell, Houghton Conquest, Houghton Regis, Hunwick, Kempston, Keysoe, Langford, Leighton Buzzard, Lower Gravenhurst, Luton, Melchbourne, Northill, Pertenhall, Poddington, Potton, Turvey, Renhold, Shefford, Shelton, Southill, Stotfold, Streathley, Tilbrook, Tingrith, Toddington, Turvey, Woburn, and Wrestingworth.

Table 8: Mortality amongst Husbands and Wives Enumerated In Bedfordshire Censuses, 1841-1851

	Professional, Merchants, Gentlemen	Labourers
Number Grooms and Brides	250	250
Number Traced Cases	165	182
Number of Traced Cases Dead	26	27
Proportion Traced Cases Dead	16%	15%
Number Years at Risk	1531	1738
Average Age Traced Cases (Years)	39.8	40.7

A total of 250 married couples were included in the sample – 125 from elite families and 125 from labourers' families. Of the 250 husbands and wives in the elite category, 165 were traced (66 per cent) either in the census of 1851 or the burial register; the equivalent figure for the labourers' sample was 182 out of 250 (73 per cent). Most of the untraced cases were probably due to migration, as they involved the disappearance of both husband and wife. It is unlikely that burials of both husband and wife were not registered, given the high quality of the burial registers in these rural parishes at this time. Of 32 widows and widowers identified in the census of 1851, 30 of their spouses were located in Anglican burial registers between 1841 and 1851, indicating a high degree of burial registration reliability.

26 of 165 elite husbands and wives (16 per cent) died in the decade between 1841 and 1851, whereas the number amongst the 182 labourers' husbands and wives was 27 (15 per cent). This slightly higher mortality among elite families was in spite of a lower average age of husbands in 1841, and a shorter period at risk. Among wives, mortality was also higher in elite than in labourers' families: 13 out of 79 traced cases died (17 per cent)

as against 10 out of 83 (12 per cent). However, the sample sizes are small, and Table 9 suggests no significant difference in overall adult mortality between elite and labourers' families in Bedfordshire at this time.[692]

Reliable figures for a wider range of occupations were published by the Registrar-General at the end of the nineteenth century. There was little or no correlation between social group and adult mortality in 1860-61 and 1871, although the white-collar group had the lowest adult expectation of life in this period.[693]

Research carried out on civil registers of deaths linked to censuses for Ipswich in the period 1871-1910 indicates that there was little or no difference in adult mortality by socio-economic status in the period 1871-81, but that a social class gradient began to emerge at the end of the nineteenth century. Adult mortality was measured by tracking families in the two decades 1871-81 and 1891-1901, analysing the mortality of husbands and wives where at least one of them survived to be enumerated at the end of the decade. Elite families employing a domestic servant were compared to labourers' families, with a total of 500 husbands and wives being selected in sequence from the census at the beginning of the decade.

---

[692] See also P. Razzell, E. Grundy, 'Socio-economic status and adult mortality in England: a historical study, 1881-91', for further evidence of a lack of a class gradient in adult mortality in the 1880s.

[693] R. Woods, *The Demography of Victorian England and Wales*, 2000, p. 86.

Table 9 Percentage Mortality among Ipswich Elite and Labourer Husbands and Wives, in 1871-81 and 1891-1901: (Number of Cases in Brackets).[694]

Period	Elite Husbands and Wives		Labourer Husbands and Wives	
	Age Group	Mortality Rate Percentage	Age Group	Mortality Rate Percentage
1871-81	20-44	6.4% (290)	20-44	7.9% (303)
	45-69	17.5% (194)	45-69	16.9% (183)
1891-1900	20-44	6.0% (285)	20-44	8.4% (356)
	45-69	11.8% (169)	45-69	17.7% (175)

There was little or no gradient in the 1870s but by the 1890s differences in mortality – particularly for the age group 45-69 – were beginning to emerge. In order to establish the validity of this finding, it will be necessary to analyse much larger samples from the Ipswich study, and to carry out a random study of individual families in England and Wales.[695]

The aggregative statistics for England and Wales indicate that since the beginning of the twentieth century, a social class gradient in adult mortality has been progressively established, and the socio-economic adult mortality differential has widened significantly during the last few decades.[696]

The Role of Nutrition and Physical Activity

Given that elite families were much wealthier than other members of the population, and that they had access to much

---

[694] P. Razzell, E. Garrett, R. Davies, *The Sociological Study of Fertility and Mortality in Ipswich, 1872-1910*, 2006, online peter.razzell.co.uk.
[695] See Razzell and Grundy, 'Socio-economic status'.
[696] R.G. Wilkinson, 'Class mortality differentials, income distribution and trends in poverty 1921-82', *Journal of Social Policy*, Volume 18, 1989, p. 308; G. Davey Smith, D. Dorling, M. Shaw (eds.), *Poverty, Inequality and Health in Britain, 1800-2000: a Reader*, 2001, p.348.

better provision of food, good housing and medical care, why were their adult mortality rates the same or even higher than the rest of the population? The issue becomes even more puzzling in the light of the relatively low adult mortality among labourers and other poor groups. There is much evidence of the inadequate diet of labourers' families in the late eighteenth and early nineteenth centuries, culminating in the 'hungry forties'.[697] Chadwick and others described the insanitary quality of much of their housing, and the poverty of labourers – particularly in rural areas – has been very widely documented.[698] Recently, Bernard Harris has argued that nutrition did play a significant historical role in shaping mortality,[699] and there is some evidence that extreme poverty did significantly increase mortality in certain historical periods.[700] These findings increase the puzzle of a lack of a socio-economic gradient in adult mortality before the twentieth century.

However, there is a contemporary literature on wealth and health, which stresses the hazards of wealth rather than poverty. Thomas Tryon in 1683 wrote:

Great drinking of *Wine* and *strong Drinks* after full Meals of *Flesh* and *Fish* … do often wound the Health … which many of the richest sort of People in this Nation might know by woeful Experience, especially in London, who do yearly spend many Hundreds, (I think I may say Thousands) of Pounds on their *Ungodly Paunches* … for their *Bellies* are swollen up to their *Chins* … their *Brains* are sunk in their *Bellies; Injection* and *Ejection* is the business of their Life, and all their precious hours are spent between the *Platter* and the *Glass*, and the *Close-stool* and *Piss-pot*.[701]

---

[697] J. Burnett, *Plenty and Want: a Social History of Diet in England from 1815 to the Present* Day, 1968.
[698] Ibid; R. Heath, *The English Peasant*, 1893; P. Razzell and R. Wainwright, *The Victorian Working* Class, 1973, pp. 4-11.
[699] B. Harris, 'Public health, nutrition, and the decline of mortality: the Mckeown thesis revisited, *Social History of* Medicine, Volume 17, 2004.
[700] Davey Smith, et.al., *Poverty*.
[701] T. Tyron, *The Way to Health, Long Life and Happiness*, 1683, pp. 313-14.

Tryon stressed that it was not just eating and drinking that was responsible for obesity, but also physical inactivity, which varied not just between individuals but among different socio-economic groups:

Suppose a man were to seek *Fat Men* and *Women,* would he go into *Country-Villages* and *poor small Towns* among *Plough-men* and *Shepherds*? ... No, no, such a Man's Errand would lie in *great Cities* and *Market-Towns,* where there is store of *strong Liquors* and *Idleness* ... [among] People that live sedentary Lives, and are easie Imployment, more especially of mature Age, as *Gentlemen* and *Citizens,* etc, who use themselves to lie long in Bed in the Morning, and to great Dinners and rich Cordial Drinks.[702]

Tryon was mainly concerned with the effect of lifestyle on the health of the wealthy, and had little to say about the ordinary population. The Puritan clergyman Richard Baxter did give a detailed account of the lives of the rural poor at the end of the seventeenth century:

For by the advantage of their labour and health, their browne bread and milk and butter and cheese and cabbages and turnips and parsnips and carrots and onions and potatoes and whey and buttermilk and pease pies and apple pies and puddings and pancakes and gruel and flummery and furmety, yea dry bread, and small drinke, do afford their appetites a pleasanter relish and their bodyes more strength and longer life than all the varieties and fullness of flesh and wines and strong drinkes do, to the idle gluttonous and voluptuous rich men ... The worst of the poore mans case as to health, is that they are put to goe through raine and wett, through thick and thin, through heat and cold and oft want that which nature needeth.[703]

---

[702] Ibid, pp. 320, 341.
[703] F.J. Powicke (ed.), *Richard Baxter's the Poor Husbandman's Advocate to Rich Racking Landlords,* 1926, pp. 22-26.

Baxter understood that the poor were able to enjoy relatively good health as long as they had an adequate diet of fresh vegetables, fruit, dairy and grain products, and engaged in vigorous activity through their working life. He may have exaggerated the quality of the diet of the poor, although he acknowledged that they suffered from the ill-effects of wet and cold.

An understanding of the link between diet, drink, exercise and health had become very general by the early eighteenth century. George Cheyne established his medical reputation through the publication in 1724 of his *Essay on Health and Long Life*, which ran to nine editions, and was translated into a number of different European languages. Cheyne summarised the main argument of this work by quoting Sir Charles Scarborough's advice to the Duchess of Portsmouth: 'you must eat less, or use more exercise, or take physic, or be sick'.[704]

Cheyne himself had suffered from obesity which he described in his autobiography:

Upon my coming to London, I all of a sudden changed my whole Manner of Living; I found the Bottle Companions, the younger Gentry, and Free-Livers' to be the most easy of Access. I soon became caressed by them and grew daily in bulk and friendship with these gay gentlemen ... and thus constantly dining and supping ... my health was in a few years brought into great distress, by so sudden and violent a change. I grew excessively fat, short-breathed, lethargic and listless ... My appetite being insatiable I sucked up and retained the juices and chyle of my food like a sponge and thereby suddenly grew plump, fat, and hale to a wonder, but ... every dinner necessarily became a surfeit and a debauch, and in ten or twelve years I swelled to such an enormous size that upon my last weighing I exceeded 32 stone.[705]

---

[704] G. Cheyne, *Practical Rules for the Restoration and Preservation of Health and the Best Means for Invigorating and Prolonging Life*, 1823, p. 64.

[705] R. Porter, 'Cleaning up the Great Wen: public health in eighteenth century London', in W.F. Bynum, R. Porter (eds.), *Living and Dying in London*, 1991, pp. 325-26, 342.

Although Cheyne acknowledged that his obesity was partly a family characteristic, he understood that it was also a function of his lifestyle. The pattern of consumption of food and drink by the fashionable was partly the result of economic prosperity and the importation of luxuries:

> Since our wealth has increased and our navigation has been extended we have ransacked all the parts of the globe to bring together its whole stock of materials for riot, luxury, and to provoke excess. The tables of the rich and great (and indeed those who can afford it) are furnish'd with provisions of delicacy, number, and plenty, sufficient to provoke, and even gorge, the most large and voluptuous appetite.[706]

Cheyne summarised his general conclusions as follows:

> If any man has eat or drank so much, as render him unfit for the duties and studies of his profession ... he has overdone ... It is amazing to think how men of voluptuousness, laziness, and poor constitutions, should imagine themselves able to carry off loads of high-seasoned foods, and inflammatory liquors, without injury or pain; when men of mechanic employments, and robust constitutions, are scarcely able to live healthy and in vigour to any great age, on a simple, low, and almost vegetable diet.[707]

Three years after Cheyne published this work, Short wrote his *Dictionary Concerning the Causes and Effects of Corpulency*, in which he concluded that 'lean People generally enjoy a far greater Measure of Health' than those who were over-weight.[708] This theme of the damaging effects of excess and obesity became commonplace in eighteenth and nineteenth century medical writings.

---

[706] Ibid, pp. 49-50.
[707] Cheyne, *Practical*, p. 65.
[708] T. Short, *A Dictionary Concerning the Causes and Effects of Corpulency*, 1727, p.39.

One of the most popular eighteenth-century books on medicine was Buchan's *Domestic Medicine* which was first published in 1769, and was frequently reprinted in new editions through to the middle of the nineteenth century. Buchan summarised his view on activity, exercise and health as follows:

> Those whom labour obliges to labour for daily bread, are not only the most healthy, but generally the most happy ... Tis now below any one to walk who can afford to be carried. How ridiculous would it seem to a person unacquainted with modern luxury ... to see a fat carcase, over-run with diseases occasioned by inactivity, dragged through the streets by half a dozen horses.[709]

The ill-health of the wealthy was sometimes linked to the incidence of gout, although contemporaries had a broader conception of the disease than would be the case today.[710] The awareness of the ill-effects of over-eating does not appear to have greatly influenced the behaviour of the wealthy in the eighteenth century. Parson Woodforde detailed in his diary his dietary excesses almost on a daily basis. For example, on the 14 February 1791, he wrote, 'we had for Dinner Cod and Oyster Sauce, a fillet of Veal rosted, boiled Tongue, stewed Beef, Peas Soup and Mutton Stakes. 2nd Course, a rost Chicken, Cheesecakes, Jelly-Custards &.'[711]

Evidence of this sort is of course only anecdotal, and may not be typical of the gentry's and aristocracy's consumption of food at this time. However, there are general accounts that suggest that their food consumption may have been excessive. When La Rochefoucald visited England in 1784, he described the dining customs of country houses as follows:

---

[709] W. Buchan, *Domestic Medicine: or the Family Physician,* 1769, pp. 100-01.

[710] See for example W. Black, *An Arithmetical and Medical Analysis of the Diseases and Mortality of the Human Species,* 1973, p. 87.

[711] J. Beresford (ed.), *James Woodforde: the Diary of a Country Parson,* 1999, pp. 262-63.

Dinner is one of the most wearisome of English experiences, lasting, as it does, for four or five hours. The first two are spent in eating and you are compelled to exercise your stomach to the full order to please your host. He asks you the whole time whether you like the food and presses you to eat more, with the result that, out of pure politeness, I do nothing but eat from the time that I sit down until the time when I get up from the table ... All the dishes consist of various meats either boiled or roasted and of joints weighing about twenty or thirty pounds.[712]

Fogel has estimated that the wealthiest tenth of the population consumed more than 4000 calories per adult per day at the end of the eighteenth century.[713] This is similar to Seebohm Rowntree's finding of 4,039 calories amongst the servant-keeping class in York at the end of the nineteenth century.[714] Commenting on the findings of a survey of the budgets of six of these families, Seebohm Rowntree concluded that:

> considering these six diets as a whole, it is clear that the amount of food consumed is in excess of requirements ... it is doubtful whether the work done by the six families here considered is more than 'light industrial work', the food requirements ... [for which are] 3000 calories of fuel energy.[715]

Seebohm Rowntree's sample was very small and there is little direct evidence of the effect of diet on obesity levels among the rich at this time. Information was collected on the weight of the wealthy and fashionable when they were weighed at Berry's wine merchants in St James's Street, London, and weight registers have survived from 1756 to the present day. This, of course, is a self-selected sample, and the consumption of wine is likely to have increased the incidence of obesity amongst this

---

[712] F. La Rochefoucald, *A Frenchman in England in 1794*, 1995, pp. 29-31.

[713] R. Fogel, 'Second thoughts on the European escape from hunger: famines, price elasticities, entitlements, chronic malnutrition and mortality rates' in S.R. Osmani (ed.), *Nutrition and Poverty*, 1992, p. 269.

[714] B. Seebohm Rowntree, *Poverty: a Study of Town Life,* 1901, p. 253.

[715] Ibid, p. 254.

wealthy group. Nevertheless, the information in the registers provides some useful background data, and was used by Francis Galton in his biometric research. He analysed the weights of 139 members of the aristocracy born between 1740 and 1829, and aged 27 to 70.[716] Many aristocrats had their weights taken several times a year, and Galton compiled charts of weight by age for each individual.

He divided his sample into three birth cohorts – 1740-69, 1770-99 and 1800-29 – and found that weight fluctuated much more significantly in the first cohort, concluding that 'there can be no doubt that the dissolute life led by the upper classes about the beginning of [the nineteenth century] … has left its mark on their age-weight traces'.[717] Although sample sizes were small, Pearson calculated mean weights for the different cohorts, and the overall average declined from 179 pounds for those born in 1740-69 to 171 pounds for those born in 1800-29.[718] The mean average of all the weights taken for the whole sample of 139 individuals is 174 pounds – 12 stone 6 pounds.

There is no information on the heights of the peerage, but there are some data on German aristocratic students aged 21 for the period 1772-96. Sixty young aristocrats had a mean average height of 168.8 cm, 6 to 7 cm less than today's equivalent.[719] Galton quoted figures of weight by age for professional men in the early 1880s, ranging from 161 pounds for 27 year-olds to 174 pounds for 60 year-olds. No heights were recorded, but there are such data on Sandhurst recruits – perhaps representative of the professional group – which indicate an average height of 68 inches for men over the age of 21 born during the middle of the

---

[716] F. Galton, 'The weights of British noblemen during the last three generations', *Nature,* 1884.

[717] Ibid, p. 267.

[718] Ibid.

[719] J.M. Tanner, *A History of the Study of Human Growth,* 1981, pp. 111-12.

nineteenth century.[720] This can be compared to data on the weight and height of contemporary working-class populations. For example, Liverpool convicts weighed an average of 143 pounds with a mean height of 66 inches during the mid-nineteenth century.[721] This indicated that working-class men were significantly leaner than their wealthy aristocratic and professional contemporaries.[722]

The association between wealth, dietary excesses, lack of exercise and ill-health continued to be documented into the nineteenth century.[723] The influence of these factors on longevity was summarised by Sinclair in 1833:

> It has been justly observed, that it is not the rich and great, nor those that depend on medicine, who attain old age, but such as use much exercise, breathe pure air, and where food is plain and moderate.... Hence it would appear, that the situation of the middle, and even the lower classes of society, is particularly favourable to longevity.[724]

Sinclair somewhat romanticised the condition of the poor, and perhaps a more realistic account is the following description of the life of agricultural labourers at the end of the nineteenth century:

> ... wages are for labourers 8s. or 9.s. a week ... In wet weather or in sickness his wages entirely cease so that he seldom makes a full week. The cottages, as a rule, are not fit to house pigs in. The

---

[720] R. Floud, K. Wachter, A. Gregory, *Height, Health and History: Nutritional Status in the United Kingdom, 1750-1980,* 1991, p.178.

[721] J.T. Danson, 'Statistical observations relative to the growth of the human body (males) in height and weight, from eighteen to thirty years of age, as illustrated by the records of the borough gaol of Liverpool' *Journal of the Statistical Society of London,* Volume 23, 1862, pp. 20-26.

[722] Most evidence points to a U-shaped relationship between body mass index and adult mortality. This suggests that both the malnourished and the over-nourished were at higher risk of mortality. See Fogel, 'Second thought', p. 24.

[723] See for example W. Wadd, *Comments on Corpulency,* 1829, p. 164; W. Banting, *Letter on Corpulence, Addressed to the Public,* 1864.

[724] J. Sinclair, *The Code of Health and Longevity,* 1833, p. 404.

labourer breakfasts on tea-kettle broth, hot water poured on bread and flavoured with onions; dines on bread and hard cheese at 2d. a pound, with cider very washy and sour, and sups on potatoes or cabbage greased with a tiny bit of fat bacon. He seldom more than sees or smells butcher's meat. He is long lived, but in the prime of life 'crippled up', i.e. disabled by rheumatism, the result of wet clothes with no fire to dry them by for the next morning, poor living and sour cider.[725]

Other descriptions of labourers' lifestyles suggest a more generous diet, although most accounts indicate that food was often in short supply.[726] Heath noted at the end of the nineteenth century the difference in stature between the farmer and agricultural labourer: 'Compare the shapely forms of the young farmers with those of the stunted young labourer, and ... compare the stalwart, jovial forms of the elderly farmers with the rheumatic, misshapen forms of the old labourers, and the evil result, not only of over-early work, but of a lifetime of poor and insufficient food and bad lodging, will be manifest.'[727] It may be that poor diet and poverty had a stronger impact on morbidity than mortality among labourers, although as we will now see, other factors may have influenced mortality levels.

The Role of Alcohol and Tobacco Consumption

Thomas Tryon summarised the changes that had taken place in the smoking of tobacco during the seventeenth century:

It is not above sixty or seventy years ago since that only *Gentlemen,* and but a few of those took *Tobacco,* and then so moderately, that one Pipe would serve four or five, for they handed it from one to another ... but now every Plow-man has his Pipe to himself.[728]

---

[725] Quoted in Burnet, *Plenty*, p. 166.
[726] Ibid.
[727] R. Heath, *The English Peasant*, 1893, p. 129.
[728] T. Tryon, *The Way to Health, Long Life and Happiness*, 1863, p. 168.

However, he acknowledged that among ordinary working families 'the Expenses which this smoking generally draws with it, have half starved their poor Families'.[729] He indicated that wealth played a role in the consumption of tobacco and other luxuries:

> Are not those that live in the most Remote parts of *England,* and far from *Cities* and *Sea-Ports,* where *Money* is scarce, and such things dear, that the common People cannot buy them, most healthful and freest from Diseases? But now these *Out-landish Ingredients* begin to be so much admired, that the *good Dame, viz the Farmers Wife* will sell her *Eggs, Butter, Cheese* and *Wheat* to buy *Sugar, Spice* and *Tobacco.*[730]

More than 60 years later, Hogarth made a similar distinction between the destructive gin-drinking of Londoners and the more healthy habits of the rural poor:

> ... go into some Country Village, where that Fiery Dragon Gin has not yet spread her Poison, and you will find their Children, though in Rags, yet of a goodly and healthful Look. Their Diet indeed is coarse, but yet it's wholesome; their Drink, though better than small Beer, answers the Ends of Nutrition better than the finest Spirituous Liquors in the World.[731]

He also drew a distinction between the habits of the wealthy and the poor in the countryside:

> The Squire, who does not keep his Cellar full of the best Liquor, is but little regarded by the Farmers and Neighbours; and if the Farmer has not a Tub of the best ready breach'd, or Brandy and other Ingredients for Punch when the 'Squire is pleas'd to honour him with his own and his Friends Company, he must never expect to be invited to the noble Sport of Hunting ... And all of them are

---

[729] Ibid, p. 171.

[730] Ibid, p. 223.

[731] W. Hogarth, *A Dissertation on Mr Hogarth's Six Prints Lately Published, Viz Gin Law, Beer Street, and the Four Stages of Cruelty,* 1751, p. 32.

unanimously of Opinion in one Thing, that is, that they never think they make a Friend welcome unless they make him drunk.[732]

La Rochefoucald, in his account of life in English country houses, commented on the amount of alcohol consumed during dinner:

> After the sweets ... the table is covered with all sorts of wine, for even gentlemen of modest means always keep a large stock of good wine. On the middle of the table there is a small quantity of fruit, a few biscuits (to stimulate thirst) and some butter, for many English people take it at dessert ... One proceeds to drink − sometimes in an alarming measure. Everyone has to drink in his turn, for the bottles make a continuous circuit of the table and the host takes note that everyone is drinking in his turn.[733]

The dangers of alcohol were well known to eighteenth-century writers and artists. One of the most vivid of Rowlandson's satires was 'Death in the Bowl', showing the skeletal figure of Death drinking with a group of obese-looking gentlemen crouched over a bowl of alcohol.[734] Another of his satires showed Death wheeling an obese man away in a wheel-barrow from a tavern, outside of which two portly gentlemen and a farmer are depicted drinking and smoking tobacco, with Death telling the dead man's wife, 'Drunk and alive, the man was thine, But dead & drunk, why − he is mine.'[735]

There is very little systematic evidence on the consumption of alcohol by different socio-economic groups, but the cost of alcohol probably constrained the amount consumed by the poor. The budgets published by Eden, Davies and others during the eighteenth and nineteenth centuries, showed that the

---

[732] Ibid, p. 6.
[733] La Rochefoucald, *A Frenchman*, pp. 29-31.
[734] A.P. Oppe, *Thomas Rowlandson: His Drawings and Water-Colours,* 1923, plate 44.
[735] W. Combe, *The English Dance of Death*, 1815, p. 97.

labouring poor bought little alcohol.[736] However, the budgets did not reveal the full story, partly because they took no account of home brewing, but also because they did not adequately measure expenditure on alcohol at taverns and public houses. Eden attempted to summarise the overall position in 1797 as follows:

> Purchased liquor is an article of expenditure particularly prevalent in the South... [although] if taxed, at any time, with drinking too much, he [the labourer] thinks it sufficient ... to allege, that, excepting on a Saturday evening, or occasions of festivity, he rarely allows himself more than a pint, or at most, a pot of beer a day ... This is not the case in the North; where, besides the pure limpid stream, the general drink of the labouring classes is either whey or milk, or rather milk and water; or, at best, very meagre small beer.[737]

A hundred years later, Richard Heath came to similar conclusions. He noted the prevalence of taverns and beer-shops in rural areas, but writing about the Weald of Sussex concluded:

> ... it would be a good thing if ... the little beer shops would be shut up, and a vast amount of misery prevented. Not that the peasant of the Weald is a drunkard. He is far too poor for that. It is only on club days, and occasionally on Saturday night, that he gives way. Habitual drinking in the country is the vice of a class in a superior social position.[738]

Seebohm Rowntree, at the end of the nineteenth century, also found a relatively small consumption of alcohol amongst the respectable poor: 'the families studied [earning under 26

---

[736] F.M. Eden, *The State of the Poor, or, an History of the Labouring Classes in England from the Conquest to the Present Period*, 1797; D. Davies, *The Case of Labourers in Husbandry*, 1796; W. Neild, 'Comparative statement of the income and expenditure of certain families of the working classes in Manchester and Dunkenfield in the years 1836 and 1841', *Journal of the Statistical Society of* London, Volume 4, 1841; B.S. Rowntree, *Poverty: A Study of Town* Life, 1901.
[737] Eden, *The State*, p. 542.
[738] Heath, *The English Peasant*, p. 187.

shillings a week] represent the steady, respectable section of the labouring classes, who spend practically nothing upon drink'.[739] However, he echoed Heath when he concluded:

There is more drinking in Class B [the second poorest group] than in Class A [the poorest group], but this does not imply a lower moral standard. People in Class A are for the most part so absolutely destitute that they could not get much drink even if they wished. And in Class B, as we have seen ... the money for drink can only be found, in the great majority of cases, by foregoing some other expenditure which is necessary for maintaining the family in a state of physical efficiency.[740]

More prosperous working-class groups did, however, consume alcohol, and Seebohm Rowntree estimated that the average expenditure on drink was six shillings a week, absorbing 'more than one-sixth of the average total family income of the working classes of York.'[741] There is plenty of evidence that alcohol was consumed in large quantities in the second half of the nineteenth century. Samuel Smiles estimated in 1875 that the working classes spent £60,000,000 on drink and tobacco.[742] As John Burnett has pointed out, 'when allowance is made for the growing number of teetotallers, it means that many families must have spent a third, and some half or more, of all their income on drink'.[743] A degree of prosperity was required for the consumption of drink, and growing real incomes of working-class families after the middle of the nineteenth century made this possible.

This was also true of tobacco consumption which increased significantly after the middle of the nineteenth century, and appears to have been influenced by changes in per capita

---

[739] Rowntree, *Poverty.*, p. 237.
[740] Ibid, p. 58.
[741] Ibid, p. 143.
[742] S. Smiles, *Thrift*, 1905, p. 114.
[743] Burnett, *Plenty*, p. 199.

income during the period 1791-1938.[744] Budgets compiled by Eden, Davies, Seebohm Rowntree and others showed virtually no consumption of tobacco in respectable working-class families, similar to the pattern of alcohol consumption.[745] Tobacco cost about three pence an ounce, and where family incomes were less than ten shillings a week, it would have been impossible for the working poor to sustain a significant consumption of tobacco over extended periods.[746]

The literary evidence indicates that wealthy men smoked tobacco fairly regularly. Smoking rooms were introduced into some country houses as early as the 1720s, and by the middle of the nineteenth century 'smoking rooms had become an integral part of most gentlemen's country houses, and guests who did not appear in them for a convivial smoke or game after the ladies had retired were liable to be dragged out of bed to conform to a recognised social convention'.[747] The habits of the royal family are illuminating in this respect:

> [Queen Victoria] disliked the habit intensely ... Even Prince Albert had not presumed to smoke in her presence; and at Osborne House ... a special smoking room was built ... The queen could always detect the smell of tobacco on documents which were sent up to her; and her Assistant Private Secretary, Frederick Ponsoby ... and his colleagues took to carrying peppermints in their pockets in case a summons to the queen came at a moment when their breath was sure to offend her. [748]

---

[744] The annual per capita consumption of tobacco was as follows: 1791-1815: 1.11 pounds; 1816-40: 0.84 pounds; 1841-65: 1.06 pounds; 1866-90: 1.42 pounds; 1891-1915: 1.92 pounds; 191-38: 3.13 pounds. These patterns of consumption are similar to changes in per capita income. See B.R. Mitchell, P. Deane, *Abstract of British Historical Statistics*, 1971, pp. 343-35, 355-58.

[745] Eden, *The State*; Davies, *The Case*; Neild, 'Comparative'; Rowntree, *Poverty*.

[746] C. Hibbert, *The English: A Social* History, 1987, p. 559. See also the budgets quoted in Eden, *The State*; Davies, *The Case*; Neild, 'Comparative'; Rowntree, *Poverty*.

[747] Hibbert, *The English*, p. 554.

[748] Ibid, p. 553.

The economic capacity to consume tobacco – along with an excessive consumption of food and alcohol – undoubtedly damaged the health of the wealthy. These patterns of consumption along with a lack of physical activity may have been largely responsible for the high adult mortality of the rich, a theme which can be further explored through the work of the eminent Victorian actuary, Frederick Neison.

The Work of Francis Neison

Neison was an actuary who worked for one of the leading insurance companies, and had a life-long interest in the causes of ill-health and mortality. He was sceptical about the emphasis on sanitation and poverty by his contemporaries Farr and Chadwick, and produced a range of evidence to show the importance of personal behaviour, in particular the role of physical activity and the consumption of alcohol.[749] His starting point was evidence on socio-economic status and adult mortality:

> In the year 1843, a report was made, by a committee of actuaries, on the mortality among persons assured by seventeen of the principal assurance companies of this country, and these persons may be fairly considered to belong to the middle and upper classes of society; and at various periods since the year 1824, inquiries have been made into the mortality rate among the members of friendly societies, including the more industrious and prudential of the working and the labouring portion of the people. One important result derived from these investigations is, that … [the] information clearly proves the mortality of the middle and upper classes to be above, and that of the industrious working classes to be below, the ratio for the country generally.[750]

---

[749] F.G.P. Neison, *Contributions to Vital* Statistics, 1864.
[750] Ibid, p. 151.

In attempting to explain this unexpected finding, Neison pointed out the importance of the characteristics of members of friendly societies:

> Their incomes are very limited, affording but the scantiest and simplest means of support. Their habitations are of an inferior order, being of the cheapest kind, and consequently in the worst streets ... For an individual to remain a Member of a Friendly Society, it is required that he should make his weekly or monthly contribution to its funds; and although a few pence is all that is needed, it presumes on a certain amount of frugality and industrial habit, sufficient to separate him from the reckless and improvident, who are more openly exposed to the vicissitudes – poverty, distress, destitution and disease.[751]

Neison recognised that poverty did play a role in creating ill-health, but argued that this was largely a function of variations in individual behaviour. He also contrasted the frugality and temperate habits of friendly society members with that of the wealthy:

> ... by tracing the various classes of society in which there exists sufficient means of subsistence, beginning with the most humble, and passing on to the middle and upper classes, that a gradual deterioration in the duration of life takes place ... this condition would seem to flow directly from the luxurious and pampered style of living among the wealthier classes, whose artificial habits interfere with the nature and degree of those physical exercises which, in a simpler class of society, are accompanied with a long life.[752]

He provided statistical evidence in support of the thesis that physical activity and alcohol were the key factors in shaping adult mortality patterns. He analysed friendly society records and showed that clerks whose occupation required minimal physical

---

[751] Ibid, p. 38.
[752] Ibid, p. 43.

exertion had a significantly lower expectation of life at all ages than plumbers, painters, bakers and miners. Clerks at age 20 had an expectation of life of 31.8 years, plumbers and painters 36.9 years, bakers 40.0 years, and miners 40.7 years.[753]

Neison classified occupations by amount of physical activity, and whether they were employed outdoors or indoors, and summarised his findings as follows:

Table 10: Expectation of Life (Years) among Friendly Society Members.[754]

Age	Indoor Occupations with Little Exercise	Indoor Occupations with Great Exercise	Outdoor Occupations with Little Exercise	Outdoor Occupations with Great Exercise
20	41.9	42.0	37.8	43.4
30	35.1	34.5	30.1	36.6
40	27.9	27.8	23.0	29.1
50	20.5	21.2	17.3	22.0
60	14.0	15.1	11.0	15.6
70	8.6	10.4	4.6	9.3

The unhealthiest occupations were those carried out outdoors with little exercise, followed by indoor occupations with little or great exercise. The healthiest occupations were those involving great exercise but carried out outdoors. Table 10 suggests that working outside did carry some health penalties – presumably through the effects of cold and damp – but that outdoor occupations with much physical activity conferred significant health benefits.

Neison carried out a special survey of mortality among those with 'intemperate habits' through sending out questionnaires to insurance companies, asking for information on insured members from medical personnel. He found a very strong mortality gradient, with those having 'intemperate habits'

---

[753] Ibid, pp. 54, 55.
[754] Source: Ibid, p. 456

– presumably mainly those addicted to alcohol – having much higher levels of mortality.

Table 11: Mortality among Persons of Intemperate Habits Compared to that in England and Wales.[755]

Agee	Number Exposed to Risk	Died	Mortality Per Cent	England & Wales Mortality Per Cent	Proportion of Intemperance Mortality to that of England & Wales
16-20	74.5	1	1.342	.730	1.8
21-30	949.0	47	4.953	.974	5.1
31-40	1861.0	86	4.620	1.110	4.2
41-50	1635.5	98	5.992	1.452	4.1
51-60	966.0	62	6.418	2.254	2.9
61-70	500.5	40	7.992	4.259	1.9
71-80	110.0	20	18.182	9.097	2.0
81-90	15.0	2	20.000	19.904	1.0

There are problems with the interpretation of Table 11 – the nature of the sample, its socio-economic and geographical composition – but its findings are plausible: those who drank large quantities of alcohol – and probably smoked tobacco – suffered levels of mortality in some age groups four or five times higher than the general population.

Neison assumed that he had largely refuted the arguments of Farr, Chadwick and other sanitarians, but there is no inconsistency between the importance of disease environment on the one hand, and the role of lifestyle on the other. There is evidence for the importance of both, and the relative role of these variables will depend upon particular historical and social circumstances.[756] Additonally, the wealthy have been known to have avoided certain childhood diseases, such as plague and

---

[755] Ibid, p. 204.
[756] J. C. Riley, *Rising Life Expectancy: a Global History,* 2001.

smallpox,[757] and been vulnerable as adults increasing their later mortality.

Wealth and Mortality among Women

The small amount of available evidence on female adult mortality is ambiguous before the twentieth century. Tryon claimed at the end of the seventeenth century that women's health suffered because of their lifestyle:

> ... there being hardly any Women in the known-World that are such great Drinkers and lovers of strong liquors as the *English* ... the too frequent drinking of *Wine* and *strong Drinks,* which ... makes her lose her way ... [and the] Inconveniences the Mother suffers, the Child partakes thereof, both in the time of Pregnancy (or breeding) and whilst it sucks.[758]

He claimed that wealthy women were less healthy than the poor, resulting from their physical inactivity:

> Women ought *not to lie too long in* Bed, as most of them that are of any Quality or Ability do ... if they do but use any kind of Exercises, and hereby their Travail in Child-bearing is tenfold more burthensom than otherwise it would be, witness many ordinary Country People, who have nothing the trouble such times as our *fine lazy sluggabed Dames.*[759]

There is no systematic evidence on lifestyle of women in wealthy families. Certainly many of the fashionable women depicted in contemporary pictorial satires were depicted as obese and over-weight.[760] Both Pepys and Parson Woodforde describe in their

---

[757] See 'The geography of smallpox in England before vaccination: a conundrum compounded', online peter.razzell.co.uk

[758] Tryon, *The Way*, pp. 278, 283-84.

[759] Ibid, pp. 288-89.

[760] Oppe, *Thomas Rowlandson*; V. Murray, *High Society: a Social History of the Regency Period, 1788-1830*, 1998.

diaries female guests consuming very generous quantities of food and drink.[761] Woodforde also makes reference to female alcoholics of his acquaintance.[762] Dobson quotes Dr George Buxton's diary for the year 1770, in which 'he claimed to have seen many women die miserably' of alcoholism.[763]

Gronow, writing in the Regency period, described how women along with men consumed large quantities of food and alcohol during dinner parties:

> ... a perpetual thirst seemed to come over people, both men and women, as soon as they had tasted their soup; as from that moment everybody was taking wine with everybody else, till the close of the dinner; and such wine that produces that class of Cordiality which frequently wanders into stupefaction. How all this eating and drinking ended was obvious, from the prevalence of gout, and the necessity of every one making the pill-box their constant bedroom companion.[764]

Irvine Loudon has presented evidence to show that maternal mortality was as high or even higher among middle-class as it was working-class mothers during the nineteenth and early twentieth centuries, and this was probably partly due to the delivery of babies by medical practitioners with inadequate obstetric practices.[765] Judith Lewis has argued that there were similar problems with the treatment of pregnant aristocratic women, although her research indicates that only about five per cent of women in peerage families died in childbirth in the period before the mid-nineteenth century, similar to estimated levels in

---

[761] R.C. Latham, W. Matthews (eds.), *The Diary of Samuel Pepys,* 11 Volumes, 1995; Beresford, *James Woodforde.*
[762] Beresford, *James Woodforde,* pp. 20, 99.
[763] M. Dobson, *Contours of Death and Disease in Early Modern England,* 1997, p. 246.
[764] Murray, *High Society.*
[765] I. Loudon, *Death in Childbirth: an International Study of Maternal Care and Maternal Mortality, 1800-1950,* 1992, pp. 243-46.

the general population.[766] However, there was a marked drop in maternal mortality among aristocratic women in the nineteenth century, much more rapid and significant than that which occurred amongst the general population, which may have been linked to the development of the anti-sepsis movement in the mid-nineteenth century.[767]

Conclusion

The link between socio-economic status and adult male mortality probably did not become fully established until the twentieth century.[768] Given the known association between poverty and mortality, this contradiction represents an historical puzzle which warrants further investigation. Given the provisional nature of the evidence, the central aim of the paper is not to provide definitive answers to the questions raised, but rather to stimulate a debate about the potential hazards of wealth to health and mortality in the pre-twentieth-century period. The data we present are limited in scope, both in the size of samples and the geographical areas covered, and suffer from a lack of randomness due to the self-selected nature of much of the source material. However, the data are from a number of independent sources which suggest certain provisional conclusions, providing the basis for more systematic and comprehensive research in the future.

A review of literary evidence suggests that the ownership of wealth carried its own risks. Medical authorities and other writers described in detail the hazards of wealth: the excessive consumption of food, alcohol, and tobacco, linked to physical inactivity and other lifestyle factors. The research reviewed in

---

[766] J. Lewis, "'Tis a misfortune to be a Great Ladie': Maternal mortality in the British aristocracy, 1559-1959', *Journal of British Studies*, Volume 37, 1998.
[767] Lewis, 'Tis a misfortune'; Loudon, *Death*.
[768] See P. Razzell, 'Population growth and the increase in socio-economic inequality in England, 1550-1850'.

this paper suggests that lifestyle may have been primarily responsible for the high adult mortality of wealthy men.

However, there are still a number of unresolved issues and the role of nutrition and poverty in shaping adult mortality still requires further clarification. A more detailed analysis of adult mortality by occupational group would partly help achieve this aim. The method of calculating mortality by tracking married couples between censuses, used with Bedfordshire and with selected English samples, is possible for all parts of England with surviving census schedules and parish registers. [769] For example, a comparison between farmers and agricultural labourers for individual parishes would further clarify the role of poverty in determining mortality. Evidence quoted earlier in Table 4 and from late nineteenth-century national censuses indicates that there was no significant difference in mortality between these two occupational groups.[770]

We have seen earlier that the life-long poverty of labourers led to physical stunting compared to farmers. It is possible that the effects of poverty among labourers were counter-balanced by the hazards of wealth among farmers – the consumption of alcohol, tobacco and an excess of food. Both groups lived in rural areas and led physically active lives, and explanations of their mortality patterns will require further research into other aspects of lifestyle and cause of death.

The overall evidence considered in this paper provides only minimal support to Wilkinson and Marmot's thesis that social inequality per se leads to higher mortality in adults. The absence of a social-class gradient in this type of mortality before the twentieth century indicates that other factors were more significant. We have suggested that lifestyle – excessive consumption of food, alcohol and tobacco, and a lack of physical activity – was central to high adult mortality among wealthy men and women. Additionally, the avoidance of certain childhood diseases by the rich may have taken their toll in later adulthood.

---

[769] For the latter see Razzell and Grundy, 'Socio-economic status'.
[770] Ibid.

The data reviewed suggest that there were significant health hazards attached to the ownership of wealth, but given the provisional nature of the evidence, much further research is going to be required before the complex relationship between wealth and mortality can be fully resolved.

Chapter 10: Introduction to Mayhew's Morning Chronicle Survey.[771]

On Monday, September 24th, 1849 *The Morning Chronicle* published an account of a visit to the cholera districts of Bermondsey – the first of a series of articles on the London poor by Henry Mayhew. The area he concentrated on was Jacob's Island, one of the few districts surviving the great fire of London. The island was surrounded by a tidal ditch which had become one vast open sewer and Mayhew described a part of the area as follows:

> We then journeyed on to London-street, down which the tidal ditch continues its course. In No. 1 of this street the cholera first appeared seventeen years ago, and spread up it with fearful virulence; but this year it appeared at the opposite end, and ran down it with like severity. As we passed along the reeking banks of the sewer the sun shone upon a narrow slip of the water. In the bright light it appeared the colour of a strong green tea, and positively looked as solid as black marble in the shadow – indeed it was more like watery mud than muddy water; and yet we were assured that this was the only water that the wretched inhabitants had to drink. As we gazed in horror at it, we saw drains and sewers emptying their filthy contents into it; we saw a whole tier of doorless privies in the open road, common to men and women, built over it; we heard bucket after bucket of filth splash into it, and the limbs .of the vagrant boys bathing in it seemed, by pure force of contrast, white as Parian marble. And yet, as we stood doubting the fearful statement, we saw a little child, from one of the galleries opposite, lower a tin can with a rope to fill a large bucket that stood beside her. In each of the balconies that hung over the stream the same-self tub was to be seen in which the inhabitants put the mucky liquid to stand, so that they may, after it has rested a day or two, skim the fluid from the solid particles of filth, pollution and disease. As the little

---

[771] Published in P. Razzell (ed.), *The Morning Chronicle Survey of Labour and the Poor: The Metropolitan Distracts*, 2007,

thing dangled her tin cup as gently as possible into the stream, a bucket of night soil was poured down from the next gallery.[772]

The impact of the article was considerable; as a result of it for example, Charles Kingsley and the Christian Socialists pressed for sanitary reform.[773] Mayhew's great skill lay in his ability to vividly recreate scenes and events encountered – we feel as we read his account that we are there in Bermondsey, seeing what he saw, 170 years ago. Mayhew also achieved the impact that he did through pioneering what we would now call oral history – or in his words, 'the first attempt to publish the history of the people, from the lips of the people themselves.'[774]

There was nothing new of course in the concern for the conditions under which the poor lived – 'The Condition of England' question was long-standing, and had been probed and investigated, since the beginning of the century in a series of medical, poor law and other government reports. Perhaps what was new was a sharpening of the concern of the propertied classes for the stability of the social order in which they so clearly had an overwhelming vested interest; *The Morning Chronicle* in its editorial, announcing the commencement of the national survey of labour and the poor argued

the starving or mendicant state of a large portion of the people ... if suffered to remain unremedied many years longer, will eat, like a dry rot, into the very framework of our society, and haply bring down the whole fabric with a crash.[775]

The Chartist agitation of the previous year had left its mark, and the 'dangerous classes' is a phrase which appears frequently in *The Morning Chronicle* – although Mayhew only used it to rebut

---

[772] *The Morning Chronicle,* September 24, 1849.
[773] A. Humphreys (ed.), *Voices of the Poor: Selections from Henry Mayhew's The Morning Chronicle Labour and the Poor, 1849, 1850,* 1971, p. ix.
[774] H. Mayhew, *London Labour and the London Poor,* Volume 1, 1968, p. xv.
[775] *The Morning Chronicle,* October 18, 1849.

the assumptions and fears which it concealed. A secondary concern revealed by *The Morning Chronicle* editorial was the injustice of society as it was then constituted – 'No man of feeling or reflection can look abroad without being shocked and startled by the sight of enormous wealth and unbounded luxury, placed in direct juxtaposition with the lowest extremes of indigence and privation.'[776]

But again none of this was new – the middle class public had long been aware through novels as well as government reports of the existence of the poor – what was new was that a man of great sensitivity of language and feeling, was about to embark on one of the greatest surveys of human life ever undertaken; and this 'factual' survey was to have an impact on contemporaries that no other writing on the poor had ever had. To understand how Mayhew achieved this impact is one of the aims of this introduction.

Mayhew himself claimed that he had been responsible for suggesting the national survey to *The Morning Chronicle*, but this was disputed by the newspaper in an editorial after Mayhew had broken with them.[777] Whatever the origin of the survey, Mayhew's first letter appeared in the newspaper on October 19th, 1849, and a series of eighty two letters by him continued until December 12th, 1850. Just over a third of this material was incorporated in Mayhew's later study, *London Labour and the London Poor*, but the bulk of it has never been newly published (although selections have appeared in the last few years.[778]) The survey covered many regions of England and Wales, and was divided between three types of area – the rural, manufacturing and metropolitan.

---

[776] Ibid.

[777] *The Morning Chronicle,* October 31, 1850.

[778] Humphreys, *Voices*; E.P. Thompson, Eileen Yeo, *The Unknown Mayhew,* 1971; P. Razzell, R. Wainwright (eds.), *The Victorian Working Class: Selections from the Morning Chronicle*, 1973.

Mayhew was appointed the metropolitan correspondent and he appears to have been helped by his brother Gus, as well as by Charles Knight and Henry Wood, along with assistants, stenographers and general helpers.[779] It was Mayhew's contribution that soon attracted attention and the great majority of letters to the newspaper concerned his accounts of the London poor, rather than those on the countryside or industrial areas. Not only was there great general interest, but novelists of the day were clearly influenced by what they read – Charles Kingsley incorporated some of Mayhew's work into his novel *Alton Locke* and someone of the stature of Thackeray wrote in the March 1850 issue of *Punch*:

> A clever and earnest-minded writer gets a commission from *The Morning Chronicle* newspaper, and reports upon the state of our poor in London; he goes amongst labouring people and poor of all kinds – and brings back what? A picture of human life so wonderful, so awful, so piteous and pathetic, so exciting and terrible, that readers of romances own that they never read anything like to it; and that the griefs, struggles, strange adventures here depicted, exceed anything that any of us could imagine.[780]

Mayhew achieved this effect on his readers by combining the survey side of his work with illustrations drawn from vivid individual autobiographical histories. It was this latter approach which gave his work such emotional force; people could identify for the first time with the poor, not just as depicted in a novel, but through the words of individuals whose lives were being laid out before the reader. No amount of statistical and official information on the poor could come near to Mayhew's work for emotional impact. He may have arrived at his method partly through his journalistic experience; but ironically, it was probably his literal tendering of the evidence given to him by the

---

[779] Thomson and Yeo, *The Unknown*, pp. 60, 61.
[780] Humphreys, *Voices*, p. ix.

people he interviewed. But also Mayhew understood the poor: there were elements in his character and experience which led him to ·sympathize and identify with them, as we will now see.

He was born in London in 1812 the son of a self made solicitor, and was educated at Westminster Public School. The evidence we have suggests his father was both tyrannical and unsympathetic to all his children, particularly to his sons; he also appears to have been violent with his wife. Mayhew wrote a satire on his father, suggesting that he had a particular dislike for the front of respectability that his father presented to the world.[781] Although Mayhew appears to have been a brilliant pupil, his indolence and rebelliousness led him to leave the school at an early age. He refused to be flogged by the headmaster for a minor misdemeanour and immediately left the school never to return. Similarly, after a brief period of apprenticeship in his father solicitor's business, he caused his father some embarrassment by forgetting to lodge legal papers, and fled the house not to see his father for several years.

Mayhew's brilliance, indolence and humour led him to adopt the life of a literary bohemian, writing for satirical magazines (he claimed to be one of the co-founders of Punch), newspapers, as well as his own plays, short stories and novels. Much of this writing had a radical edge which was probably linked with his reaction against the conservative respectability of his father, although his work was also characterized by some of the middle-class assumptions of the day, showing that he had not escaped the influence of his bourgeois background.[782]

One aspect of Mayhew's character which perhaps has not been sufficiently stressed in other commentaries on his work, was his interest in the natural sciences. According to

---

[781] Thomson and Yeo, *The Unknown*, p. 13.
[782] See Humphreys, *Voices*, pp. xv, xvi.

one account, he had unsuccessfully tried to persuade his father to allow him to become an experimental chemist,[783] and when he left home, he spent much of his time on such experiments – he is reputed to have nearly blown up his brother's house on one occasion![784] – and his interest in natural science clearly influenced the way he approached *The Morning Chronicle* survey. He wrote to the editor of that paper in February 1850 explaining his approach:

> I made up my mind to deal with human nature as a natural philosopher or a chemist deals with any material object; and, as a man who had devoted some little of his time to physical and metaphysical science, I must say I did most heartily rejoice that it should have been left to me to apply the laws of inductive philosophy for the first time, I believe, in the world to the abstract questions of political economy.[785]

Although this stress on science and political economy would seem a far cry from Mayhew the great originator of working class oral history, with all its moving and vivid writing, the contradiction is not as great as it might seem. Mayhew always stressed he was presenting a *factual* picture of the London poor as he found them; when in dispute with the editor of *The Morning Chronicle* about the content of some of his articles – the editor had removed some passages antipathetic to free trade – Mayhew insisted that the original report of the speech of a boot-maker be restored on the grounds that he was 'a person collecting and registering facts.'[786] His notion of natural science was essentially that it was an inductive discipline, with factual information being collected in great detail before valid

---

[783] Ibid, p. xi.
[784] Ibid.
[785] *Report of the Speech of Henry Mayhew and the Evidence Adduced at a Public Meeting ... Convened by the Committee of the Tailors of London*, 1856, p. 6
[786] Ibid.

generalizations could be reached. It was partly on these grounds that he was critical of 'the political economists of the day'; he believed that they constructed their theories without familiarising themselves with the complexities of the situations they were trying to explain.

An obvious weakness in Mayhew's method was that he did not use a strict process of random sampling in selecting informants – his work was carried out before this had been developed – but he did attempt wherever possible to avoid undue bias. This is illustrated by the dispute that arose over the reliability of his evidence on Ragged Schools. His assistant R. Knight gave the following account of the method of selecting informants in a letter to *The Morning Chronicle*:

> I was directed by your Special Correspondent to obtain for him the addresses of some of the boys and girls who attended the Ragged School in Westminster, so that he might be able to visit them at their homes. Your correspondent desired me to take the names of the first parties that came to hand, so that neither particularly good nor bad cases might be selected, but such as might be presumed to be fair average examples of the practical tendency of the school in question.[787]

Mayhew comes near here to a random sampling method, but elsewhere he was too dependent on special sources of information to be able to achieve this aim. Frequently he used key informants 'doctors, clergymen, trade union leaders' to both provide on a subject and introduce him to other informants on the area that he was interested in. The disadvantages and potential bias in this method is obvious, but in practice it seems to have been remarkably successful. All of Mayhew's key informants appear to have been intelligent and well-informed men, and were able to provide him with a range and depth of information that would have been unavailable elsewhere (this is

---

[787] *The Morning Chronicle*, April 25 1850.

perhaps a method that social scientists today might benefit from rediscovering). A check on the reliability and objectivity of the information given was the public nature of the survey. Errors were open to correction through the letter column of the newspaper – and that there were only one or two corrections of this kind,[788] bears testimony to the high overall accuracy of Mayhew's work.

The major theme of the survey was of course poverty, and an introduction of this kind can only touch upon some of the more important aspects of the subject as it was treated by Mayhew. One of the things which he revealed to his contemporaries was the complexity of poverty, as well as its inevitability. Anything which could destroy a family's ordinary means of livelihood – illness, old age, death or accident – could throw it into the most extreme and abject poverty. I quote at some length the following account given to Mayhew of what happened to a coalwhipper (a labourer unloading coal) after an accident:

I was a coalwhipper. I had a wife and two children. Four months ago, coming off my day's work, my foot slipped, and I fell and broke my leg. I was taken to the hospital, and remained there ten weeks. At the time of the accident I had no money at all by me, but was in debt by the amount of ten shillings to my landlord. I had a few clothes of myself and wife. While I was in the hospital I did not receive anything from our benefit society, because I had not been able to keep up my subscription. My wife and children lived, while I was in hospital, by pawning my things, and going from door to door, to everyone she knowed, to give her a bit. The men who worked in the same gang as myself made up 4s: 6d. for me, and that, with two loaves of bread that they had from the receiving officer, was what they got while I was in the hospital; the landlord seized for the rent the few things that my wife had not pawned; and turned her and my two little children into the street – one was a boy three years old,

---

[788] See for example *The Morning Chronicle*, February 25, 1850, for a letter correcting errors on prices paid in the shoe trade.

and the other a baby just turned ten months. My wife went to her mother, and she kept her and my little ones for three weeks, till she could do so no longer. My mother, poor old woman, was most as bad off as we were. My mother only works on the ground out in the country at gardening. She makes about 7s. a week in summer; and in the winter she only has only 9d. a day to live upon; but she had at least a shelter for her child, and she willingly shared that with her daughter and daughter's children. She pawned all the clothes she had to keep them from starving – but at last everything was gone from the poor old woman, and then I got my brother to take my family in. My brother worked at garden work, the same as my mother in law did. He made about 15s. a week in summer; and about half that in the winter time … he had only one room, but he got in a bundle of straw for me, and we lived and slept there for seven weeks. He got credit for more than £1 of bread, and tea, and sugar for us; and now he can't pay, and the man threatens to summon him for it. After I left my brother's, I came to live in the neighbourhood of Wapping for I thought I might manage to do a day's work at coalwhipping, and I couldn't bear to live on his little earning any longer – he could scarcely keep himself then. At last I got a ship to deliver, but I was too weak to do the work, and in pulling at the ropes, my hand got sore, and festered for want of nourishment … After this I was obliged to lay up again, and that's the only job of work that I have been able to do for this last four months … I had one pennyworth of bread this morning. We altogether had half-a-quartern loaf among the four of us, but no tea nor coffee. Yesterday we had some bread, and tea, and butter, but wherever my wife got it from I don't know. I was three days, but a short time back, without a taste of food. (Here he burst out crying). I had nothing but water which passed my lips. I had merely a little at home, and that my wife and children had. I would rather starve myself than let them do so. Indeed, I've done it over and over again. I never begged – I'd die in the streets first. I never told nobody of my life. The foreman of my gang was the only one besides God that knew of my misery; and his wife came to me and brought me money and brought me food; and himself too, many a time ('I had a wife and five children of my own to maintain, and it grieved me to my heart,' said the man who sat by, 'to see them want, and I unable to do more for them.')

Anyone tempted to dismantle the welfare state would do well to ponder this passage at some length; there is no doubt whatsoever from the voluminous evidence produced by Mayhew and the other correspondents of *The Morning Chronicle,* that this man's experience of what happened in sickness and ill-health was entirely typical. It is not only the extreme poverty of the family itself, but the poverty of their neighbours, workmates and relatives which gives the report such importance in revealing the terrible conditions under which the poor of Victorian England lived. The harshness with which the family were treated by the landlord and the relieving officer obviously added considerably to their misery; only the support of neighbours, workmates and above all relatives, enabled them to survive at all.

Mayhew makes it very clear that these cases were not merely examples of individual distress, but were characteristic of whole classes of people. Poverty of this kind was the result of structural changes in society, a theme which became Mayhew's overriding concern in his *Morning Chronicle* letters. He analysed the poverty resulting from changes in the organisation of trades, and began to generalize this into an indictment of the whole of capitalist society. Before he embarked on this analysis, he gathered together a vast amount of empirical evidence on the incidence and nature of poverty, and perhaps what was so unusual about this, was his ability to write so well about what other authors had managed to make so mundane and boring. Here is his description of the hiring of labourers in the docks:

As the foreman calls from a book the names, some men jump upon the backs of the others, so as to lift themselves high above the rest, and attract the notice of him who hires them. All are shouting. Some cry aloud his surname, some his Christian name; others call out their own names; to remind him that they are there. Now the appeal is made in Irish blarney, now in broken English. Indeed it is a sight to sadden the most callous, to see *thousands* of men struggling for only one day's hire, the scuffle being made the fiercer by the knowledge that hundreds out of the number assembled must be left to idle the day out in want. To look in the faces of that hungry crowd is to see a sight that must be ever remembered.[789]

He went on to detail the poverty of the dock labourers, and illustrated this in brilliant fashion through interviews with individual dockers and their families – families that lived in one squalid, unheated and virtually unfurnished room, who were frequently subject to hunger and illness, without proper clothing – children without shoes and socks – and could only find work if they were prepared to participate in the scramble described above. Many of the people seeking dock work had previously been silk weavers living and working in the Spitalfields area. The drastic decline in the prosperity in this trade was delineated by Mayhew in one of his first letters.[790]

Although silk-weaving was the most dramatic example of an occupation falling into destitution, most of the trades covered by Mayhew were subject to something of the same process. Real wages fell amongst nearly all occupational groups, and *The Morning Chronicle* survey provides an unrivalled series of economic histories of various trades from the late eighteenth century onwards. Workers in the shoe and boot making trade had suffered severely in living standards since the prosperity of the Napoleonic wars, as was revealed by one of Mayhew's informants:

In 1812 the boot-makers received their highest wages. If an average could have been taken then of the earnings of the trade; one with another, I think it would have been about 35s. a man. The great decrease (from 35s. to 13s. 6d. a week) that has taken place is not so

---

[789] Ibid, October 26, 1849.
[790] Ibid, October 23, 1849.

much owing to the decrease of wages as to the increase of hands; and the consequent decrease of work coming to each man. I know myself that my late master used to earn £2 a week on average many years back, but of late years I am sure he has not made 15s. a week.[791]

Mayhew unfortunately did not collect systematic information on changes in prices – the evidence he did publish suggests that prices only begun to fall significantly after the mid-1840s. But the qualitative evidence on living standards more than outweighs this deficiency. Here is a description of a boot-maker's earnings and style of life in the early years of the century:

I got work in Mr. Roby's ... not long after the battle of Waterloo, in 1815, and was told by my fellow workmen that I wasn't born soon enough to see good times; but I've lived long enough to see bad ones. Though I wasn't born soon enough; as they said I could earn, and did earn £150 a year, something short of £3 a week; and that for eight years when trade became not so good ... I could then play my £1 a corner at whist. I *wouldn't* play at that time for less than 5s. I could afford a glass of wine, but was never a drinker; and for all that, I had my £100 in the Four per Cents for a long time (I lent it to a friend afterwards), and from £40 to £50 in the savings bank. Some made more than me, though I *must* work. I can't stand still. One journeyman, to my knowledge, saved £2,000. He once made 34 pairs of boots in three weeks. The bootmen then at Mr. Hoby's were all respectable men; they were like gentlemen – smoking their pipes in their frilled shirts, like gentlemen – all but the drunkards. At the trade meetings, Hoby's best men used to have one corner of the room to themselves, and were called the House of Lords. There was more than one hundred of us when I became one; and before then there were an even greater number. Mr. Hoby has paid five hundred pounds a week in wages. It was easy to save money in those days; one could hardly help it. We shall never see the like again.[792]

---

[791] Ibid, February 4, 1850.
[792] Ibid, February 7, 1850.

Contrast this with the life-style of a boot-closer who assured me that he had dealt with his baker for fourteen or fifteen years and had never been able to get out of debt lately ... As for a coat, he said: 'Oh, God bless my soul, sir, I haven't bought one for this six or seven years, and my missus has not been able to purchase a gown for the same time; to do so out of my earnings *now* is impossible. If it wasn't for a cousin of mine that is in place, we shouldn't have a thing to our backs, and working for the best wages too ... Wages have been going down ever since 1830. Before that time my wife attended to her domestic duties only ... Since that period my wife has been obliged to work at shoe binding, and my daughter as well ... My comforts have certainly not increased in proportion with the price of provisions. In 1811 to 1815 bread was very high – I think about 1s.10½d, the best loaf – and I can say I was much more comfortable then than at present. I had a meat dinner at that time every day, but now I'm days without seeing the sight of it. If provisions were not as cheap as they are now we should be starving outright ...'[793]

These were men who worked in the 'honourable' part of the trade — working on the premises of their employer for fixed hours, their conditions of work regulated by agreement with their trade union. Although increasingly impoverished by the fall in wages, their situation was much better than that of people working in the 'dishonourable' sector – those who either worked for themselves as 'chamber masters' in their own homes, or were employed by them. This sector was strongly concentrated in the east end of London, whereas the more respectable part of the trade was concentrated mainly in the west end. This polarisation of the trades – with about ten per cent 'honourable' and ninety per cent 'dishonourable – was revealed by Mayhew to be common in the London trades. He summarised the markedly different life-styles of the two groups and illustrated it with reference to the tailoring trade:

[793] Ibid.

302

The very dwellings of the people are sufficient to tell you the wide difference between the two classes. In the one you occasionally find small statues of Shakespeare beneath glass shades; in the other all is dirt and foetor. The working tailor's comfortable first floor ... at the West-end is redolent with the perfume of the small bunch of violets that stand in the tumbler over the mantel piece; the sweater's wretched garret is rank with the stench of filth and herrings. The honourable part of the trade are really intelligent artisans, while the slop workers are generally almost brutified with their incessant toil, wretched pay, miserable food, and filthy homes.[794]

The sweating system at its worst could be highly dangerous to health and life, as was revealed by someone who had worked for one:

One sweater I worked with had four children, six men, and they, together with wife, sister-in-law, and himself lived in two rooms, the largest of which was about eight feet by ten. We worked in the smallest room and slept there as well – all six of us. There were two turn-up beds in it, and we slept three in a bed. There was no chimney, and indeed no ventilation whatever. I was near losing my life there. Almost all the men were consumptive, and I myself attended the dispensary for disease of the lungs.[795]

What had brought about the terrible mass of misery and poverty that week after week filled *The Morning Chronicle's* pages? The answer of the political economists of the day was that it was largely due to an over-rapid expansion of population, and it was this Malthusian orthodoxy that Mayhew was most concerned to dispute. He did not contest that an over-supply of labour would lead to a fall in wages and living standards, but criticised the Malthusian conclusion on empirical grounds. In his later work *London Labour and the London Poor,* he argued that there had been no excessive

---

[794] Ibid, December 14, 1849.
[795] Ibid, December 18, 1849.

increase in population in the first half of the nineteenth century, stating that the demand for labour as measured by various output/production series, had more than kept pace with population increase.[796]

He did not seem to realise that this contradicted his own findings about the increasing poverty of the mass of the people, although he could have saved part of his argument by stressing the re-distribution of income from poor to rich. The re-distribution would have had to have been very dramatic to account for the depth of poverty he found in his survey, and there is no evidence that it ever reached this scale. The major problem with Mayhew's argument is that he used production series for commodities such as cotton and wool, which are known to have expanded very dramatically, the textile industry being central to the industrial revolution then taking place. The standard of living and how it changed in this period has of course become a subject of extensive scholarly debate, but this does not appear to be resolvable with existing statistical data. Mayhew's own detailed qualitative evidence seems much more useful in telling us what was happening at this time, and the conclusion from his survey must be that there was a significant increase in poverty during the first half of the nineteenth century.

How are we to reconcile the above conclusion with some of the statistical series on wages which appear to contradict it? The answer lies I believe in what the boot-maker told Mayhew in the interview quoted previously – that it was not so much a fall in wage rates of existing trades that was responsible, but a significant decrease in the amount of employment available and the growth of sweated work practices outside of the recognized (and presumably the statistically measured) regular trades. Mayhew himself stated that 'in the generality of trades the calculation is that one-third of the hands are fully employed, one-third partially, and one-third unemployed throughout the

---

[796] H. Mayhew, *London Labour and the London Poor,* Volume 2, 1968, pp. 317-321.

year.'[797] This would seem to bring the analysis back to an over-supply of labour and an expanding population, but Mayhew had a series of detailed arguments based on his empirical findings with which to counter this thesis.

For him the surplus of labour was the result of the competitiveness of contemporary capitalist society, and he brought this out in a number of separate but related themes. He recognised that the introduction of new technology had a significant impact on the creation of labour surpluses; for example, he described in some detail the effect of steam machinery on the employment of sawyers and how it had both reduced their numbers and income. But the effect of the new technology was very limited in London as most industries were labour-intensive. What Mayhew did trace however was the impact of the industrial revolution of the textile industry in Lancashire, for some of the labour displaced found its way on to the London labour market. One man who had become destitute, gave Mayhew the following account of his life:

I am thirty-eight he said, and have been a cotton-spinner, working at Chorlton-upon-Medlock. I can neither read nor write. When I was a young man, twenty years ago, I could earn £2 10s. clear money every week, after paying two piecers and a scavenger. Each piecer had 7s. 6d. a week – they are girls; the scavenger – a boy to clean the wheels of the cotton spinning machine had 2s. 6d. I was master of them wheels in the factory. This state of things continued until about the year 1837. I lived well and enjoyed myself, being a hearty man, noways a drunkard, working every day from half past five in the morning .till half-past seven at night – long hours that time, master. I didn't care about money as long as I was decent and respectable. I had a turn for sporting at the wakes down there. In 1837 the 'self actors' (machines with steam power) had come into common use. One girl can mind three pairs – that used to be three men's work – getting 15s. for the work which gave three men £7 10s. Out of one factory 400

---

[797] Ibid, p. 300.

hands were flung in one week, men and women together. We had a meeting of the union, but nothing could be done, and we were told to go and mind the three pairs, as the girls did, for 15s. a week. We wouldn't do that. Some went for soldiers, some to sea, some to Stopport (Stockport), to get work in factories where the self actors wer'nt agait.[798]

The Luddite reaction to new technology becomes completely understandable, its beneficiaries at this time being almost entirely the owners of factories and their like. The sawyers had destroyed the first mechanical mills in London (these were run by horse-power but on the same principle as the later steam mills), but had eventually succumbed to the new technology.

Mayhew realised however that technology was not the prime moving force in the early capitalist transformation of society, at least in the London area. Much more important was the 'extraction of labour-surpluses' through changes in the organisation of what Marx called the social relationships of production – in particular the development of petty capitalism in various forms. Mayhew did not of course analyse the course of events in such simple analytical terms; he gave a much more descriptive account of what he called the effects of the 'competitive system'. He analysed the increase of surplus labour under two headings: the increase in the number of labourers and the increase in the amount of labour extracted from an existing labour force. He saw six ways of increasing the number of labourers:

1. By the undue increase of apprentices. 2. By drafting into the ranks of labour those who should be other-wise engaged, as women and children. 3. By the importation of labourers from abroad. 4. By the migration of country labourers to towns, and so overcrowding the market in the cities. 5. By the depression of

---

[798] *The Morning Chronicle*, January 18, 1850.

other trades. 6. By the undue increase of the people themselves.[799]

Three, four and six are all direct effects of increasing population and belong if you like to the 'opposition argument'. One and two form a part of Mayhew's main argument (five is rather nebulous), although he does not spell this out. He grouped the means of increasing the amount of labour from a fixed labour force under seven headings: 1. By extra supervision when the workmen are paid by the day 2. By increasing the workman's interest in his work, as in piece work, where the payment of the operative is made proportional to the quantity of work done by him. 3. By large quantities of work given out at one time; as in 'lump-work' and 'contract work'. 4. By the domestic system of work, or giving out materials to be made up at the homes of the workpeople. 5. By the middleman system of labour. 6. By the prevalence of small master. 7. By a reduced rate of pay as forcing operatives to labour both longer and quicker, in order to make up the same amount of income.[800]

Many of these headings overlap as Mayhew himself was prepared to admit; categories two to six all have a strong element of increasing the capitalist principle into work situations, and in practice the prevalence of the contract system and in particular the growth of small masters (petty capitalists) seem to have been most important, at least in Mayhew's work. Headings one and seven concern the control that employers were able to exert over their work force, without having to go through indirect market forces The distinction between employer and employee becomes blurred of course in the case of the small master. A more appropriate distinction here would be between the rich capitalist and the poor worker who actually provided the labour, under whatever relationship of production.

---

[799] Mayhew, *London Labour.*, Volume 2, p. 311.
[800] Ibid, p. 328.

That employers were able to extract enormous amounts of extra labour through direct control was brought out by Mayhew in a number of places. Perhaps the most striking example was the 'strapping system' in the carpentry and joinery trade:

> Concerning this I received the following extraordinary account from a man after his heavy day's labour; and never in all my experience have I seen so bad an instance of over-work. The poor fellow was so fatigued that he could hardly rest in his seat. As he spoke he sighed deeply and heavily, and appeared almost spirit-broken with excessive labour: – 'I work at what is called the strapping shop', he said, 'and have worked at nothing else for these many years past in London. I call 'strapping', doing as much work as a human being or a horse possibly can in a day, and that without any hanging upon the collar, but with the foreman's eyes constantly fixed upon you, from six o'clock in the morning to six o'clock at night. The shop in which I work is for all the world like a prison – the silent system is as strictly carried out there as in a model gaol. If a man was to ask any common question of his neighbour, except it was connected with his trade, he would be discharged there and then. If a journeyman makes the least mistake, he is packed off just the same. A man working in such places is almost always in fear; for the most trifling things he is thrown out of work in an instant ... I suppose since I knew the trade a man does four times the work that he did formerly ... What's worse than that, the men are everyone striving one against the other ... They are all tearing along from the first thing in the morning to the last thing at night, as hard as they can go, and when the time comes to knock off they are ready to drop, it was hours after I got home last night before I could get a wink of sleep; the soles of my feet were on fire, and my arms ached to that degree that I could hardly lift my hand to my head.'[801]

---

[801] *The Morning Chronicle*, July 18, 1850.

The result of this terrible exploitation of labour was that many joiners were 'quite old men and gray with spectacles on, by the time they are forty.'[802]

It is easy now to understand current trade union practices which attempt to regulate and control the amount of work to be done independently of the 'logic of production'. Trade unions were of course active during the whole of the nineteenth century and we must ask why they were unable to prevent the extreme conditions described above. This is perhaps the crucial question that Mayhew never answered in his discussion of political-economy, yet the answer to such a question is to be found in his own survey. Unions had been very active in the protection of living standards and working conditions, even when they had not achieved legal recognition. One boot-maker described the strike of 1812 which resulted in victory for the union:

> The masters, at that time, after holding out for thirteen weeks, gave way, yielding to all the demands of the men. 'The *scabs* had no chance in those days', said my informant, 'the wages men had it all their own way; they could do anything, and there were no slop shops then. Some scabs went to Mr. Roby 'occasioning' (that is asking whether he 'had occasion for another hand'), but he said to them, 'I can do nothing; go to my masters (the journeymen) in the Parr's Head, Swallow Street' (the sign of the public-house used by the men that managed the strike).[803]

The key to the success of unions this time was provided by another of Mayhew's informants:

> I believe the reduction of wages in our trade is due chiefly the supra-abundance of workmen; that is the real cause of our prices having gone down, because when men are scarce, or work is plentiful, they *will* have good wages. From the year

---

[802] Ibid.
[803] Ibid, February 4, 1850.

1798 our wages began to increase partly because the number of hands was decreased by war, and partly because the foreign orders were much greater then than now.[804]

After the Napoleonic wars labour flooded back onto the market, and with population doubling in the first half of the nineteenth century, the supply of labour greatly began to exceed its demand. This of course is a highly complex question, much debated by economists, sociologists and historians, the critical element in the debate being the balance between supply and demand for labour, and its relationship with the distribution of real resources within an early capitalist economy. Another boot-maker put this very simply when he told Mayhew:

> The cause of the trade being so over stocked with hands is, I believe, due in great measure to the increase of population. Every pair of feet there is born, certainly wants a pair of shoes; but unfortunately, as society is at present constituted, they cannot get them. The poor, you see, sir increase at a greater rate than the rich.[805]

Several of Mayhew's artisan informants showed a remarkably good grasp of basic economics, and one or two even anticipated Marx and Keynes in their understanding of the effects of under-consumption on the capitalist economy. One man believed in particular that the new technology would have disastrous effects on the economy:

> Suppose, I say, that *all* human labour is done away by it, and the working men are turned into paupers and criminals, then what I want to know is who are to be the customers of the capitalists? The capitalists themselves, we should remember, spend little or none (comparatively speaking) of the money *they* get; for, of course, it is the object of every capitalist to save all he

---

[804] Ibid, February 7, 1850.
[805] Ibid.

can, and to increase the bulk of money out of which he makes his profits. The working men, however, spend *all* they receive – it's true a small amount is put into the savings bank, but that's a mere drop in the ocean; and so the working classes constitute the great proportion of the customers of the country. The lower their wages are reduced of course the less they have to spend, and when they are entirely superseded by machinery, of course they'll have nothing at all to spend, and then, I ask again, who are to be the capitalists' customers?[806]

These dire predictions did not come to full realisation in the hundred years or so after they were made, and this was partly because the industrial revolution had brought about an improvement of average living standards after the 1840s, mainly through a fall in prices. A number of informants told Mayhew how the fall in prices of bread, meat, fruit and vegetables, clothing and other goods, had improved their lot from the mid-1840s onwards, and this was due to a number of factors – new technology, railways, more efficient farming, foreign imports – and undoubtedly this development was the great turning point in the history of capitalism. There were of course many other factors that prevented the pauperisation of the working classes predicted by Marx – perhaps one of the most important being the development of specialization and the growth of the division of labour, which enabled the labour force through their unions to exploit the dependency of employers on small numbers of key workers. At the time that Mayhew wrote however, there was little evidence of this development, and the unions were weak and the mass of the population in a pauperised state.

What Mayhew failed to realise was the importance of the rate of expansion of the population for the conditions under which the struggle between capital and labour was conducted. (I assume here that population was expanding for other than economic reasons, and was primarily function of medical and

---

[806] Ibid, July 25, 1850.

other non-economic factors.)[807] Throughout his survey there is constant mention of a massive surplus of labour demanding work which was not there to be had.[808] This enabled employers to ruthlessly squash strikes and union activity, either by employing blackleg labour, or by sending work into non-unionized sectors and areas of the country.

What Mayhew did realise was that this surplus of labour enabled employers to extract even further surpluses through the modes of exploitation discussed above – formulated by Mayhew in the phrase, 'Over-work makes under-pay, and under pay makes over-work.'[809] A surplus of population did not operate in a vacuum, it was employed within a certain social relationship of production, and this could be crucial for the development of the economy. In the case of London during the middle of the nineteenth century, it was the growth of petty-capitalism that was crucial. This took many guises – sub-contracting, chamber-masters, sweaters, etc. – but the critical development was the exploitation of labour through a system of production which gave workers a personal but minimal interest in profitability.

A cabinet-maker gave the following explanation of why so many men became small capitalists working on their own account:

> One of the inducements ... for men to take for making up for themselves is to get a living when thrown out of work until they can hear of something better ... Another of the reasons for the men turning small masters is the little capital that it requires for them to start themselves .... Many works for themselves, because nobody else won't employ them, their work is so bad. Many weavers has took to our business of late .... Another reason for men turning little masters is because employment's more certain

---

[807] See P. Razzell, 'Malthus, mortality or marriage?: population change in eighteenth century England'.
[808] See for example *The Morning Chronicle*, October 26, 1849, November 16, 1849, January 11, 1850, January 15, 1850, July 11, 1850.
[809] *Report of the Speech*, p. 21.

like that way; a man can't be turned off easily, you see, when he works for himself. Again, some men prefer being small masters because they are more independent like; when they're working for themselves, they can begin working when they please, and knock off whenever they like. But the principal reason is because there ain't enough work at the regular shops to employ them all.[810]

These small masters were drawn into a system of ruthless competition and the money paid to them by the warehouses – the 'slaughterer' – became barely sufficient for subsistence. Many of the chamber-masters were sweaters, employing their wives and children and any other source of cheap labour, but none of them were real beneficiaries from the long and grinding hours of work – it was the owners of the warehouses and their customers who really gained from this system of exploitation. The major reason why so many small masters were prepared to tolerate these conditions was because there was no alternative – a surplus of labour through a rapidly-expanding population had thrown them out of regular work and into pauperized independence, which in turn helped destroy the power of the trade unions in the 'honourable' sector of the trade.

Although Mayhew failed to link population growth with the changes in the structure of the social relationships of production which he so effectively described, he provided in his survey nearly all that we would want to know to understand the development of contemporary capitalism. However, his survey went well beyond the confines of this major theme, and to the sociologist, his work provides a range of fascinating detail on other sociological subjects. One theme that constantly recurs is the growth of a culture of respectability during the nineteenth century, a subject which obviously fascinated Mayhew. There are frequent mentions in the survey of the decline in drunkenness

---

[810] *The Morning Chronicle*, August 22, 1850.

and brutality which characterized many English workmen of an earlier epoch; here is Mayhew's interview with a cabinet-maker on the subject of respectability:

'Within my recollection,' said an intelligent cabinet-maker, 'there was much drinking, among the cabinet-makers. This was fifteen years back. Now I am satisfied that at least seven eighths of all who are in society are sober and temperate men. Indeed, good masters won't have tipplers now-a-days' ... The great majority of the cabinet-makers are married men, and were described to me by the best informed parties as generally domestic men, living, whenever it was possible, near their workshops, and going home to every meal. They are not much of play-goers, a Christmas pantomime or any holiday spectacle being exceptions, especially where there is a family. 'I don't know a card-player,' said a man who had every means of knowing, 'amongst us, I think you'll find more cabinet-makers than any other trade members of mechanics' institutes and literary institutions and attendees of lectures.' Some journeymen cabinet-makers have saved money, and I found them all speak highly of the advantages they, as well as their masters, derive from their trade society.[811]

These respectable artisans were of course only a minority of the total of working people. We saw earlier how the members of the 'honourable' west end trade lived very different lives to those of the east end. The 'respectable' artisans were family men, living quiet private lives, markedly in contrast with the life of the 'rough' working class, which was violent, noisy and gregarious. Mayhew had a deeply ambivalent attitude towards respectability; on the one hand he admired the 'rational' sobriety, cleanliness and cultured life-style of his intelligent artisans, yet on the other was greatly attracted to the spontaneity and colour of his street folk: vagabonds, delinquents, labourers and other unrespectable inhabitants of London. The intelligence of the respectable artisan enabled him to take an active interest in union and political

---

[811] Ibid, August 1, 1850.

matters, whereas the unskilled workmen tended to passively acquiesce in the miseries of his lot:

> The transition from the artisan to the labourer is curious in many respects. In passing from the skilled operative of the West End to the unskilled workman of the Eastern quarter of London, the moral and intellectual change is so great that it seems as if we were in a new land and among another race. The artisans are sufficiently educated and thoughtful to have a sense of their importance in the state ... The unskilled labourers are a different class of people. As yet they are as un-political as footmen. Instead of entertaining violently democratic opinions, they appear to have no political opinions whatever or if they do possess any, they rather lean towards the maintenance 'of things as they are', than towards the ascendancy of the working people.[812]

Not only were the unskilled un-political, but they tended to be more addicted to violence, drunkenness and dishonesty than the rest of the population. Mayhew findings from official statistical returns of crime that the labourers of London were 'nine times as dishonest, five times as drunken, and nine times as savage, as the rest of the community.'[813]

What Mayhew most disliked about the unrespectable however was the dirt and squalor in which they lived. In discussing the importance of fish in the diet of the poor – the railway had ushered in an era of very cheap fish in London – he wrote:

> The rooms of the very neediest of our needy metropolitan population always smell of fish; most frequently of herrings. So much so, indeed, that to those, like myself, have been in the habit of visiting their dwellings the smell of herrings, even in comfortable

---

[812] Ibid, December 21, 1849.
[813] Ibid.

houses, savours from association, so strongly of squalor and wretchedness as to be often most oppressive. [814]

This echoes the passage quoted earlier, which contrasted the west end tailors comfortable apartment with flowers and pictures, and 'the sweater's wretched garret ... rank with the stench of filth and herrings.' Mayhew believed that the poor of the east end were 'brutified with their incessant toil, wretched pay, miserable food, and filthy homes' and in a number of places in his survey he uses strong moral language to condemn what he considered to be the vices of the unrespectable poor. Listen to the following account of the lives of pickpockets and note the mixture of moral disapproval and insightful sociological and psychological analysis:

> It is a singular fact that as a body the pickpockets are generally very sparing of drink. My informant never knew any one of these young pickpockets or 'gonuffs' to be drunk, or to seem in any way anxious for drink. They are mostly libidinous, indeed universally so, and spend whatever money they can spare upon the low prostitution round about the neighbourhood ... Nor can their vicious propensities be ascribed to ignorance, for we have seen that out of 55 individuals, 40 could read and write, while four could read ... Neither can the depravity of their early associations be named as the cause of their delinquencies for we have seen that, as a class, their fathers are men well to do in the world. Indeed their errors seem to have rather a physical than either an intellectual or moral cause. They seem to be naturally of an erratic and self-willed temperament, objecting to the restraints of home, and incapable of continuous application to any one occupation whatsoever. They are essentially the idle and the vagabond; and they seem generally to attribute the commencement of their career to harsh government at home. [815]

---

[814] Mayhew, *London Labour and the London Poor*, Volume 1, p. 62.
[815] *The Morning Chronicle*, November 2, 1849.

Much of this account could be applied to Mayhew himself – his own reaction against parental authority, his 'erratic and self-willed temperament', and his restlessness. Although current sociological fashion is against the kind of physiological explanation of delinquency given by Mayhew, there is probably as much evidence in its favour as with rival more widely accepted theories.

The delinquents were rebels, but rebels with energy, intelligence, humour and a love of life. It is these qualities which inform some of Mayhew's best-known work, the writing on street entertainers, costermongers, tricksters·and the host of other colourful characters which fill his pages. Listen to the marvellous account of one of the many tricks played on a gullible public:

> I've done *the shivering dodge* too – gone out in the cold weather half naked. One man has practised it so much that he can't get off shivering now. Shaking Jemmy went on with his shivering so long that he couldn't help it at last. He shivered like a jelly – like a calf's foot with the ague – on the hottest day in summer.[816]

And some of Mayhew's characters are so close in language to Dickens, that the reader finds himself unconsciously carried from one to the other. One of the Punch and Judy men told Mayhew:

> One of my pardners was buried by the workhouse; and even old Pike, the most noted showman as ever was, died in the workhouse. Pike and Porsini – Porsini was the first original street Punch, and Pike was his apprentice – their names is handed down to prosperity among the noblemen and footmen of the land. They both died in the workhouse, and, in course, I shall do the same. Something else *might* turn up, to be sure. We can't say what this luck of the world is. I'm obliged to strive wery hard – wery hard indeed, sir – now, to get a living,

---

[816] Ibid, January 31, 1850.

and then not get it after all at times – compelled to go short often.[817]

The comic quality of the language conceals of course the real suffering of the street performers – Mayhew met a street clown on the verge of starvation; minutes afterwards transformed into an apparently happy and laughing performer[818] – but their human quality shines through their sufferings, and there is almost something moving in the quaintness of their language. '

Mayhew was acutely aware of how sociological factors influenced the adoption of respectability or its opposite; he gave a great deal of space for example to the effects of the system of paying wages in public houses to men working in the coal unloading trade. For many years it had led to widespread drunkenness and brutality – many men beating their wives because of disputes over the spending of money on drink – and Mayhew summarised the effects of the system in the following passage:

> The children of the coalwhippers were almost reared in the tap-room, and a person who had great experience in the trade tells me he knew as many as 500 youths who were transported, and as many more who met with an untimely death. At one house there were forty young robust men employed about seventeen years ago, and of these are only two living at present. My informant tells me that he has frequently seen as many as 100 men at one time fighting pell-mell at King James's stairs, and the publican standing by to see fair play.[819]

Similarly amongst dockers the irregularity of work and income led to 'irregularity of habits' – drunkenness, violence and the squandering of money.[820] In the last resort, Mayhew's sympathy

---

[817] Ibid, May 16, 1850.
[818] Ibid, May 30, 1850.
[819] Ibid, December 21, 1849.
[820] Ibid, October 30, 1849.

for the poor was so great that it over-rode his own middle class prejudices. In a number of places he observed that morality was very different when viewed from the perspective of middle class comfort as against the realities of life amongst the poor:

> It is easy enough to be moral after a good dinner beside a snug sea-coal fire, and with our hearts well warmed with fine old port. It is easy enough for those that can enjoy these things daily to pay their poor-rates, rent their pew, and 'love their neighbours as themselves'; but place the self-same highly respectable people on a raft without sup or bite on the high sea, *and they would toss up who should eat their fellows* ... Morality on £5000 a year in Belgrave Square, is a very different thing to morality on slop-wages in Bethnal Green.[821]

In his speech to the tailors at a special public meeting on the 28th October, 1850, explaining his reasons for withdrawing from *The Morning Chronicle*, he passionately denounced the inequities of contemporary capitalist society, and perhaps came nearest to a socialist ethic and philosophy. He subsequently went on to write *London Labour and the London Poor,* some of which included part of his *Morning Chronicle* material. After this work, he fell into oblivion and obscurity. The poor seemed to bring out the very best of Mayhew; without them, his work sunk back into the rather pedestrian satirical plays and novels written for a middle class reading public (*The Morning Chronicle* survey was read by a wide range of social classes.)[822]

The very best of Mayhew was the material he collected on the lives of the poor, 'from the lips of the people themselves'. The range and depth of these autobiographies is so brilliant, that no amount of commentary can even come near to their quality and importance. Mayhew opened up a new history of the English people in this part of his work, as his informants had come from all parts of the country and spanned a complete age range. The reader has to read the survey itself to appreciate this part of his

---

[821] *Report of the Speech*, op. cit., p. 36.
[822] See for example *The Morning Chronicle*, June 13, 1850.

work. Dances and music at the harvest celebrations, vagabond life in the countryside and its pleasures and hardships, the problems of a country linen-draper, the harshness of convict life in Australia – the floggings and killings – the brutal conditions on board ship for emigrants (but not convicts – these were protected by their military escort), the meekness and deference of some of the poor, suffering the worst of all poverties, the colour prejudice experienced by an Indian street entertainer – this and a host of other subjects are covered in what we would now consider the beginnings of oral history. Mayhew died in July 1887, forgotten and unknown; he is now recognised as one of the great pioneers of sociological study, but above all, he was a man of deep sympathy and compassion for the suffering of the poor.

Chapter 11: Asian Population Growth and the Increase of Socio-Economic Inequality in Britain.[823]

Introduction.

There is historical evidence that English population growth in the eighteenth and nineteenth centuries increased socio-economic inequality by creating labour surpluses.[824] Thomas Piketty has recently analysed patterns of economic status, including a significant rise in inequality in Britain since the 1980s.[825] He has attributed these changes mainly to economic factors, but the present paper presents evidence to show that demographic changes linked to disease have had an independent influence on levels of inequality.

The period since the 1970s is one of economic globalisation, and inequality has been significantly shaped by global demographic and technological trends. As with the history of England, most world-wide population growth has resulted from reductions in mortality. In 1975, Preston concluded from a statistical analysis of available data that 'factors exogenous to a country's current level of income probably accounted for 75-90 per cent of the growth of life expectancy for the world as a whole between the 1930s and 1960s. Income growth *per se* accounts for only 10-25 per cent.'[826] More recently Easterlin has concluded that 'all of the modern improvement in life expectancy is due to advances in health technology, not to higher GDP per capita.'[827] This has occurred sometimes in very poor countries which have

---

[823] Unpublished paper.

[824] P. Razzell, *Mortality, Marriage and Population Growth, 1550-1850*, 2016, pp. 99-118.

[825] T. Piketty, *Capital in the Twenty-First Century*, 2014, pp. 316, 319, 323, 344.

[826] S.H. Preston, 'The changing relation between mortality and level of economic development', *Population Studies*, 29, 1975, pp. 231-248.

[827] R.A. Easterlin, 'Cross-sections are history', *Population and Development Review*, 38 Supplement, 2012, p. 304.

benefited from medical and other forms of aid.[828] Much of this diminished mortality occurred in Communist countries which had good educational and public health systems, but low per capita income growth.[829] This has invariably happened during periods of high fertility as a part of demographic transition,[830] leading to the creation of labour surpluses.

These labour surpluses allowed some developing countries to create highly competitive export industries because of the cheapness of their labour. However, the most important global demographic development was that which occurred in Asia.

Table 1: Life Expectancy and Population Growth in Asia, 1950-2001.[831]

Year	Life Expectancy	Year	Population
1950	41.6	1955	1,546,143,227
1973	57.5	1975	2,394,338,004
1990	65.5	1990	3,221,341,718
2001	67.1	2000	3,730,370,625

Life expectancy in Asia increased particularly rapidly in the period between 1950 and 1973, resulting in significant population growth in the decades between 1955 and 1990.

The most important economy in Asia was China. Its population grew rapidly after 1960, also fuelled largely by increasing life expectancy.

---

[828] J. Caldwell, 'Routes to low mortality in poor countries', *Population and Development Review*, 1986.
[829] J. Riley, *Low Income, Social Growth, and Good Health: a History of Twelve Countries,* 2007.
[830] S. Harper, *How Population Change Will Transform Our World*, 2016.
[831] World Bank Asian Data Online

Table 2: Life Expectancy and Population Growth in China, 1960-2015.[832]

Year	Life Expectancy (Years)	Population Size
1960	43.8	667,070,000
1980	66.6	981,235,000
2015	76.1	1,379,000,000

Most of the growth of China's population occurred between 1949 and 1975,[833] during a period of poverty and stagnating incomes, including the famine of 1959-61.[834] Riley has summarized the factors responsible for the decline of mortality after 1949 under three headings:

1. Communist rule opened with a crash programme of smallpox vaccination in 1949-52 ... [additionally] the Patriotic Hygiene Campaign sought to cleanse the environment by cleaning up towns and cities, managing refuse and waste in urban and rural areas, and reducing breeding and feeding opportunities for disease vectors, especially rats, snails, lice, houseflies, and mosquitoes. State authorities pushed latrine building, alerted people to the role of human faeces in disease propagation ... and in general followed a household approach to sanitation.
2. The campaign asked people to learn how to protect themselves against disease, using continuous social pressure to induce changes in individual behaviour and attitudes towards personal hygiene, environmental sanitation, and nutrition.
3. The Chinese, copying the Soviets, began a massive programme to train physicians and medical aids and to build hospitals and clinics.[835]

---

[832] World Bank China Data Online.

[833] M. Bergaglio, 'Population growth in China: the basic characteristics of China's demographic transition', CiteSeer Online, 2001.

[834] World Bank China Data Online

[835] Riley, *Low Income*, pp. 110, 111.

Much of the improved health was the result of the introduction of a cadre of 'barefoot doctors':

> Thousands of peasants – men and women who were mostly in their 20s and already had some general education – were selected for an intensive three-to-six month course in medical training. They were instructed in anatomy, bacteriology, diagnosing disease, acupuncture, prescribing traditional and Western medicine, birth control and maternal and infant care ... The barefoot doctors continued their farming work in the commune fields, working alongside their comrades. Their proximity also made them readily available to help those in need. They provided basic health care: first immunizations against disease such as diphtheria, whooping cough and measles, and health education. They taught hygiene and basic as hand washing before eating and after using latrines. Illnesses beyond their training the barefoot doctors referred to physicians at commune health centres ... there were an estimated 1 million barefoot doctors in China.[836]

Before these developments 'large numbers of people had died prematurely from malaria, tuberculosis, and faecal disease ... The methods of controlling them came to be understood through medical and public health research in western countries and partly through what western public health experts learned while working in Latin America, the Caribbean, and Asia.'[837]

These health improvements occurred in spite of China's real income per head only being a fraction of that in the United Kingdom, even after a period of significant growth between 1970 and 2016.

---

[836] V. Valentine, *Health for the Masses: China's 'Barefoot' Doctors*, NPR Online, 2006, p. 2.
[837] Riley, *Low Income*, p. 169.

Table 3: GNI per Capita (U.S.A. Dollars) in China and the United Kingdom, 1970 and 2016.[838]

Year	China	United Kingdom
1970	120	2,430
2016	8,260	42,390

The reduction in mortality and the growth of population resulted in a large surplus of cheap labour. The working population – aged 15-64 – between 1990 and 2017 in China increased by over 240 million, whereas the equivalent figure in Europe and the United States combined in the same period was less than 60 million.[839] This allowed China to develop a highly competitive manufacturing export industry: in 2004 its share of world manufacturing output was 8.7%, but by 2017 it had reached 26.6%,[840] gradually eroding the manufacturing industries of Britain, Europe and the United States.

As Nicholas Comfort has concluded, 'Over the decades that followed [from 1989 onwards] China, whose Communist Party had approved the opening up of the economy as far back as 1978, would embrace a rampant capitalism ... that would in turn generate an export-led boom giving it a near-stranglehold over the global economy.'[841]

The import of manufactured goods from Asia and China into the United Kingdom in 2016 is as follows:

---

[838] World Bank China Data Online

[839] C. Goodhart, M. Pradhan, *The Great Demographic Reversal*, 2020, p. 2.

[840] Ibid, p. 3.

[841] N. Comfort, *The Slow Death of British Industry*, 2012, p. 170.

Table 4: The Country of Origin of Imports of Selected Commodities into the United Kingdom, 2016.[842]

Imported Commodity	Asia & Oceania, Responsible for Proportion of Total Imports	China, Responsible for Proportion of Total Imports
Headgear	84.6%	71.3%
Ships & Boats	77.0%	10.6%
Toys & Games	69.1%	61.4%
Textiles	55.4%	51.9%
Footwear	53.2%	30.1%
Tools, Implements & Cutlery	40.7%	28.2%
Electrical Machinery	36.5%	23.3%
Furniture	30.9%	15.1%
Ceramics	28.0%	20.5%
Iron & Steel Products	21.4%	13.1%

The scale of exports coming from Asian countries – particularly from China – has had a major impact on Britain's economy and society. Manufacturing as a proportion of all employment in the United Kingdom fell from 22% in 1982 to 15% in 1992 and 8% in 2015.[843] In China and elsewhere, labour surpluses have been exploited for the maximisation of profit, transferring industrial production from developed to developing countries, with an increasing reliance on services in the developed world. Abhijit Banerjee and Esther Duflo have coined the phrase 'the China Shock' to describe its effect on deindustrialization in Western countries, and have summarized its impact on the areas affected in the U.S.A., Spain, Norway and Germany as follows:

---

[842] uktradeinfo@hmrc.gsi.gov.uk
[843] Manufacturing Statistics, 2015, Online.

Fewer people got married, fewer had children, and of the children born, more were born out of wedlock. Young men – in particular, young white men – were less likely to graduate from college. Deaths of despair from drug and alcohol poisoning and suicides skyrocketed. These are all symptoms of a deep hopelessness once associated with African American communities in inner cities of the United States but are now replicated in white suburbs and industrial towns up and down the Eastern Seaboard and the eastern Midwest.[844]

The impact of these changes on the UK's economy has been summarized as follows:

The UK's manufacturing sector has shrunk by two-thirds in the three decades between 1980 and 2010. Whereas a million people made cars in the UK during the 1960s, but by 2009 that number was just 180,000 ... by the 1980s the cotton industry had vanished. In 1983 there were 170 working coal mines, but by 2009, there were 4. After World War 2, manufacturing accounted for almost 40% of UK's economy. Manufacturing is now just a tenth of the UK economy ... and the service industry is now 75.8%.[845]

These changes have resulted in increases in the amount of socio-economic inequality. *The Economist* recently observed: 'When countries with lots of low-wage workers begin trading with richer economies, pay for similarly skilled workers converges. Those in poor countries grow richer while in richer countries workers get poorer.'[846] This process has a particular impact on the different regions of the wealthier countries, creating poverty in the old industrial communities but increased wealth in regions specializing in services. An example of this is to be found in

---

[844] A.V. Banerjee and E. Duflo, *Good Economics for Hard Times,* 2019, pp. 80-81, 85-86.
[845] A. Taylor, '21 Sad facts about deindustrialization of Britain' *Business Insider,* 18th November 2011.
[846] *The Economist,* 21st October 2017, p. 20.

patterns of household expenditure and property prices in different regions in England & Wales.

Table 5: Regional Gross Disposable Household Income and Property Prices in England & Wales.[847]

Region	Manufacturing as a Proportion of all Jobs, 1991	Manufacturing as a Proportion of all Jobs, 2015	Gross Disposable Annual Income Per Head, 2014 (£)	Average House Price, March 2017 (£)
West Midlands	30%	11%	15,611	180,293
East Midlands	30%	12%	16,217	176,213
Yorkshire & Humber	25%	11%	15,498	149,606
North West	25%	9%	15,776	150,250
North East	24%	9%	15,189	122,298
Wales	23%	10%	15,302	147,746
East	22%	8%	18,897	277,127
South West	19%	8%	18,144	240,222
South East	17%	6%	20,434	311,514
London	11%	2%	23,607	471,742

Although not a perfect correlation, the northern regions with the greatest historical reductions in the amount of manufacturing industry have lower household incomes and property values than elsewhere. The changing regional pattern of the social structure of England and Wales in the twentieth century has been documented by Gregory, Dorling and Southall:

The data [on the regional proportion of Social Class V] for 1911 present an intriguing pattern: the highest values were in London and particularly the East End; almost all of Southern England had higher rates than the Midlands or the North. [The data on regional changes] ... shows areas in the rural south in particular as having improved

---

[847] GovUk Online, 2017.

significantly since before the First World War, while Wales, the West Midlands, western parts of Norfolk, Nottinghamshire, Derbyshire, and southern Yorkshire, and what are now County Durham and West Cumbria have got worse. This arguably reflects major changes in the industrial bases of different areas, the northern areas losing the staple industries which employed large numbers of skilled and semi-skilled workers ... while rural southern areas were colonized by white-collar commuters. The inequality ratio for Social Class V tells a broadly similar story to our other measures of [inequality, including infant mortality].[848]

In the nineteenth century incomes were higher in the industrial regions of the north of England,[849] a pattern reversed in the twentieth century.

The impact of the process of deindustrialization has been summarized by Aditya Chakrabortty in 2011:

Before moving to Yale and becoming a bestselling historian, Paul Kennedy grew up on Tyneside in the 50s and 60s. 'A world of great noise and much dirt,' is how he remembers it, where the chief industry was building ships and his father and uncles were boilermakers in Wallsend. Last year the academic gave a lecture that reminisced a little about those days. 'There was a deep satisfaction about making things,' he said. 'A deep satisfaction among all of those that had supplied the services, whether it was the local bankers with credit; whether it was the local design firms. When a ship was launched at [the Newcastle firm] Swan Hunter all the kids at the local school went to see the thing our fathers had put together ...Wandering around Wallsend a couple of weeks ago, I didn't spot any ships being launched, or even built. The giant yard Kennedy mentioned, Swan Hunter, shut a few years back, leaving acres of muddy wasteland that still haven't lured a buyer. You still find

---

[848] I. Gregory, D. Dorling, H. Southall, *A Century of Inequality in England and Wales using Standardized Geographical Units*, 2001, p. 307
[849] B.R. Mitchell, P. Deane, *Abstract of British Historical Statistics*, 1971, pp. 346, 347; E.H. Hunt, 'Industrialisation and regional inequality in Britain, 1760-1914' *The Journal of Economic History*, 49, 1986, pp. 935-966; M. Penn, *Manchester Fourteen Miles*, 1979, pp. xvii, xviii.

industrial estates, of course ... The biggest unit on one estate is a dry cleaner; on another, a warehouse for loft insulation dwarfs all else. At a rare actual manufacturing firm, the director, Tom Clark, takes me out to the edge of the Tyne, centre of the industrial excitement remembered by Kennedy. 'Get past us and there's nothing actually being made for miles,' he says, and points down the still waterfront. At his firm, Pearson Engineering, Clark introduces me to a plater called Billy Day. Now 51, he began at the firm at 16. His 23-year-old son William is still out of work, despite applying to dozens of small factories. As the local industry's gone, so too have the apprenticeships and jobs. 'No wonder you get young kids hanging out doing whatever,' says Day. 'We've lost a whole generation.' You can see similar estates and hear similar tales across the country, from the north-west down to the Midlands and the old industrial parts of suburban London. But it's in the north-east, the former home of coal, steel, ships and not a lot else, that you see this unyielding decline at its most concentrated. It's a process I've come to think of as the de-industrial revolution, in which previously productive regions and classes are cast adrift.'[850]

These conditions have had political consequences, summarized by *The Economist*: 'Votes for Brexit and for Mr Trump were often cast as an expression of anger at a system that seems rigged. Unless policymakers grapple seriously with the problem of regional inequality, the fury of those voters will only increase.'[851]

These problems are unlikely to diminish in the short-run, but a part of the long-run solution will only occur if falling fertility in developing countries reduces population increases to levels found currently in the developed world. This is likely to happen according to demographic transition theory,[852] although this raises speculative issues beyond the scope of the present paper.

---

[850] *The Guardian*: 15th November, 2011.
[851] *The Economist*, October 21st, 2017, p. 24
[852] Harper, op. cit., 2016.

CONCLUSION

Demography has been seen traditionally by economists and other social scientists as a function of economics, but this book presents detailed evidence to show that it has acted as an independent force influencing England's economic and social development through changes in disease patterns. Several essays in the book also illustrate the historical link between population growth and economic inequality, as well as the complex relationship between wealth, marriage and fertility

It was established through a number of independent sources – censuses, apprenticeship indentures, and marriage licences – that there had been major fall in adult mortality from the early eighteenth century onwards, approximately halving between the beginning and end of the century. The reduction in mortality occurred in all socio-economic groups and in all areas of the country, suggesting an autonomous fall in overall disease mortality. Infant and child mortality reduced first among the wealthy from the middle of the eighteenth century onwards, indicating that life-style changes such as improved personal hygiene and midwifery practices, along with smallpox inoculation, may have been partly responsible for the mortality reductions.

The essays in the book have been written on the assumption that sociology is a natural science, but in recent years there has been a growth in phenomenological sociology rejecting the deterministic assumptions of natural science. Work on disease and demography led to an examination of the problem of determinism which forms chapter 1 of this book. This research confirmed sociology as a natural science, providing the foundation for a discussion of Weber's *Protestant Ethic* thesis in the second essay.

Recently Thomas Piketty has criticized the 'immoderate use of mathematical methods', stressing that 'historical experience remains our principle source of knowledge.' The essays in this book are based on this approach, but with an emphasis on direct statistical and contemporary literary evidence. The principle of triangulation has been applied to demographic analysis by assessing the accuracy of the registration of births, marriages and deaths. This has been achieved through comparing independent measures of these events, and has led to the conclusion that population growth in England during the eighteenth century was largely shaped by the reductions of mortality rather than by increases in fertility

In addition to demography, an exploration has been made to the role of geography in political, economic and cultural life. Geography like demography can be seen as an objective factor in shaping historical change. Triangulation has been used in the sociological analysis of the English civil war, citing evidence from both supporters of parliament and their royalist enemies. Traditionally England did not rely on a standing army, but used the navy as the chief form of defence against external attacks. This was because of its geographical position as an island, which had a major influence on its political history. On the continent of Europe standing armies had been developed because of the threat of land-based attacks, which strengthened authoritarian regimes and the power of monarchies. In the absence of land-based threats, English kings were forced to rely on militias which resulted in a limited ability to impose taxes and control the economy. As a consequence, a culture of individualism developed in England, particularly in areas outside the manorial control of the aristocracy and gentry. Science flourished in England because of its individualistic culture, reflected in the Royal Society's slogan, "*Without Authority*".

During the late sixteenth and first half of the seventeenth century population had grown largely as a result of the gradual disappearance of plague. This led to increasing property prices due to a greater demand for food and other consumer goods. There was a marked rise in the wealth of yeomen farmers at this time, and along with tradesmen they became increasingly literate. These groups formed the backbone of Cromwell's New Model Army, playing a major role in the English civil war.

The later Regency period also saw a relationship between population growth and socio-economic inequality. Not only was there an increase in the pauperization of labourers as a result of growing surplus labour, but the increase in life expectancy amongst the gentry and aristocracy meant that they increasingly monopolized elite occupations.

Although relating to recent times, the last essay in this book describes the influence of Asian population growth on inequality in England. Chinese population had increased in spite of famines in 1959-61, and this was due to the application of state sponsored medicine and improved personal and public hygiene. Chinese companies have exploited the surplus labour resulting from these changes to create cheap manufactured goods, which they exported to England, America and Europe. This has led to the erosion of manufacturing industries in these countries, resulting in economic inequality and the rise of populism in rustbelt areas.

The essays in this book illustrate the way that sociological analysis can provide an understanding of historical topics, as well illuminating major issues in contemporary life.